Microsoft®

Working with Windows® Small Business Server 2011 Essentials

Charlie Russel
Sharon Crawford
Andrew Edney

Published with the authorization of Microsoft Corporation by:
O'Reilly Media, Inc.
1005 Gravenstein Highway North
Sebastopol, California 95472

ISBN: 978-0-7356-5670-3

1 2 3 4 5 6 7 8 9 M 6 5 4 3 2 1

Printed and bound in the United States of America.

Microsoft Press books are available through booksellers and distributors worldwide. If you need support related to this book, email Microsoft Press Book Support at *mspinput@microsoft.com*. Please tell us what you think of this book at *http://www.microsoft.com/learning/booksurvey*.

Acquisitions and Development Editor: Ken Jones
Production Editor: Teresa Elsey
Editorial Production: Online Training Solutions, Inc.
Technical Reviewer: Robert Pearman
Indexer: Ellen Troutman Zaig
Cover Design: Twist Creative • Seattle
Cover Composition: Karen Montgomery

Dedicated to the SBS MVPs for their ongoing service to the community.
– Charlie Russel and Sharon Crawford

*For Katy, thank you for putting up with the hours upon hours I spent
in my office working on yet another book.*
– Andrew Edney

Contents at a Glance

Part V Appendices

Table of Contents

What do you think of this book? We want to hear from you!

Microsoft is interested in hearing your feedback so we can continually improve our
books and learning resources for you. To participate in a brief online survey, please visit:

microsoft.com/learning/booksurvey

Introduction

Small businesses make up the economic engine that moves a nation forward, and all small businesses must deal with a highly competitive marketplace, unpredictable economic cycles, time pressures, and technological demands that are constantly exerting pressure on the bottom line.

Your business needs the same technologies that large companies do. You need the ability to share information with customers, partners, and employees. You have the same worries about spam, malware, and security. And you have the same need to manage resources and employee access to those resources.

The major difference is that you probably don't have the luxury of an in-house IT staff.

Windows Small Business Server 2011 Essentials (SBS 2011 Essentials) allows small businesses to operate at the same technology level as much larger organizations, but without the added costs of maintaining a network administration department.

Working with Windows Small Business Server 2011 Essentials is a reference, assistant, and coach for the busy network administrator, whether the administrator is on the scene or accessing the network from another location.

Organization of This Book

This book is divided into five parts, each of which focuses on a different aspect of using Windows Small Business Server 2011 Essentials. Part I, "Getting Started with Windows Small Business Server 2011 Essentials," provides a quick overview of SBS 2011 Essentials, reviews hardware and network planning, and walks you through installation and getting started with SBS 2011 Essentials. Part II, "Using Windows Small Business Server 2011 Essentials," gets you using SBS 2011 Essentials, covering storage, sharing, and backups. Part III, "Enhancing, Optimizing, and Maintaining Windows Small Business Server 2011 Essentials," gives you still more skills, for such things as handling updates, installing printers, and managing remote access. Troubleshooting, disaster planning, and server recovery are the subjects of Part IV, "Advanced Tasks and Windows Small Business Server 2011 Essentials." Finally, the five appendices in Part V cover migrating from previous versions of Windows Small Business Server, provide background on topics key to SBS 2011 Essentials, and point you to additional resources.

Conventions and Features in This Book

Even though SBS 2011 Essentials has automated many, many of the tasks associated with configuring and securing a network, this book is required when you want to do something slightly out of the ordinary—or when you need additional understanding of what a wizard is doing.

Look for book elements such as these:

> ## Real World
>
> Everyone can benefit from the experiences of others. "Real World" sidebars contain elaboration on a particular theme or background based on the adventures of other users of SBS 2011 Essentials.

 Note Notes include tips as well as alternative ways to perform a task or some information that needs to be highlighted.

 Important Information marked Important shouldn't be skipped. (That's why it's called Important.) Here you'll find security notes, cautions, and warnings to keep you and your network out of trouble.

 Best Practices When there's a best way to do something, we'll let you know. The experience of those who have done this before is distilled into Best Practices.

 Planning Planning information gives you a heads-up when forethought about something now can make your life easier later.

 More Info More Info boxes provide just that, pointing you to resources that offer more detail about something being described in the main text.

Acknowledgments

No book comes together without the efforts of many people.

During the writing of this book, Charlie and Sharon were fortunate to have the use of an excellent Hewlett-Packard StorageWorks X1500 server running Windows Storage Server 2008 R2. This fine machine gave us great flexibility to quickly and easily deploy test environments. The server loan was made possible by Joel Garcia from Microsoft and Jim Hankins from Hewlett-Packard. We're deeply appreciative of the use of the server and only wish we could have kept it.

More thanks are due to:

Jonas Svensson of Microsoft for his support of the SBS MVP Community, and his outstanding assistance with software builds when we needed them.

Greg Starks of Hewlett-Packard for his unstinting efforts to support the SMB (Small to Midsize Business) community.

Kevin Beares of Microsoft for his years of supporting SBS and the SBS Community, as well as his critical hardware support.

Paul Fitzgerald of Microsoft for years and years of SBS expertise and help, plus some key answers around GPT (GUID Partition Table) when we needed them.

Of course, the people at Microsoft Press are the ones who really made the book possible—in particular, senior editor Ken Jones, production editor Teresa Elsey, and technical editor Robert Pearman.

Errata & Book Support

We've made every effort to ensure the accuracy of this book and its companion content. Any errors that have been reported since this book was published are listed on our Microsoft Press site at oreilly.com:

http://go.microsoft.com/FWLink/?Linkid=225907

If you find an error that is not already listed, you can report it to us through the same page.

If you need additional support, email Microsoft Press Book Support at *mspinput@microsoft. com*.

Please note that product support for Microsoft software is not offered through the addresses above.

We Want to Hear from You

At Microsoft Press, your satisfaction is our top priority, and your feedback our most valuable asset. Please tell us what you think of this book at:

http://www.microsoft.com/learning/booksurvey

The survey is short, and we read every one of your comments and ideas. Thanks in advance for your input!

Stay in Touch

Let's keep the conversation going! We're on Twitter: *http://twitter.com/MicrosoftPress*.

Part I

Getting Started with Windows Small Business Server 2011 Essentials

Chapter 1
Introducing Windows Small Business Server 2011 Essentials

If you have a business with thousands of users and a large IT budget, solution providers will line up outside your door as if you were handing out free World Cup tickets. However, when your needs and resources are more modest, your choices are, too. Now with the introduction of Windows Small Business Server 2011 Essentials (SBS 2011 Essentials), a cost-effective and robust solution designed for smaller networks is available.

SBS 2011 Essentials is a new first-server solution for small businesses (up to 25 users) that can seamlessly integrate into online services such as Microsoft Office 365, cloud backup solutions, and cloud management solutions. No separate user licenses are required, and only minimal IT knowledge is needed.

 Note *Cloud computing* means using multiple server computers via a digital network, as though they were one computer.

Features of SBS 2011 Essentials

A great "feature" of SBS 2011 Essentials is that it's built on Windows Server 2008 R2. You get security, reliability, report and management tools, enhanced access to the Internet, and business applications—all in a single, integrated, low-maintenance package. In addition to great hardware and scaling features and easier virtualization, you'll also have:

- A straightforward interface designed for small businesses.
- An easy installation.
- Remote access for simple access almost anywhere.
- A health-monitoring infrastructure that analyzes both server and client well-being.
- On-premises as well as cloud-based support for software.

The Dashboard

When you install SBS 2011 Essentials, you'll immediately notice that the interface includes the Windows Small Business Server 2011 Dashboard (shown in Figure 1-1), a central organizational point from which you can perform many administrative tasks associated with SBS 2011 Essentials.

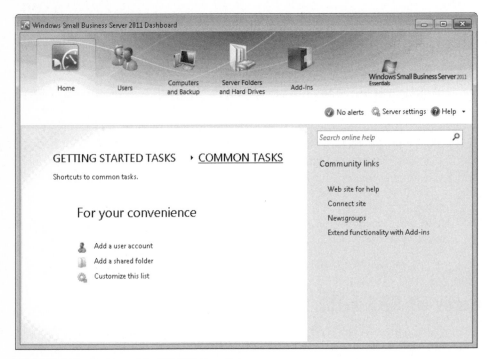

FIGURE 1-1 The Dashboard for SBS 2011 Essentials.

The Dashboard makes adding users, sharing folders, scheduling backups, and other routine chores a matter of a few clicks. From the Dashboard, you have a comprehensive view of the health and security of client computers and servers in the network, making it easy to manage common IT tasks and address technology issues before they occur.

User Management

Managing the users on an SBS 2011 Essentials network is simply a matter of opening the Dashboard and selecting the Users tab. As you can see in Figure 1-2, all users are listed, and adding, removing, or configuring user accounts takes only a few clicks of the mouse.

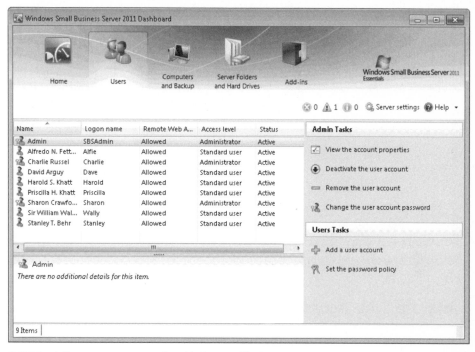

FIGURE 1-2 User accounts are easily added or modified.

Improved File Management

Find and access your files faster and utilize your network sbetter and more efficiently than ever before. SBS 2011 Essentials makes it easy to organize and maintain your business file structure—saving time, expense, and reducing the risk of lost productivity. Shared folders are easily added and configured in the Dashboard, as shown in Figure 1-3.

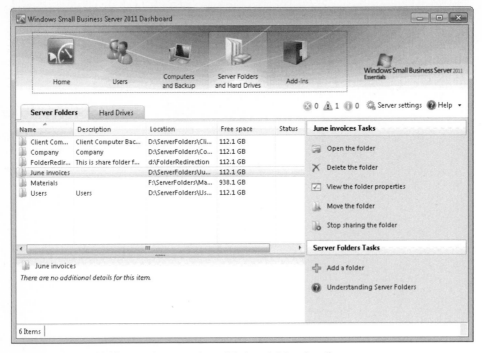

FIGURE 1-3 Shared folders can be created, modified, and deleted easily.

Remote Web Access

Remote Web Access (RWA) has many pluses, a few of which are:

- The ability to remotely access shared folders.

- Secure, anywhere access to your files and documents through any common web browser.

- The ability to connect to the PCs in your network and even run applications from virtually any location.

- A new interface that administrators can reorganize without programming knowledge.

Chapter 14, "Managing Remote Access," covers the features and uses of Remote Web Access.

Data Protection

Everyone agrees that the easiest way to protect your data is to back it up at frequent intervals. SBS 2011 Essentials makes this chore much easier than before by conducting automatic, daily backups of every computer on the network. A click in the Dashboard shows the backup status of all computers (see Figure 1-4).

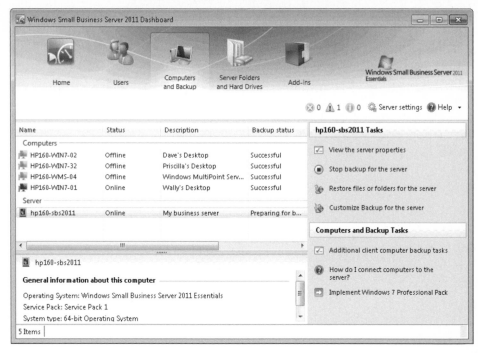

FIGURE 1-4 Checking the backup status for all computers.

Restoration of individual files, folders, or an entire computer is easily done by using the uncomplicated disaster recovery tools included with SBS 2011 Essentials.

The full story on setting up and using the backup features is found in Chapter 9, "Backing Up and Restoring."

Installation and Migration

Installation could hardly be easier. In addition to the familiar Windows interface, you'll also get:

- A much simplified setup procedure with complete guidance for configuring the server, as well as improved Internet and domain configuration.
- The ability to let users connect their own PCs—without requiring an administrator.
- Automatic administration of your Internet domain name.

Installation details are in Chapter 4, "Installing Windows Small Business Server 2011 Essentials." The procedures for migration are in Appendix A.

Summary

This chapter is a brief summary of some of the features of SBS 2011 Essentials. The next chapters cover planning your hardware and planning your network. Following the recommendations in these chapters will simplify and speed your installation.

Chapter 2
Planning Hardware

Before you start buying hardware or installing software for your Windows Small Business Server 2011 Essentials network, you should spend time planning what that network will look like. Time spent now will be repaid later, with interest, by saving time, energy, and complications.

In this chapter, we help you identify the hardware your network will require. By understanding the requirements, and what the tradeoffs are among cost, functionality, security, and robustness, you'll be in a position to make informed choices when implementing SBS 2011 Essentials.

Server Hardware Requirements

If you have a server that can meet the capacity needs of the network or can be upgraded to do so while allowing for future growth, by all means use this server. But realistically, because there is no upgrade path to SBS Essentials, you should plan to buy a new server as part of your implementation. The good news is that SBS 2011 Essentials doesn't have particularly stringent hardware requirements, allowing the costs of your new server to remain reasonable.

Processor, RAM, and Networking

The official minimum requirements for an SBS 2011 Essentials server are a single processor core, 2 GB of RAM, and an Ethernet card. The more realistic requirements, however, are a minimum of a dual-core processor, 4 GB of RAM, and at least a 100 Mb Ethernet card. At the upper end of the SBS 2011 Essentials range, for 20-25 users, the realistic requirements are a quad-core processor, 8-12 GB of RAM, and a 1 gigabit Ethernet card.

Minimum requirements, and even our best estimates of realistic requirements, should always be viewed with skepticism. We obviously have no knowledge of exactly how you'll be using your network, or what kinds of users you have and what kinds of workloads will run on the server or the network as a whole. These variables can have a substantial impact on the hardware requirements of your server. If you have doubts about what your requirements are, we urge you to consult a qualified Small Business Server specialist. This should be a Microsoft partner who has the Small Business Specialist Community (SBSC) competency.

Real World: Server-Class Hardware

The first, and foremost, hardware requirement for SBS 2011 Essentials is that the server actually be a real server, not a workstation or a desktop PC. The reason for this is simple, really—you're going to run your *business* on this server, and you don't want your business to be unable to function because of a hardware failure.

A client or workstation computer is used by one person at a time and is designed to function well in that scenario. It generally does not have a redundant power supply and usually has a single hard disk that isn't designed to run under continuous load. The networking and I/O subsystems are designed to work well with one user accessing the network and the disk at a time. And in the event of a failure, only one person's work is affected.

By comparison, a server computer is used by multiple people running different tasks, all at the same time. A server computer should have a redundant power supply, a fault-tolerant disk array (redundant array of independent disks, or RAID) that will continue to function without data loss in the event of a disk failure, and an I/O subsystem that is designed to handle the load from multiple users simultaneously. Furthermore, server-class hardware is designed to be used 24 hours a day, seven days a week.

Your SBS server is the most important part of your network, and it must always be up and running. Although SBS 2011 Essentials doesn't require a particularly powerful server, your server computer should still have as much redundancy as possible to ensure that your network stays up even when a part of it fails.

> **Note** For a list of hardware supported for Windows Server 2008 R2, see the Windows Server catalog at *http://www.windowsservercatalog.com/*.

Storage

The minimum storage requirement for SBS 2011 Essentials is a single 160 GB hard disk—which is, frankly, hopelessly inadequate. This is (barely) sufficient to install SBS 2011 Essentials but provides no room for user files or company files, backups of client workstations, or future growth. And it also doesn't provide any redundancy whatsoever.

Basic Requirements

We think that a more realistic minimum is a mirrored (RAID 1) installation volume of 200–400 GB and a RAID 5 data volume of 1 terabyte. This allows a reasonable amount of room for the growth of operating system files, and provides enough space for essential company files and for client backups. However, depending on the number of clients workstations, and the number of users, the size of that data volume might well need to be larger. Adding more hard disk space when you purchase your server is fairly cheap, but adding it later can be quite a bit more expensive, so it's a good idea to err on the high side. Some hardware RAID controllers allow you to add additional disks to the RAID array without rebuilding the array from scratch, but not all do. And you'll also need to consider the physical needs of the disk array. If you've bought a server that has slots for five disks, and you've used them all for your current server, then adding additional disks will usually mean adding an external disk cabinet, which is never a simple or inexpensive option.

Client Backups

One of the key features of SBS 2011 Essentials is *client backup*. When you join your user's Windows client computer to the SBS network, that computer is automatically configured to back up the entire computer to the server. This protects the client computer from both catastrophic failures and inadvertent or maliciously caused misconfiguration or loss of data. You can restore individual files and folders, or restore the entire computer to a previous state. With Mac computers, you can configure your SBS 2011 Essentials server as a *Time Machine* endpoint for backups.

SBS 2011 Essentials uses a form of single-instance storage (SIS) to minimize the amount of disk space that is used to back up your client computers. This ensures that if you have ten client computers, each with a 500 GB disk, you don't need 5 terabytes of storage on your SBS 2011 Essentials server just for one day's worth of client backups. The exact amount you need will depend entirely on how similar your client computer configurations are, and how much actual data they have stored on them.

Although we're normally strong believers in RAID arrays and redundancy wherever possible, a strong argument can be made that client backups do not require redundancy. The reasoning is that they are backups, not the primary storage of the data, and that in the event of a failure of the disk holding client backups, a full set of backups will be completed in the space of a few days after the failed disk is replaced. Furthermore, if the server is being backed up regularly, and this backup includes the volume on which the client backups were being stored, there is a tertiary source of the data there in the event of a catastrophic failure of both a client disk, and the volume on which the client backups are being stored.

The advantage of using a single disk for storage of client backups is that this configuration makes it easy to move to a larger disk as disk technologies and data needs change. Simply plug in the new, larger disk, and use the built-in Move A Folder Wizard to move the Client Computer Backups folder to the new disk. The old disk can then be removed or repurposed.

All things being equal, we would still prefer that client backups be stored on a RAID 5 array. RAID 5 provides redundancy with a minimal disk space overhead. (A three-disk RAID 5 array has an overhead of 33 percent, and each disk you add to a RAID 5 array reduces the percentage of overhead.) But if you choose to use RAID 5 for this, we strongly urge you to choose a RAID controller that allows you to add disks to the array without having to delete the array and recreate it.

> **Note** As a single point of reference, three generations of client backup of three Windows 7 computers (two 64-bit and one 32-bit) with minimal data storage on them require slightly less than 20 GB of total storage on our test network.

Server Backup

In addition to the internal storage requirements of your SBS 2011 Essentials server, you also need to plan on providing external storage that allows you to back up the server itself. The preferred form for this is one or more USB disks of sufficient size to hold a full backup of the server. This might not include all of the client backups, depending on how you configure the server backup.

It is technically possible to configure the server backup by using the native Windows tools instead of the SBS wizards. If you do this, you can configure your backup to use a network storage location. However, we do not recommend this because it doesn't allow you to keep multiple generations of backup. For more on both client and server backups, see Chapter 9, "Backing Up and Restoring."

Physical Security

An often overlooked consideration when you're planning your server hardware purchase is the physical security of your server. If your server is not protected from access by unauthorized personnel, you have a serious security issue. Anyone with physical access to the server has the potential to damage the server or steal its contents, including any critical business data that is stored on the server.

Your server should be in a locked area. This can be as involved or as simple as you want to make it, but it should provide a reasonable assurance that only authorized personnel have physical access to the server. We've seen high-security rooms, with biometric access control, and we've seen simple, very sturdy wire cages with stout padlocks on them. Both worked well, and both accomplished the goal. But one solution was a lot cheaper than the other. From our perspective, elegance is less important than the actual presence of physical security for the server.

Second-Server Requirements

SBS 2011 Essentials supports the Small Business Server 2011 Premium Add-on. The Premium Add-on includes a full copy of Windows Server 2008 R2 Standard and a full copy of Microsoft SQL Server 2008 R2 for Small Business. No additional client access licenses (CALs) are required for using the copy of Windows Server 2008 R2 included in the Premium Add-on, but Premium CALs are required for connecting to SQL Server if you deploy that.

The Premium Add-on is an ideal and cost-effective solution for small businesses that require a copy of SQL Server for a line-of-business (LOB) application. If your only need is for a second Windows Server license, either for virtualization or for another use that doesn't require SQL Server, then it is usually more cost effective to purchase a stand-alone copy of Windows Server 2008 R2 Standard. Or, if your primary need for that second server is as a Remote Desktop Services (RDS) computer, we think that Windows MultiPoint Server 2011 is an excellent RDS solution and integrates into the SBS 2011 Essentials dashboard. For more on second servers, including Windows MultiPoint Server 2011, see Chapter 13, "Extending Your Network with a Second Server."

However you choose to obtain a second copy of Windows Server, the requirements for that server are the requirements for any other copy of Windows Server 2008 R2, as described at *http://www.microsoft.com/windowsserver2008/en/us/system-requirements.aspx*.

Virtualization

When we wrote *Microsoft Windows Small Business Server 2003 R2 Administrator's Companion* (Microsoft Press, 2006), virtualization was one of those things that folks talked about doing, but rarely did. The industry, such as it was, was dominated by VMware, and Microsoft had only recently jumped into the market with Virtual PC and Virtual Server. Fast-forward to today: virtualization is an everyday tool of most system administrators, and Microsoft is now a significant factor with their Hyper-V virtualization available either as a stand-alone feature or built into Windows Server.

With all the hype and promise of virtualization, however, it is not a *solution*, but a *tool*. Before you decide to virtualize SBS 2011 Essentials, you really should think about what you're trying to accomplish, and why—and whether you want to pay the overhead for increasing your network complexity.

Real World: Why Is Virtualization So Popular?

Why has virtualization suddenly become such a compelling scenario? What has changed? We think that two very important changes are driving the move to virtualize: official support from Microsoft and the move to 64-bit hardware.

Official support means that if you have an issue with Windows or just about any of the Microsoft server applications and you're running in a virtualized environment, you're still supported, and Microsoft support won't say, "Sorry. Please reproduce that problem on a physical server, and we'll be happy to help you." This is an important concern for anyone using virtualization in a production environment.

The wide availability of multicore, 64-bit processors and larger RAM densities is also driving the move to virtualization. The biggest limiting factor for running virtualization on 32-bit Windows is the RAM limitation—you just can't virtualize very many server workloads on a server that is limited to 4 GB of RAM. With Windows Server 2008 R2, which is available *only* in a 64-bit version and includes native Hyper-V, running many server workloads on a single physical server is easy. For example, while writing this book, we've been using an HP DL160 G6 server with 24 GB of RAM and two quad-core processors. That lets us easily run two copies of Windows Small Business Server 2011 Essentials, along with a copy of Windows Small Business Server 2011 Standard in virtual machines. We're also running a Premium Add-On server, a Windows MultiPoint Server 2011 virtual machine, and several Windows 7 and Windows Vista virtual machines on that same physical server. And if we needed more, the server will easily handle four times that amount of RAM.

The reality, however, is that very few businesses running SBS 2011 Essentials need anywhere near the number of servers we do, and virtualization probably doesn't make much sense for the typical SBS 2011 Essentials network. However, as your needs grow, it might well become a compelling option to consolidate your physical server(s) onto a single virtualization host.

The basic hardware and software requirements for virtualizing SBS 2011 Essentials are listed here.

- **A virtualization host**   This is the physical computer that runs the virtualization. This should be a high-quality, server-grade computer with good redundancy and excellent I/O.

- **Virtualization software**   This can be Windows Server 2008 R2 with the Hyper-V role enabled, the Microsoft Hyper-V Server 2008 R2, or some third-party virtualization solution.

- **Processor, RAM, and disk**   Each virtual machine will have the same processor, RAM and disk requirements as an equivalent physical computer. Add up the requirements for each of your virtual machines and add whatever is required for the virtualization operating system itself. For the free Microsoft Hyper-V Server 2008 R2, add an additional 384 MB.

- **Networking**   You need one physical network interface card (NIC) for each virtual machine, plus one that is used only for managing the host.

The key thing to keep in mind if you plan to virtualize is that there's no magic. If you were planning on having a quad-core processor and 4 GB of RAM for your SBS 2011 Essentials server, you still need to plan on the same level of resources for a virtualized version of it. In addition, all the caveats about server-grade hardware we discussed earlier in this chapter are even more compelling if you virtualize. Now you have multiple servers running on one physical computer. If something fails on that physical computer, you don't lose just one server—you lose all the virtual machines running on that server until you can repair or replace the server.

Client Requirements

Regardless of what operating system your current client computers are running, there's a high likelihood that they will work with SBS 2011 Essentials.

SBS 2011 Essentials supports client computers running Windows XP (Service Pack 3), Windows Vista, and Windows 7. It even supports Home editions of Windows, though there are some limitations on the functionality of Home editions. SBS 2011 Essentials supports clients running both 32-bit and 64-bit versions of Windows, with the exception of Windows XP Professional, x64 Edition. Finally, SBS 2011 Essentials supports Mac clients running at least OS/X 10.5 (Leopard).

Other operating systems might well be able to work with SBS 2011 Essentials and use the resources of the SBS 2011 Essentials network but will not be supported scenarios. Because this is your business' network, we think it's important that you be running a fully supported environment.

Summary

In this chapter, we've covered the basic hardware requirements for running Windows Small Business Server 2011 Essentials, including the hardware requirements for adding another server or for virtualization. The most important requirement is to use hardware that is designed for server use, with built-in redundancy to reduce the time your network is unavailable due to hardware failure.

In the next chapter, we'll cover the planning of your physical SBS 2011 Essentials network, including routers, wiring, switches, and security.

Chapter 3
Planning Your Network

The time you spend planning your network before you actually start building it, and installing Windows Small Business Server 2011 Essentials, is time well spent that will save money and inconvenience later. It is far easier to make changes to the network design when it's still on paper than once you've actually implemented it and found out that there's a problem.

Planning the Network Infrastructure

The first task in designing a network for your company is evaluating your computing needs. This includes making decisions about the type of Internet connection you need and the kind of local networking you want to use and support. Before starting, though, let's review some basics about networks and network operating systems.

Network Operating Systems

On a typical home computer, the role of the operating system is to manage the file system, handle the running of applications, manage the computer's memory, and control the input and output to attached devices such as cameras, printers, and scanners. A network operating system expands that role, managing all of those tasks plus handling the following:

- Centralized security

- Remote access

- Remote file systems

- Shared applications

- Input and output to shared network devices

- CPU scheduling of networked processes

When multiple computers are connected in a *workgroup*, as shown in Figure 3-1, the result is called a *peer-to-peer network:* a network without a central server and with no network operating system. Even when one or more of these computers runs Windows Server, the workgroup is still an essentially unmanaged peer-to-peer network.

Replacing that Windows Home Server with an SBS 2011 Essentials server, as shown in Figure 3-2, creates a *client/server-based network*—one or more servers and multiple clients, all sharing a single security policy. The servers provide both the resources and the security policy for the network, and the clients are the computers that use the resources managed by the server.

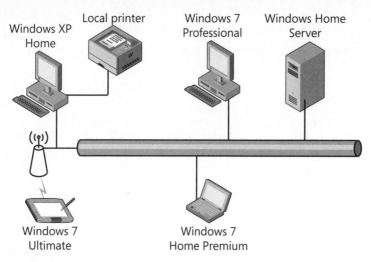

FIGURE 3-1 A peer-to-peer network, which has no central management.

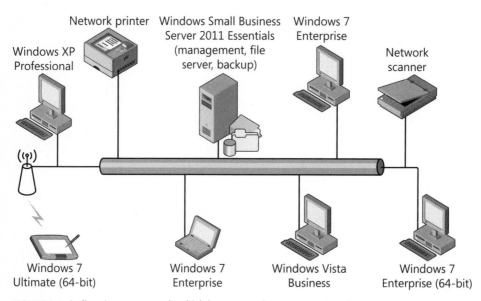

FIGURE 3-2 A client/server network, which has a central management and resource server.

Servers Use Network Operating Systems

Because SBS 2011 Essentials has to supply services to as many as 25 users, and you're depending on it to run your business, a stable and reliable operating system running on good-quality hardware is essential. Your users depend on the server to get their work done, and you need to be able to depend on that server being up and available.

In addition to supplying file, print, or other services, the network operating system must provide network security. Different businesses and organizations have varying security needs, but *all* must have some level of data protection. Therefore, the system must offer a range of configurable security levels, from the relatively non-intrusive to the very stringent.

Clients Use Workstation Operating Systems

Like other computers, client computers on a network need an operating system. However, a client operating system doesn't need to manage the resources for other computers or manage security for the network. Rebooting a workstation can be an annoyance for the user but doesn't usually disrupt anyone else's work.

On a Windows SBS 2011 Essentials network, clients can run Windows XP, Windows Vista, or Windows 7. We think Windows 7 provides the best experience. And though it is possible to join a Home Edition of Windows to the Windows SBS 2011 Essentials network, we think that businesses should be running a business edition of Windows for full support of network security policies and to allow for remote access.

Determining Your Needs

Before designing a network, you should sit down and make some decisions about which features of Windows SBS 2011 Essentials your business will use now, and which ones you're likely to need in the future. Of course, guessing about the future is always a risky business, but doing some planning now, before you implement your network, will save time, expense, and headaches later. You should consider how Windows SBS 2011 Essentials will help you accomplish your business goals, and which technologies you plan to use in the next two to five years. The key areas to consider are

- Centralized user account management.
- Centralized update management.
- Web and email access for employees.
- File sharing and centralized file storage.
- Database storage using Microsoft SQL Server.
- Printer sharing.
- Centralized backup.
- Remote access to the internal network via the Internet, including remote access directly to the user's desktop from the web.
- Management of remote computers.
- Collaboration and document management.

You should also be thinking about four key areas that affect how much money you spend now, and what tradeoffs you need to make.

- Performance

- Expandability

- Reliability

- Security

Finally, think about both your "normal" day-to-day workload, and any special workloads you might have. For example, is there a periodic report or business requirement that arises every month or every quarter? If that special workload is important and time critical, you will probably want to size your server and network to handle the load comfortably without affecting normal user operations.

Choosing an Internet Service Provider

After determining the preferred connection type and bandwidth, it's time to actually find an Internet service provider (ISP). Two websites to check are *http://www.cnet.com/internet-access/* and *http://www.dslreports.com*. In addition to speed and cost, look for the following features:

- **Static IP address**   To enable remote access, you need either a static IP address or a way to manage DNS records automatically for a dynamic IP address. Windows SBS 2011 Essentials will automatically configure your remote access name and IP address even if your ISP only provides a dynamic IP address, so having a static IP address isn't really critical. Alternatively, you can manage your external DNS with a DNS service that supports dynamic updates, such as the service available from ZoneEdit (see *http://www.zoneedit.com*).

- **Terms of service and ports**   Many ISPs have terms of service (TOS) on consumer-grade accounts that prohibit hosting email servers, or they have a policy that blocks specific ports such as ports 80 and 443. Be sure to ask *before* you buy.

- **Transfer limitations**   If the ISP has a monthly data transfer limit, make sure that the limit isn't lower than your anticipated usage—charges for going beyond the limit can be significant.

- **Web hosting**   If you want the ISP to host your organization's Internet website, look for virtual hosting (so that your organization can use its own domain name) with enough disk space on the ISP's web servers.

■ **Backup Internet connection**   If your business is dependent on always being connected to the Internet, choose a secondary Internet connection with sufficient bandwidth to allow you to limp along in case the primary Internet connection fails. This second Internet connection should use a different ISP and a different connection technology than your regular connection. You can use a dual wide area network (WAN) router to use both connections simultaneously.

Choosing a Network Type

The next step in designing a network is to choose a network type (see Table 3-1). Start by looking at where your computers are physically located. If you can easily run cable between all computers, the choice is simple: Gigabit Ethernet (GigE). If you're installing new cabling, hire a professional cabling expert. Spending money on good wiring now can save you a *lot* of problems in the future. If you're reusing existing cabling, make sure it is rated at least Cat 5. If it is not, plan to replace it, or consider wireless connectivity as an option.

If your company's computers are widely scattered or mobile, or your wiring isn't up to at least a Cat 5 rating, consider including one or more *wireless access points* (WAPs). WAPs are network devices that permit wireless clients to access a wired network. The real-world speeds of the fastest current wireless standard (802.11n) are acceptable for most uses, but not nearly as fast or as reliable as a wired network. For this reason, use a wireless network to supplement a wired network, not to replace it.

Note that most consumer-grade routers that include wireless access really aren't up to protecting your critical business assets. For example, avoid the consumer-focused HomePNA and HomePlug network types. They're more expensive, slower, less secure, and less reliable than Ethernet or a properly configured 802.11n wireless network. Consider using a combination firewall and router designed to support small to mid-sized businesses; some options are those from SonicWALL, Fortinet or NETGEAR. These should support Remote Authentication Dial In User Service (RADIUS) authentication and provide full firewall functionality, including virtual private networking (VPN). For more information about wireless access points, see "Choosing a Wireless Standard: 802.11a/b/g/n" later in this chapter.

Important   All wireless technologies have the potential to introduce security risks. When using wireless networking, always use appropriate security measures, such as Wi-Fi Protected Access (WPA) 2 (802.11i), or 802.1x. For more information, see "Planning for Security" later in this chapter.

TABLE 3-1 Common Network Types

Technology	Speed	Speed (Real World)	Cabling	Maximum Distance	Comments
Fast Ethernet	100 Mbps	94 Mbps	Cat 5, Cat 5e, or Cat 6	328 feet from hub or switch	Requires Fast Ethernet (100 Mbps) switch.
Gigabit Ethernet	1000 Mbps	327 Mbps	Cat 5e or Cat 6	328 feet from hub or switch	Requires GigE switch.
802.11b (WiFi)	11 Mbps	4.5 Mbps*	Wireless	1800 feet (60–150 feet typical indoors)	Not really up to business class use.
802.11a	54 Mbps	19 Mbps*	Wireless	1650 feet (50–100 feet typical indoors)	Not widely supported. Different frequency from 802.11b/g.
802.11g	54 Mbps	13 Mbps*	Wireless	1800 feet (60–150 feet typical indoors)	Minimum level for most businesses.
802.11n	540 Mbps	130 Mbps*	Wireless	7200 feet (100–500 feet typical indoors)	Recommended. Dual-band now becoming widely available.

*Wireless speeds vary greatly depending on distance from the access point, and the number and type of walls, floors, and other interference between the access point and the client device.

Choosing the Right Network Cable

Choosing the right cable for a wired Fast Ethernet (100 Mbps) network is easy—Cat 5 cable. If there is existing wiring, have it checked by a qualified network cabling professional to ensure that it is at least Cat 5. If you expect to run GigE networking, you should have at least Cat 5e cabling. Unfortunately, most existing wiring in buildings is at most Cat 5 and might not support GigE networking.

New construction should run several strands of Cat 5e or, ideally, Cat 6. Although Cat 5 cable can be used with Gigabit Ethernet, it is marginal at best. Cat 5e and Cat 6 cables are more reliable and provide headroom for 10-gigabit Ethernet standards. Cables should converge at a reasonably clean, centrally located wiring closet with adequate power, ventilation, and security for all servers and network devices. (Be sure to leave room for future growth.)

Shielded Cat 5, Cat 5e, and Cat 6 cables are available for situations that potentially involve high levels of electromagnetic interference (such as antennas). You should use plenum-grade cable any time wiring is placed in a drop ceiling. (Before running cable in a drop ceiling, talk to the building manager.)

Choosing a Wireless Standard: 802.11a/b/g/n

Currently you can choose from four wireless standards: 802.11b, 802.11a, 802.11g, and 802.11n. Here's what you need to know about each (also see Table 3-1 earlier in this chapter):

- **802.11b**   802.11b is the most widely deployed standard, though the speed is limited (11 Mbps theoretical; 5 Mbps or even less in the real world). 802.11b supports a maximum of 32 users per access point and a maximum of three simultaneous channels in use in the same location. *Channels* separate wireless networks, with each channel providing 11 Mbps of bandwidth. If you currently have 802.11b equipment, it's time to upgrade.

- **802.11g**   802.11g is faster than 802.11b (54 Mbps theoretical; 13 Mbps real-world) and backward compatible with 802.11b. 802.11g supports a maximum of 32 users per access point and a maximum of three simultaneous channels in use in the same location.

- **802.11a**   802.11a is faster than 802.11g (54 Mbps theoretical; 19 Mbps real-world) and is more tolerant of microwave interference and network congestion because it uses the 5-gigahertz (GHz) frequency band. 802.11a supports a maximum of 64 users per access point and a maximum of eight channels in use simultaneously in the same location. 802.11a is not compatible with either 802.11b or 802.11g. 802.11a was never widely adopted.

- **802.11n**   802.11n is faster than 802.11g (up to 540 Mbps theoretical; 100-130 Mbps real-world) and backward compatible with 802.11g and 802.11b. Most 802.11n equipment is in the same frequency band (2.4 GHz) as 802.11b/g, but dual-band equipment is now becoming widely available that can also use the 5-GHz range of 802.11a. This dual-band equipment provides the greatest flexibility and compatibility, and is especially good at avoiding interference from other equipment. Choosing dual-band equipment from a single OEM is the safest choice for compatibility at the highest speeds. If you're buying new wireless equipment, we strongly recommend 802.11n, and prefer dual-band 802.11n where possible.

Choosing Network Devices

After selecting a network type and Internet connection method, the next step is to create a network diagram to visually show which network devices are needed, and then select the necessary devices for the network, such as switches, wireless access points, firewalls, and network adapters.

 Best Practices Choose a single brand of network hardware, if possible. This ensures greater hardware compatibility, simplifies administration, and makes obtaining vendor support easier.

Diagramming the Network

Creating a diagram of the network can quickly show which devices you need and where they should be located, as shown in Figure 3-3.

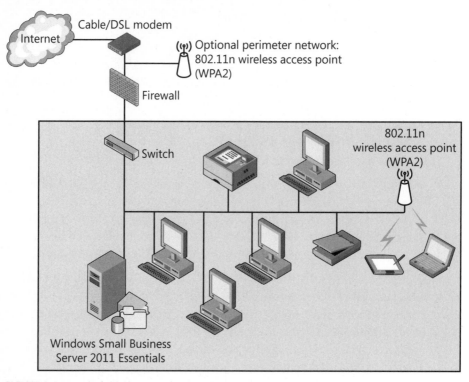

FIGURE 3-3 A typical Windows Small Business Server 2011 Essentials network.

Use the following list as a guide when creating the network diagram:

- **Internet connection**   The Internet connection is usually in the form of a telephone or coaxial cable that connects to a DSL or cable modem that also acts as a router. It is traditionally represented by a cloud at the top of the drawing and a line that connects to the router or firewall.

- **DSL or cable modem**   The Internet usually enters the organization through a telephone or cable line that plugs into a DSL or cable modem.

- **Firewall**   The DSL or cable modem is then plugged into the firewall or router. Some modems are combined with built-in routers that have basic firewall capabilities. Consumer-grade routers or DSL modems are not sufficient protection for a business network.

- **Perimeter network**   This is an optional area of the network between the DSL or cable modem and the firewall, where low-security devices such as public wireless access points can be placed.

- **Internal network**   The internal network includes the Windows SBS 2011 Essentials computer, the Premium Add-on computer if you're running the Premium Add-on, your client computers, and any network-connected devices, such as printers.

> **Planning**   Wireless access points should be on the internal network and use 802.11i (WPA2) encryption. You can also place access points in the perimeter network when you want to provide Internet access to the general public (such as in a coffee shop, conference room, or lobby). When you have a publicly accessible WAP, you should ensure that it is completely segregated from the internal network.

Choosing a Network Switch

Ethernet networks use the *star* network topology (also known as *hub and spoke*). In a star network, all network devices are plugged into a central hub or switch. Consider the following factors when deciding which switch or switches to buy:

- **Switch or hub**   Don't buy a hub unless you have a specialized need and understand why you're doing it. Get a switch instead. Switches are inexpensive, provide additional performance, and facilitate mixing 10 Mbps, 100 Mbps, and 1 Gbps devices on the same network segment.

- **Number of ports**   Make sure that the switch provides more than enough ports for all computers, access points, network printers, and network-attached storage (NAS) devices on the network, along with spare ports for expansion or in the event of a port failure.

- **Speed**   Fast Ethernet (100/10 Mbps) switches offer basic performance for small businesses, but GigE (1000/100/10 Mbps) switches, which are almost equivalent in price, provide extra bandwidth for improved performance of file servers and high-quality video streaming (where the network cabling supports it).

- **Management**   Managed switches provide the ability to view and manage the status of attached devices from a remote connection, which can be useful for off-site technicians. In many cases, they also have additional security features. But they're generally significantly more expensive than simple unmanaged switches, and in a small business network they aren't usually worth the expense.

Choosing Wireless Access Points

Wireless access points enable devices to wirelessly connect to a wired network. Access points are often integrated into routers, but they are also available as stand-alone devices that must be plugged into a switch like any other network device. Avoid wireless "gateway" or router products for connecting to your internal network—they will complicate your network management and TCP/IP configuration. They're fine for externally connected wireless access points. Some wireless routers can be reconfigured to be simple access points.

> **Note** Business-grade access points are more expensive than consumer-oriented access points; however, they are usually more reliable and full featured.

When choosing an access point, consider the following features:

- Routers with built-in access points are often no more expensive than stand-alone access points and are useful when you are creating a perimeter network. But be sure that the router you choose can be used as a pure access point—many can only function as routers, which won't work with an SBS network.

- Access points should support 802.11i (WPA2). WEP and WPA security do not provide any realistic protection against intruders and should not be connected to your SBS network.

- Access points should support 802.1x (RADIUS) authentication if you want to provide the highest level of security and ease-of-use to a wireless network.

> **Important** Two "features" that are often suggested to improve wireless security are the disabling of service set identifier (SSID) broadcasts and the use of media access control (MAC) address filtering. Don't bother. They are a significant and ongoing administrative burden, and a hacker with a port scanner can easily defeat them anyway.

- Some access points have two or more antennas that can be adjusted for better coverage; others support external antennas that can be mounted on a wall for better placement.

- Stand-alone wireless bridges (often referred to as wireless Ethernet bridges) and some access points provide the ability to wirelessly bridge (connect) two wired networks that can't be connected via cables. There are a number of different types of bridging modes, including point-to-point and AP client. Point-to-point mode uses two wireless bridges to link two wired networks. AP client uses an access point on the main network (to which wireless clients can connect) and a wireless bridge in AP client mode on the remote network segment, acting as a wireless client.

Clients on the other side of a wireless bridge will experience slower performance to the main network segment because of the shared wireless link, so use wireless bridges with discretion, and always use bridges and access points made by the same manufacturer.

■ Don't include "turbo" or other high-speed modes offered by some manufacturers in your buying criteria. They provide little performance gain, if any, in the real world, and can have a deleterious effect on compatibility.

Real World: Placing Access Points for the Best Coverage

Wireless access points have a limited range, especially in the environment of a typical office. The indoor range of 802.11g access points is usually around 60–100 feet at the highest connection speed. That said, 2.4-GHz cordless phones, microwave ovens, and Bluetooth devices can cause serious interference with 802.11g when they are turned on. Fluorescent lights, metal walls, computer equipment, furniture, and someone standing too close to the access point can also reduce the range of wireless networks. Unfortunately, there is no reliable way to quantify these variables—trial and error is the best way to position access points. With 802.11n, and especially with dual-band 802.11n, the effective distance is at least double that of 802.11g, but this still requires full 802.11n deployment and optimal conditions.

In our tests, 802.11n does appear to provide a more stable and reliable signal at a significantly greater distance than our previous 802.11a/g equipment. This is good news if you've got a large office and a lot of walls to deal with, but is actually a significant security issue for most small businesses. The greater the useful range, the more likely someone is going to try to hack into your network. There are some useful guidelines when selecting access point locations:

■ Place the access point and wireless network card antennas as high as possible to get them above objects that might attenuate the signal.

■ If you place access points in the plenum (the space inside a drop ceiling or raised floor), make sure you obtain access points or enclosures certified for plenum installation.

■ Place the access point in the center of the desired coverage area to provide the best coverage while also reducing the publicly exposed "surface area" of the network.

■ Only use the minimum signal strength (power) required to provide coverage for your office. Most WAPs have multiple levels of signal strength but are set to a default of maximum strength out of the box.

- Use multiple access points as necessary to cover multiple floors or large offices, or to serve a large number of clients simultaneously. Twenty clients per one 802.11n WAP is a reasonable maximum, with an average of no more than two to four simultaneously active users per access point yielding the best network performance.

- Use wireless bridges to place another Ethernet network segment (or another wireless access point) in a location unreachable by cables. Wired clients on this segment communicate with other wired devices on this segment at the speed of the wired network (1000/100/10 Mbps); however, communication with the main network segment takes place at the speed of the wireless network (10-100 Mbps real-world bandwidth).

- When selecting channels for access points, *sniff* (search by using a wireless client) for the presence of other networks, and then choose an unused channel, preferably one that is four or more channels separated from other channels in use. For example, channels 1, 6, and 11 can be used simultaneously without interference.

Choosing a Firewall Device or Router

Windows SBS 2011 Essentials is designed to connect directly to a firewall and does not provide any direct protection for the rest of the SBS network. Windows SBS 2011 Essentials includes the Windows Firewall that is part of Windows Server 2008 R2 to protect the server, but your network should be protected by an additional, separate firewall that will also act to protect the computers on the internal network.

You should look for the following features on your network firewall device:

- **Packet filtering**   Firewalls should support inbound packet filtering and stateful packet inspection (SPI).

- **Protection from specific attacks**   Firewalls should support protection from denial-of-service (DoS) attacks and other common attacks such as ping of death, SYN flood, LAND attack, and IP spoofing.

- **Network address translation (NAT)**   NAT is the backbone of most firewall devices, providing basic security and Internet connectivity to internal clients.

- **IPv6 support**   As IPv6 becomes more pervasive, and as the pool of available IPv4 addresses approaches exhaustion, the need to directly support IPv6 for Internet connections becomes more compelling. Choosing a firewall device that fully supports IPv6 now will save money and time later.

- **VPN pass-through**   To allow properly authenticated Internet users to establish VPN connections with a Windows SBS 2011 Essentials computer behind a firewall, you must ensure that the firewall supports the VPN pass-through of the VPN protocol (PPTP, L2TP, and/or IPsec).

- **VPN tunnels**   Some firewall devices provide direct support for establishing VPN connections. If you do choose to use a firewall device to establish VPN connections with clients and servers in remote offices, make sure that the firewall supports the necessary number of simultaneous VPN tunnels.

- **UPnP support**   Windows SBS 2011 Essentials can automatically configure firewalls that support the UPnP architecture. UPnP support can be found in most consumer firewall devices as well as in some business firewalls.

> **Note** Enabling UPnP support on a dedicated firewall device makes configuring the device to work with Windows SBS 2011 Essentials easy, but it does have security implications. We suggest using the UPnP architecture to do the initial setup of the firewall device, if the device supports it, but then disabling UPnP support completely.

- **Dual-WAN support**   Some firewalls come with support for two WAN connections to increase speed and reliability, which is a great solution for networks that require a reliable Internet connection. Other firewalls provide a serial port so that an external dial-up modem can be used as a backup connection, but this connection is much slower.

- **Content filtering**   Most firewalls allow administrators to block certain websites, such as websites that contain specified keywords. Many businesses use this feature to reduce their employees' ability to visit objectionable websites, although most content filters are largely ineffective.

- **Built-in wireless access points**   Firewalls with built-in access points and switched, GigE wired ports combine several functions and can be a cost-effective solution. However, their primary function is to protect the network, and that should be the first and most important evaluation criterion.

- **RADIUS support**   RADIUS support on your firewall enables additional functionality and security, which includes making it easy to integrate two-factor authentication (TFA) into your remote access configuration.

Planning for Security

It is far easier to implement effective security measures to protect your SBS network if you plan for security *before* you actually start buying hardware or installing software. In the following sections, we'll cover some of the most common attack vectors and the preliminary steps you can take in this planning stage to prepare your defenses. The most common attack vectors are:

- **Careless or disgruntled employees and former employees**   The single most common attack vector for any network is *people*. Internal users and former users are the biggest risk factors to data loss and data theft. Whether from laziness, disregard of security policies, outright malice, or simply the desire to help someone having trouble, the internal user is often the most dangerous on your network. See "Ensuring Physical Security" later in this chapter for guidelines.

- **Internet hackers**   All computers and devices attached directly to the Internet are subject to random attacks by hackers. According to the Cooperative Association for Internet Data Analysis (CAIDA), during a random three-week time period in 2001 more than 12,000 DoS attacks occurred: 1200–2400 were against home computers, and the rest were against businesses. If your organization has a high profile, it might also be subject to targeted attack by hackers who don't like your organization or who are engaging in corporate espionage.

  For more information about securing a network against Internet hackers, see "Securing Internet Firewalls" later in this chapter.

- **Wireless hackers and theft of service**   Wireless access points are exposed to the general public, some of whom might be looking for free Internet access, and to mobile hackers. To reduce this risk, refer to the "Securing Wireless Networks" section later in this chapter.

- **Viruses and worms**   Networks are subject to virus exposure from email attachments, infected documents, and worms such as Code Red and Blaster that automatically attack vulnerable servers and clients. Refer to the "Securing Client Computers" section later in this chapter for more information.

Ensuring Physical Security

Although security is not something that can be achieved in absolute terms, it should be a clearly defined goal. The most secure operating system and network in the world is defenseless against someone with physical access to the computer. Evaluate your physical environment to decide what additional security measures you should take, such as the following:

- Place servers in a locked server room. And control who has the keys!
- Use case locks on your servers, and don't leave the keys in them.
- Place network hubs, routers, and switches in a locked cable room or wiring closet.
- Install case locks on client systems or publicly accessible systems.

- Use laptop locks when laptops are used in public.

- Use BitLocker to encrypt the data on all laptops.

Securing Client Computers

Even a highly secure network can be quickly compromised by a poorly secured client computer—for example, a laptop running an older version of Windows with sensitive data stored on the hard drive. To maximize the security of client computers, use the following guidelines:

- **Use a secure operating system**   Use Windows Vista or Windows 7 on all client computers, with a strong preference for Windows 7 on laptops.

- **Use NTFS, file permissions, BitLocker, and EFS**   Use NTFS for all hard drives, and apply appropriate file permissions so that only valid users can read sensitive data. Encrypt sensitive files on laptop computers by using the Encrypting File System (EFS), and encrypt at least the system drive on laptops by using BitLocker. (BitLocker is only available on Enterprise and Ultimate editions of Windows Vista and Windows 7.)

- **Keep clients updated**   Use the Automatic Updates feature of Windows to keep systems updated automatically. Set all client computers to automatically download and install updates, and also configure them to update all Microsoft products, not just Windows.

- **Enforce password policies**   Require all passwords to be a minimum of eight characters, with not less than three of the four types of characters (lowercase alphabetic, uppercase alphabetic, numerals, and symbols).

> **Note** Remembering passwords has become an increasingly difficult prospect, leading to the resurgence of the yellow-sticky-note method of recalling them. It's important to discourage this practice, and encourage the use of distinctive but easy-to-remember passphrases. See the Real World sidebar, "Beyond Passwords: Two-Factor Authentication," for an alternative to annoyingly complex passwords.

- **Install antivirus software**   Antivirus software should be installed on the Windows SBS 2011 Essentials computer as well as on all clients. The best way to do this is to purchase a small-business antivirus package that supports both clients and the server. There are good third-party solutions specifically designed for the SBS market available from several vendors.

- **Install antispyware software**   Antispyware software should be installed on all client computers on the network and configured for real-time monitoring and daily full scans.

- **Keep web browsers secure**   Unupdated web browsers are a significant security issue. Always keep web browsers updated with the latest security updates.

Real World: Beyond Passwords—Two-Factor Authentication

Password policies are a difficult subject for many small businesses. Serious security using only passwords requires long and complex passwords that must be changed regularly and never repeated. That's a nice goal, but it's also not something that users are going to be all that happy with. If your network contains sensitive information—and whose doesn't, these days—you should consider providing an additional layer of security beyond simple passwords. Windows SBS 2011 Essentials can be set to reasonable, if somewhat minimal, password policies, but even the best of password policies is a balancing act between making the passwords difficult to crack and making the passwords easy for users to remember and use so that they aren't tempted to write them down on the back of their keyboards.

Passwords are a form of authentication, but they're only one of four kinds of authentication. The four kinds of authentication methods or factors are:

- Something you know (password)
- Something you have (token or physical key)
- Something you are (biometric)
- Somewhere you are (location)

Of these, only the first three are realistic and usable in a small business environment, though the fourth—location—is starting to be used by banks as one factor to be sure that the person trying to access your bank account is actually you.

Passwords alone are a single-factor authentication method, which in this case is something you know. Two-factor authentication requires two of the main three factors, and provides a definite improvement in ensuring that the person authenticating to your network is really who he or she claims to be. By enabling a second authentication factor, your need for draconian password policies is greatly reduced.

For a second authentication factor, we like the simplicity, moderate cost, and effectiveness of a one-time password (OTP). Generated automatically by a token you carry around with you, the combination of the token, a PIN, and your SBS password provides an additional level of security. Requiring administrators and all remote users to use two-factor authentication is a good way to improve the overall security of the sensitive data on your network.

Third-party OTP tokens include AuthAnvil (*http://www.authanvil.com*), CRYPTOCARD (*http://www.cryptocard.com*) and RSA SecurID (*http://www.rsa.com*). Of these, only AuthAnvil is focused on the small business market; AuthAnvil Essentials is specifi-cally designed for Windows SBS 2011 Essentials and integrates into the Dashboard. Additionally, the AuthAnvil soft tokens run on users' phones, greatly simplifying token management and deployment. We use AuthAnvil for all laptops and servers, and for all remote access.

Securing Wireless Networks

Wireless networks using the 802.11b, 802.11a, 802.11g, and 802.11n standards are certainly convenient, but they can also introduce significant security vulnerabilities if not properly se-cured. To properly secure wireless networks, follow these recommendations:

- Change the default password of all access points.

- Change the default SSID. Pick a name that doesn't reveal the identity or location of your network.

- Enable 802.11i (WPA2-Enterprise) encryption on the access points.

- If the access points don't support WPA2, don't use them on your internal network.

Note WPA2 provides two methods of authentication: an Enterprise method that makes use of a RADIUS server, and a Personal method known as WPA2-Personal that uses a pre-shared key (PSK) instead of a RADIUS server. The Enterprise method is strongly preferred, but it does take more initial configuration. Once it has been set up, however, it is transpar-ent to users.

- Disable the ability to administer access points from across the wireless network.

A wireless network should always be considered a potential threat vector, and should be pro-tected as completely as you can. We have good friends who are security geeks who simply won't allow wireless on their networks.

Securing Internet Firewalls

Most external firewall devices are secure by default, but you can take some additional steps to maximize the security of a firewall:

- Change the default password for the firewall device! We know this seems obvious, but unfortunately, it is all too often ignored.

- Disable remote administration, or limit it to respond to a single IP address (that of your network consultant).

- Disable the firewall from responding to Internet pings. OK, we admit that this is controversial. It's certainly a best practice, but it can also make troubleshooting a connectivity issue remotely a lot harder.

- Enable SPI and protection from specific attacks such as the ping of death, Smurf, and IP spoofing.

- Leave all ports on the firewall closed except those needed by the Windows SBS 2011 Essentials server.

- Regularly check for open ports by using trusted port-scanning sites.

- Require two-factor authentication for all access to the firewall.

- Keep the firewall updated with the latest firmware versions, available for download from the manufacturer's website.

Summary

In this chapter, we covered how to design and prepare a network prior to installing Windows Small Business Server 2011 Essentials. We also covered how to plan for adequate network security. In the next chapter, we'll cover the actual installation of Windows Small Business Server 2011 Essentials.

Chapter 4
Installing Windows Small Business Server 2011 Essentials

Installing Windows Small Business Server 2011 Essentials is a straightforward process. If you have purchased a computer with SBS 2011 Essentials already installed, you can skip this chapter.

Performing the Setup

Before starting the setup, review Chapter 2, "Planning Hardware."

1. Place the Windows Small Business Server 2011 Essentials installation DVD into your computer's DVD drive. The Installing Windows dialog box appears, as shown in Figure 4-1.

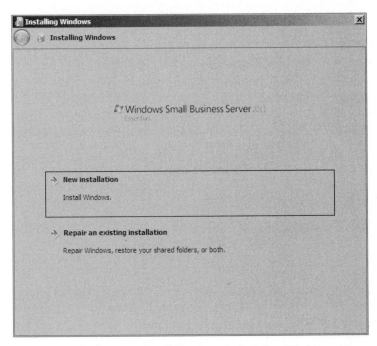

FIGURE 4-1 Selecting a new installation from the Installing Windows screen.

2. Click New Installation to continue. The next screen is the available hard drive verification screen, as shown in Figure 4-2.

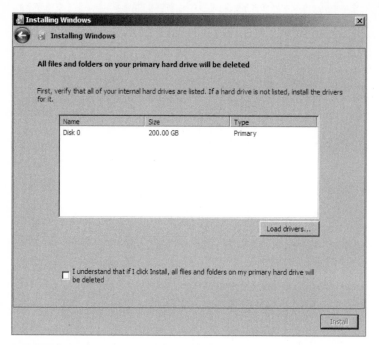

FIGURE 4-2 Confirming that all of your internal hard drives are listed and available.

Important If you have any external hard drives connected, remove them now and reconnect them after you've installed SBS 2011 Essentials, otherwise they will be erased.

Repairing an existing SBS 2011 Essentials installation or reinstalling SBS 2011 Essentials is covered in Chapter 16, "Disaster Planning and Server Recovery."

3. Select the I Understand That If I Click Install, All Files And Folders On My Primary Hard Drive Will Be Deleted check box, and then click the Install button.

Important This will completely erase all of the hard disks listed in the dialog box. Be sure you have a complete and up-to-date backup for everything on the hard disks. This step cannot be undone.

4. When you see the first configuration screen, as shown in Figure 4-3, the installation of SBS 2011 Essentials is complete.

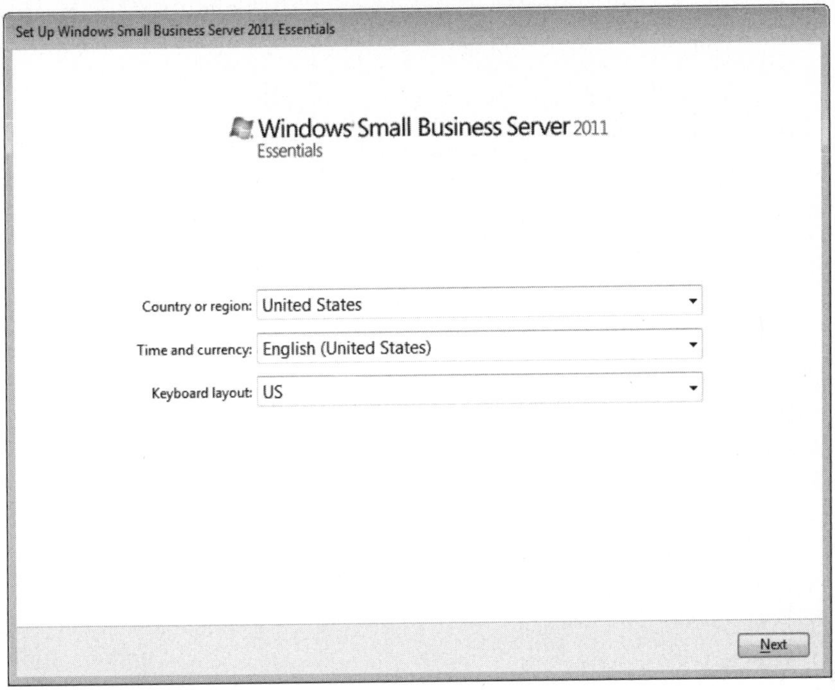

FIGURE 4-3 The end of installation and the start of configuration.

Completing the Setup Process

Provide the information about your location and language preferences on the configuration screen shown in Figure 4-3. Click Next to continue, and then follow these steps.

1. On the Verify The Date And Time Settings page, shown in Figure 4-4, click Change System Date And Time Settings if you need to change them. This includes the time zone.

2. Click Next. The next page displays the software license terms. Read the terms and conditions, select the I Accept The License Terms check box, and then click Next.

3. Enter the SBS 2011 Essentials product key that came with your copy of SBS 2011 Essentials. Choose whether or not to activate Windows automatically when you are next online. Click Next.

4. Next is the Personalize Your Server page, as shown in Figure 4-5. Here you can enter your company name, your internal domain name, and the name you want to give the server. (If you don't have an internal domain name, just enter anything—for example, **SBS.local** is often used.)

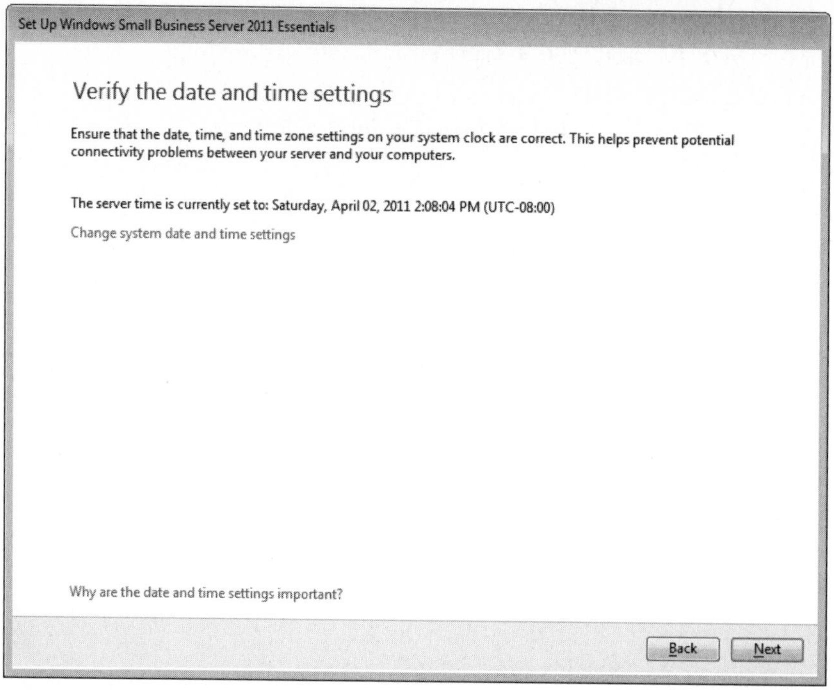

Set Up Windows Small Business Server 2011 Essentials

Verify the date and time settings

Ensure that the date, time, and time zone settings on your system clock are correct. This helps prevent potential connectivity problems between your server and your computers.

The server time is currently set to: Saturday, April 02, 2011 2:08:04 PM (UTC-08:00)

Change system date and time settings

Why are the date and time settings important?

Back   Next

FIGURE 4-4 Verifying the date and time settings for your SBS 2011 Essentials installation.

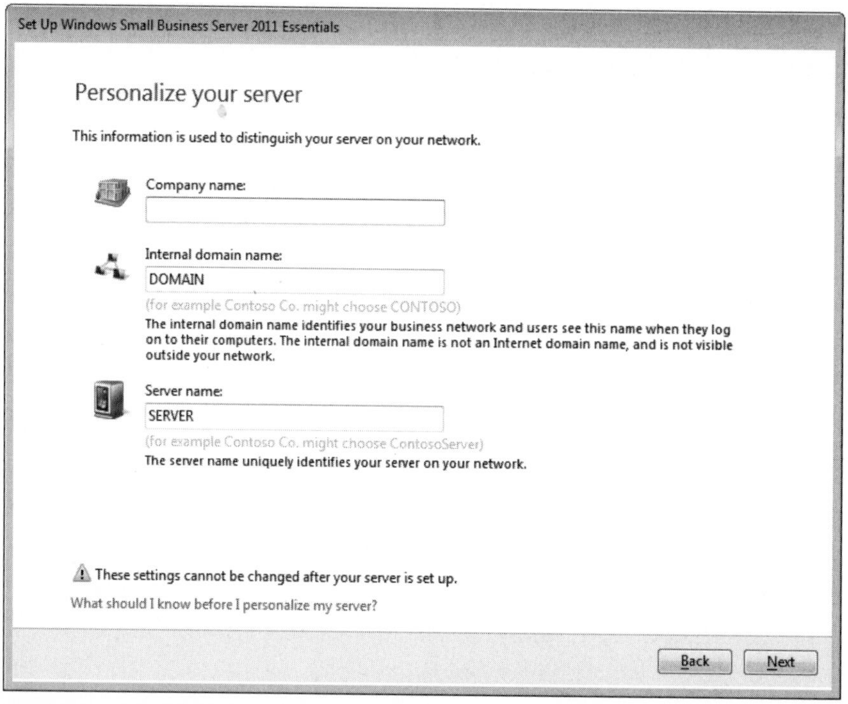

Set Up Windows Small Business Server 2011 Essentials

Personalize your server

This information is used to distinguish your server on your network.

Company name:

Internal domain name:

DOMAIN

(for example Contoso Co. might choose CONTOSO)

The internal domain name identifies your business network and users see this name when they log on to their computers. The internal domain name is not an Internet domain name, and is not visible outside your network.

Server name:

SERVER

(for example Contoso Co. might choose ContosoServer)

The server name uniquely identifies your server on your network.

⚠ These settings cannot be changed after your server is set up.

What should I know before I personalize my server?

Back   Next

FIGURE 4-5 Personalizing your server name and setting a password.

Real World: Choose a Generic Domain Name

You might be tempted to choose a simple domain name that somehow reflects the name of the company that will be using the SBS server. This makes perfect sense, and no one will question it. In fact, this is what we used to do when we set up networks for our customers. And it seemed to work fine, until the first time one of those customers merged with another small company and changed their company name to reflect the new company. And we had to tell them that there wasn't any way to change the domain name.

The only solution was to rebuild the network from scratch—with all the pain and risk that's involved. We learned an important lesson, however. Although it's important to choose a name that makes sense to users—because they'll see it every time they log on to their workstations—make it a generic name that reflects function, not the specific company name.

5. Click Next to move on to the next page, shown in Figure 4-6. Enter an administrator account name and password. This is the account that you will use to log on to and manage your SBS 2011 Essentials server.

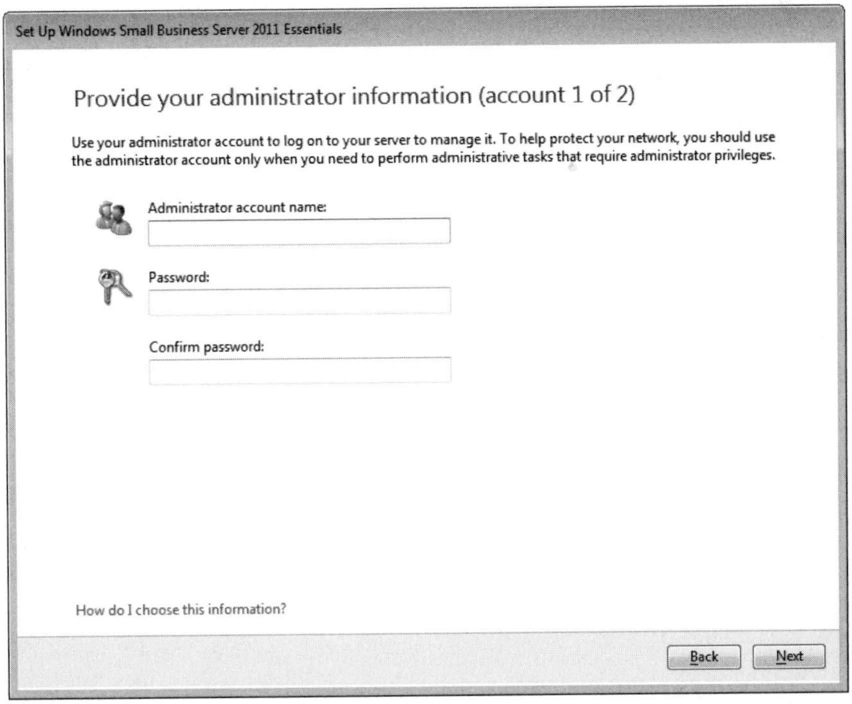

Set Up Windows Small Business Server 2011 Essentials

Provide your administrator information (account 1 of 2)

Use your administrator account to log on to your server to manage it. To help protect your network, you should use the administrator account only when you need to perform administrative tasks that require administrator privileges.

Administrator account name:

Password:

Confirm password:

How do I choose this information?

Back   Next

FIGURE 4-6 Providing your administrator information.

6. Click Next to continue to the page shown in Figure 4-7. Enter a standard user account name and password. This account is the one you'll use for normal daily tasks, not for administration.

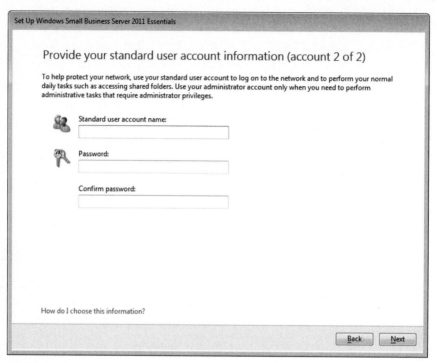

FIGURE 4-7 Providing your standard user account information.

7. Click Next to continue. Choose a method for keeping SBS 2011 Essentials up to date, as shown in Figure 4-8. When you click a selection, you will continue to the next page.

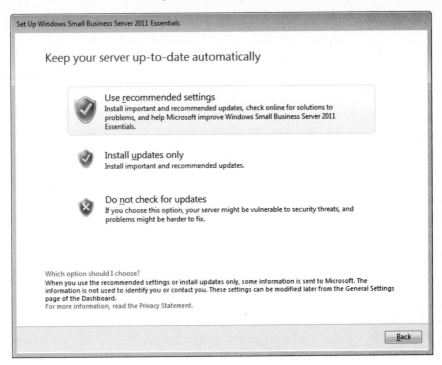

FIGURE 4-8 Choosing how to keep your server up to date.

Note The recommended setting is Use Recommended Settings (hence the name). This setting will keep SBS 2011 Essentials up to date with all relevant security updates and fixes, it will make your Internet browsing safer, it will check online for solutions to problems, and it will also report any problems and help Microsoft improve SBS 2011 Essentials. For more information on managing updates, see Chapter 11, "Managing Updates."

8. When the server preparation has completed, the page shown in Figure 4-9 is displayed. When you click the Close button, the post-installation configuration phase will be complete.

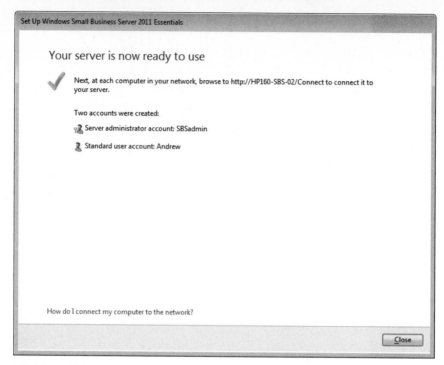

FIGURE 4-9 The server configuration process is now complete.

Installing by Using a USB Flash Drive

If your server lacks a DVD drive, you can use a USB flash drive to install Windows Small Business Server 2011 Essentials.

Note You will need a flash drive with more than a 4 GB capacity, so an 8 GB flash drive works very well. If you are purchasing a flash drive for this installation, get the fastest one you can find.

Using the Windows 7 USB/DVD Download Tool

Using the Windows 7 USB/DVD Download Tool involves downloading a piece of software from Microsoft, running it, and selecting the source material—in this case, an SBS 2011 Essentials installation DVD ISO image.

> **Note** Even though the tool is called the Windows 7 USB/DVD Download Tool, it can be used to create a bootable USB flash drive for any Microsoft operating system, including Windows 7 or SBS 2011 Essentials; all you need is an ISO image of the installation DVD.

You must be an administrator on the computer onto which you are installing the Windows 7 USB/DVD Download Tool. The tool requires the Microsoft .NET Framework 2.0 or higher.

The system requirements for the tool are as follows:

- Windows XP SP2, Windows Vista, or Windows 7 (32-bit or 64-bit)
- A Pentium 233-megahertz (MHz) processor or faster (300 MHz is recommended)
- 50 MB of free space on your hard drive
- A DVD-R drive or 4 GB removable USB flash drive (but this is the requirement for a Windows 7 installation from a USB flash drive, not for a Small Business Server 2011 Essentials installation)

Downloading the Tool

To download the Windows 7 USB/DVD Download Tool, follow these steps.

1. Enter the following address in your Windows Internet Explorer address bar:
   http://images2.store.microsoft.com/prod/clustera/framework /w7udt/1.0/en-us/Windows7-USB-DVD-tool.exe

2. When prompted, choose Run to run the file. Click Next to start the Windows 7 USB/ DVD Download Tool Setup Wizard (shown in Figure 4-10).

3. Click Next, and then click Install.

4. When the tool has been installed, click Finish.

FIGURE 4-10 The Windows 7 USB/DVD Download Tool Setup Wizard.

Using the Tool

To use the tool, follow these steps.

1. Click the Start button on the taskbar, and select Windows 7 USB/DVD Download Tool in the All Programs list to open the Windows 7 USB/DVD Download Tool. The dialog box shown in Figure 4-11 appears.

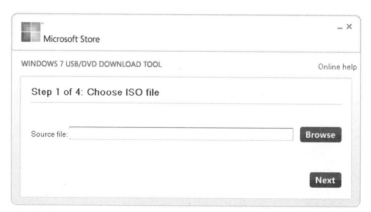

FIGURE 4-11 Choosing the ISO file.

2. In the Source File box, type the name and path of your Small Business Server 2011 Essentials ISO file, or click Browse and select the file from the Open dialog box. Click Next to continue to the next dialog box, shown in Figure 4-12.

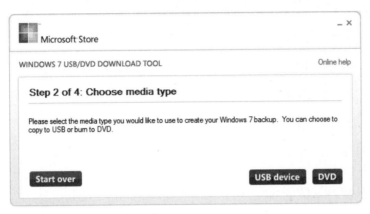

FIGURE 4-12 Selecting the media type.

3. Click USB Device to create a copy on a USB flash drive. The dialog box shown in Figure 4-13 appears.

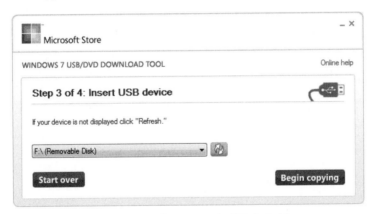

FIGURE 4-13 Preparing to start the copy to the USB flash drive

4. Select your USB device from the drop-down list, and click Begin Copying. If your USB flash drive is not listed, click the Refresh icon and try again.

5. When you see the Bootable USB Device Created Successfully message, you can close the tool and remove the flash drive.

To use the flash drive to install Windows Small Business Server 2011 Essentials, follow the installation instructions earlier in this chapter, substituting the flash drive for the DVD in the steps involving the SBS 2011 Essentials installation DVD.

Note The other method for preparing a USB flash drive is to use an application called diskpart, which is a command-line application included in Windows. For all the necessary steps, see Charlie's blog posting at *http://msmvps.com/blogs/russel/archive/2010/03/03 /making-a-bootable-usb-disk-stickdrive-pendrive-flashdrive.aspx.*

Summary

In this chapter, we covered the installation and initial configuration of SBS 2011 Essentials. The next chapter details the post-installation tasks.

Chapter 5
Getting Started Tasks

After you have installed Windows Small Business Server 2011 Essentials, there are some typical chores to be completed and services to be set up before your network is complete. Not
all of these chores need to be done at once, and some don't need to be done at all, but you
do need to review the list.

Start by opening the Windows Small Business Server 2011 Dashboard. On the Home page,
as shown in Figure 5-1, you'll see a list of tasks to be completed. Some might already have
check marks next to them, but all can be modified.

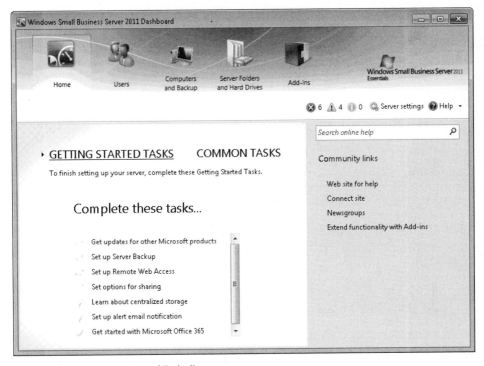

FIGURE 5-1 The Getting Started Tasks list.

Getting Updates for Other Microsoft Products

To change or verify the settings for updates, click Server Settings (near the top of the screen). On the Server Settings General page (shown in Figure 5-2), you'll see a section for Windows Update and error reporting.

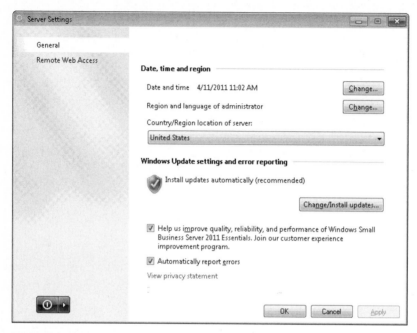

FIGURE 5-2 The Server Settings General page.

Click Change/Install Updates to open the Windows Update dialog box (as shown in Figure 5-3). From here you can check for updates, change update settings, review update history, and more.

Real World: Customer Feedback Options

Customer feedback is an area of considerable importance to Microsoft and even to us end users—in the long run. In the short term, you might wonder why you should participate in a program unlikely to be of direct benefit to you.

Well, it's something like paying taxes for schools when you have no children or your children are all adults. We pay those taxes because an educated populace is a greater social good. On a less lofty level, the Microsoft Customer Experience Improvement Program should result in better software in the future. And because this is software used by hundreds of millions of people, some considerable social good should therefore emerge.

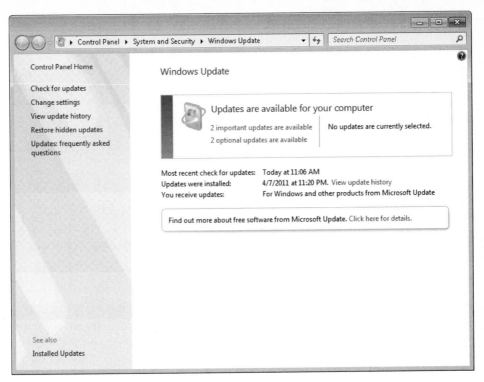

FIGURE 5-3 Checking Windows Update.

Note As you can see from the address field at the top, you can also get to this page by navigating to System And Security in Control Panel.

For more on configuring your system for updates, see Chapter 11, "Managing Updates."

Setting Up Server Backup

In the Getting Started Tasks list on the Dashboard, click the Set Up Server Backup link to start the backup wizard. This is a task that you can postpone now, but it must be completed as soon as your server is completely configured.

For step-by-step instructions on configuring backups, see Chapter 9, "Backing Up and Restoring."

Setting Up Remote Access

The initial setup of Remote Web Access (RWA) for your SBS 2011 Essentials server should be done immediately after the initial installation of SBS 2011 Essentials. This initial setup will set your Internet domain name, configure DNS, and configure your router to forward the required ports to your SBS 2011 Essentials server. Additional configuration and customizations beyond the initial setup can be done at any time and are covered in Chapter 14, "Managing Remote Access."

Real World: Manual Router Configuration

SBS 2011 Essentials is designed to work with routers that support UPnP. When UPnP is enabled, all the configuration of your router is managed and controlled by the SBS 2011 Essentials server. This simplifies configuration significantly and allows everything to work as SBS 2011 Essentials expects it to.

However, if your router doesn't support UPnP, you can configure it manually by using whatever interface it provides. (We'd give you specific steps, but every brand of router is a bit different.) If you are going to manually configure your router, we recommend that you configure the SBS 2011 Essentials server to have either a fixed IP address or at least a Dynamic Host Configuration Protocol (DHCP) reservation on the router. Then, at the router, configure *virtual servers* to forward ports 80 and 443 (HTTP and HTTPS protocols) to the IP address of the SBS 2011 Essentials server. You should configure the router *before* you run the Set Up Remote Web Access Wizard.

To set up RWA, use the following steps:

1. Click Set Up Remote Web Access on the Getting Started Tasks page of the Dashboard (shown previously in Figure 5-1) to open the Getting Started page of the Turn On Remote Web Access Wizard, shown in Figure 5-4.

2. If your router doesn't support UPnP, see the "Manual Router Configuration" sidebar earlier in the chapter and configure your router before proceeding, then select the Skip Router Setup check box on the Getting Started page.

3. Click Next to continue to the Turn On Remote Web Access page. SBS 2011 Essentials will do a lot of configuration here, and when it completes it will provide additional information. For example, if there's an issue with enabling RWA, you will see a report of the problem, as shown in Figure 5-5.

4. If you received an error report, either correct the cause of the error and click Retry, or select the I Want To Skip The Listed Issues For Now And Run The Wizard Again Later check box and click Next.

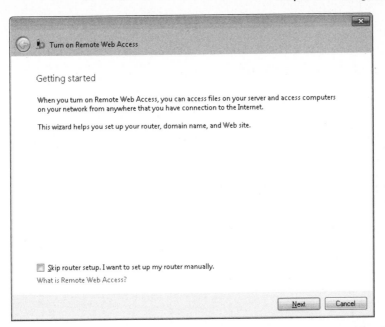

FIGURE 5-4 The Getting Started page of the Turn On Remote Web Access Wizard.

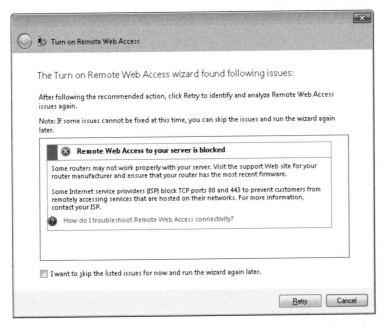

FIGURE 5-5 Failure report for the Turn On Remote Web Access Wizard.

If you don't yet have an Internet domain name for your company, skip ahead to the "Setting Up a New Domain Name" section later in this chapter.

Setting Up an Existing Domain Name

If you already have an Internet domain name, you can continue with the Set Up Your Domain Name Wizard by using the following steps:

1. Click Set Up Your Domain Name to open the Getting Started page of the Set Up Your Domain Name Wizard.

2. Click Next to continue to the Do You Own A Domain Name? page shown in Figure 5-6.

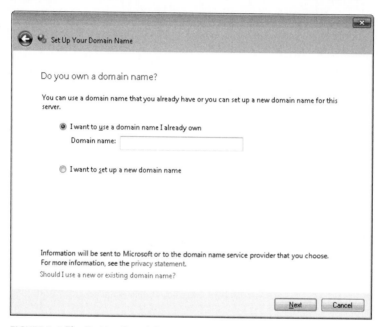

FIGURE 5-6 The Do You Own A Domain Name? page of the Set Up Your Domain Name Wizard.

3. Enter your domain name in the Domain Name box, and click Next. The wizard will check to see who your domain name registrar is, as shown in Figure 5-7.

4. Click the Go To button (this is Go To eNomCentral for our domain, but yours might be different). You'll be warned that you're being redirected to the web. Click Yes, and your browser will open on the website of your domain name registrar. From here, you can purchase or download an SSL Certificate for your domain. Follow the instructions from your registrar to configure your RWA site with the certificate.

5. When you've finished at the registrar's site, close Internet Explorer and return to the Set Up Your Domain Name Wizard. Click Next to continue to the Store Your Domain Name Information page, shown in Figure 5-8.

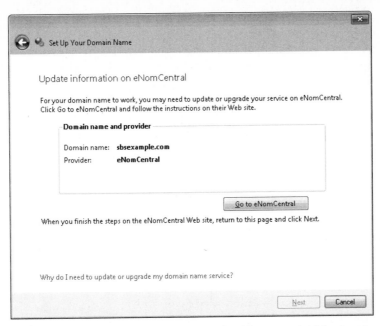

FIGURE 5-7 The Set Up Your Domain Name Wizard has recognized the domain.

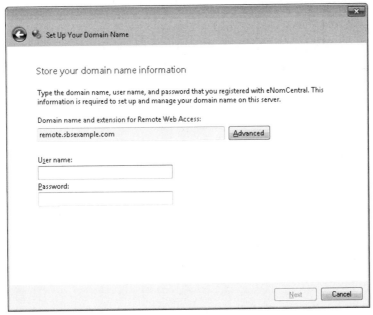

FIGURE 5-8 The Store Your Domain Name Information page of the Set Up Your Domain Name Wizard.

6. Fill in the required information and complete the wizard to configure the RWA site.

Setting Up a New Domain Name

If you don't already have a domain name, you can buy and register a new one, or use a third-level domain provided by Microsoft for free. These third-level domains will be in *yourcompanyname*.remotewebaccess.com form. The steps are similar for both types, except that if you buy a new domain name, you'll have to go to the regulator's site to purchase the domain and the SSL Certificate for it. In this example, we use the wizard to set up a third-level domain. Third-level domains aren't as pretty as second-level domains (*sbsexample.com*, for example), but if all you're doing is setting up RWA for your employees to connect to the office, a third-level domain such as *sbsexample.remotewebaccess.com* works just fine. And third-level domains are free. Just use the following steps:

1. On the Do You Own A Domain Name? page of the Set Up Your Domain Name Wizard (shown earlier in Figure 5-6), select I Want To Set Up A New Domain Name.

2. Click Next to continue to the What Kind Of Domain Name Do You Want? page, shown in Figure 5-9.

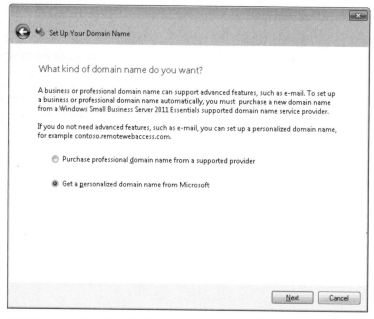

FIGURE 5-9 The What Kind Of Domain Name Do You Want? page of the Set Up Your Domain Name Wizard.

3. Select the Get A Personalized Domain Name From Microsoft option, and click Next to continue to the Sign In To Windows Live page. Enter your Windows Live account information (or create a new Windows Live account).

4. Click Next to continue to the Privacy Statement And Agreement page. You don't have a choice; you have to accept the agreement if you want to use the *remotewebaccess.com* third-level domain.

5. Click Accept to continue to the Create A Domain Name page shown in Figure 5-10.

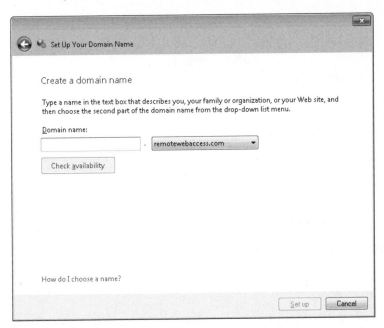

FIGURE 5-10 The Create A Domain Name page of the Set Up Your Domain Name Wizard.

6. Type in the domain name you want (we used **SBSExample**), and click Check Availability. If your name hasn't been used before, you'll see confirmation below the Check Availability button, as shown in Figure 5-11.

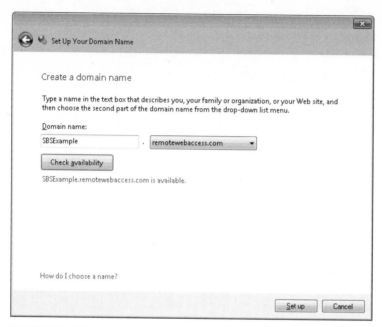

FIGURE 5-11 *SBSExample.remotewebaccess.com* is available.

7. Click Set Up. When the wizard completes, you'll see a confirmation page like that shown in Figure 5-12.

8. You can confirm that everything is set up correctly by clicking Visit Remote Web Access. This opens your browser and navigates to the logon page of RWA, as shown in Figure 5-13.

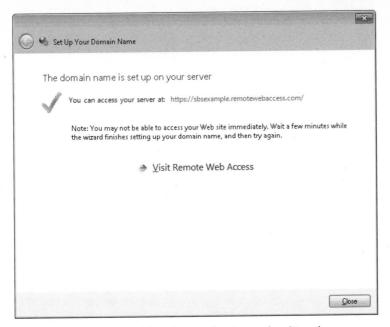

FIGURE 5-12 The third-level domain name is set up and registered.

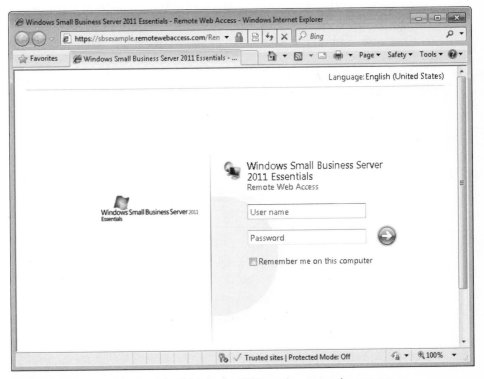

FIGURE 5-13 The logon page of the RWA site for *SBSExample.remotewebaccess.com*.

Setting Options for Sharing

Click the Set Options For Sharing link in the Getting Started Tasks list to open the dialog box shown in Figure 5-14.

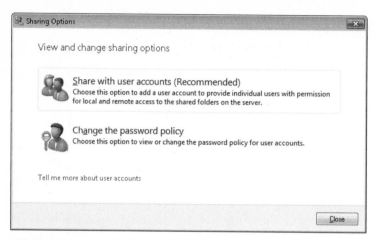

FIGURE 5-14 The Sharing Options dialog box.

Click Share With User Accounts to add a user who will have local and remote access to shared folders on the server. As shown in Figure 5-15, as you add a user, the system confirms that the password is of sufficient length and fulfils the password complexity requirement.

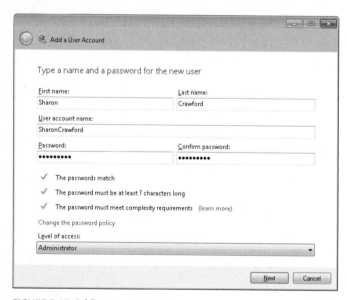

FIGURE 5-15 Adding a user account.

Click the Change The Password Policy link to alter the password requirements for all users.

Learning About Centralized Storage

Click the Learn About Centralized Storage link to view the dialog box shown in Figure 5-16. For information on file storage, see Chapter 7, "Configuring and Maintaining Storage."

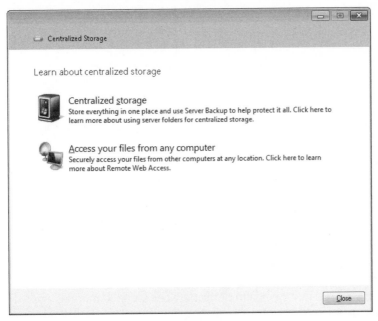

FIGURE 5-16 The Centralized Storage dialog box.

To access your files from any computer, see Chapter 14, "Managing Remote Access."

Setting Up Alert Email Notification

SBS 2011 Essentials monitors its own health status and the status of the computers in your network, and notifies you of issues or problems that might occur, such as problems with your backups, or server storage and low disk space. These issues are displayed as alerts in the Alert Viewer, which can be launched from the server's Dashboard or a client computer's Launchpad. However, to make sure that alerts get faster attention, you can configure email alerts.

Click Set Up Alert Email Notification in the Getting Started Tasks list, and then click Enable to open the dialog box shown in Figure 5-17. Fill in the fields using the information provided by your mail service.

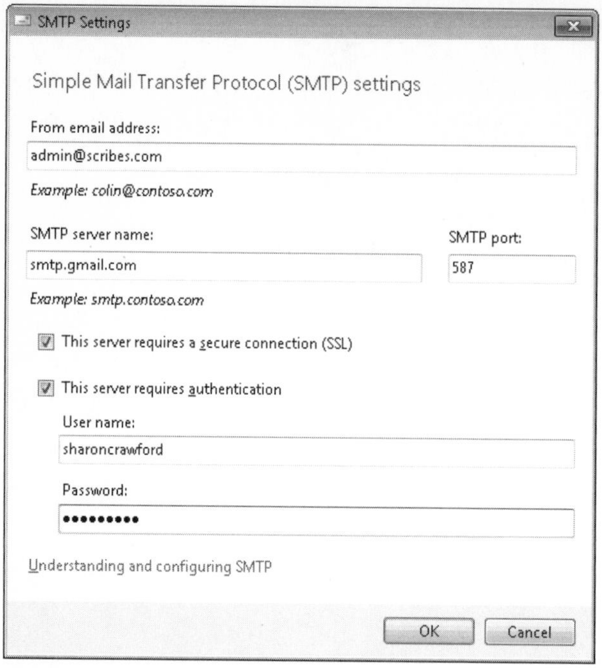

FIGURE 5-17 Configuring email for alerts.

By default, the server evaluates the health of the network every 30 minutes. For more on configuring alerts, see Chapter 15, "Troubleshooting."

Getting Started with Microsoft Office 365

SBS 2011 Essentials is designed to work with cloud-based services such as Microsoft Office 365. With Office 365, you can have a rich collaborative environment that includes Microsoft Exchange Online and Windows SharePoint Online. The intent is that SBS 2011 Essentials will directly integrate with Office 365, allowing you to manage users, email messages, and application access directly from the Windows Small Business Server 2011 Dashboard. Unfortunately, at the time of this writing, that plug-in has not yet been released or made available for beta use, and we can't show it to you. But stay tuned to the book's website and we'll try to provide updated information there after that add-in becomes available.

Summary

In this chapter, we covered the steps that you need to take after you install SBS 2011 Essentials. In the next chapter, we'll cover the steps for configuring and connecting your users' computers to the server.

Chapter 6
Adding User Accounts

Now that you have Windows Small Business Server 2011 Essentials installed and configured, the next tasks are to create user accounts and then install the SBS 2011 Essentials Connector on each client computer. During the installation process, the computer will be joined with the SBS 2011 Essentials server.

A user account (or network account, as it is also sometimes called) is required for every user. SBS 2011 Essentials allows up to 25 user accounts.

Adding a User Account

To add a user account, open the SBS 2011 Essentials Dashboard and follow these steps.

1. Click Common Tasks on the Users tab.

2. Click Add A User Account and complete the user account details, as shown in Figure 6-1. In the Level Of Access list, select Standard User or Administrator.

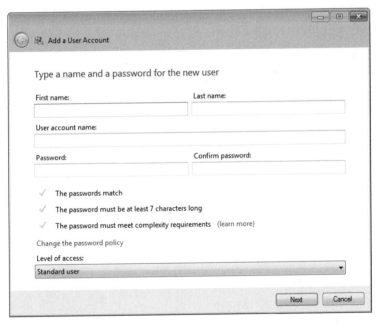

FIGURE 6-1 Completing the user account details to add a new user.

3. Click Next to continue. Select the shared folder access you want to grant that user, and click Next.

4. Enable or disable Remote Web Access for the user, and then click Create Account. You are now done.

Chapter 14, "Managing Remote Access," has more information on Remote Web Access.

The SBS 2011 Essentials Connector

Installing the SBS 2011 Essentials Connector not only joins client computers to the SBS 2011 Essentials server but also enables the following additional functions:

- Automatic daily backup of computers running Windows (the Mac Connector doesn't provide backup or restore capability)

- Health monitoring of your computers

- The ability to configure and remotely administer your SBS 2011 Essentials server from any computer

Prerequisites for Connection

Several requirements must be met before you can install the SBS 2011 Essentials Connector on a computer:

- The computer must be running one of the supported operating systems. (See the next section for the list of supported operating systems.)

- The computer must be on the same IP subnet as SBS 2011 Essentials.

- The computer must have 1 GB of free hard disk space.

- The computer cannot already be connected to another SBS server or an Active Directory domain.

Supported Operating Systems

The SBS 2011 Essentials Connector can be installed on all of the following operating systems and their variants (x86 and x64):

- Windows 7, all editions

- Windows Vista, all editions with SP2

- Windows XP, all editions with SP3 (the x64 edition is not supported)

- Mac OS X 10.5 or later

Installed Components and Changes Made to the Computer

When you install the SBS 2011 Essentials Connector, several other changes are also made to the computer to enable it to communicate with SBS 2011 Essentials and to give you a better user experience:

- The Microsoft .NET Framework 4 is installed, if it is not already present (on computers running Windows).

- Windows Firewall is configured to allow the Core Networking and Remote Desktop features to work.

- The SBS 2011 Essentials Health Agent is installed to detect problems and to create alerts that will appear as alert notifications on the computer and on the SBS 2011 Essentials dashboard.

- Scheduled tasks are created for recurring health assessments and to synchronize health alert definitions.

- Scheduled tasks are created to run automatic backups (for Windows only).

- Services are added to allow the computer to communicate with the SBS 2011 Essentials server.

- Services are installed to manage backup operations (for Windows only).

Installing the Connector on a Computer Running Windows

You can install the SBS 2011 Essentials Connector on any of your supported computers running Windows in one of two ways. Either download the Connector software and install it from a CD or a USB flash drive, or connect directly to the SBS 2011 Essentials server from each computer.

 Best Practices Installing the SBS 2011 Essentials Connector directly from the server means that you don't need to keep a copy of the software on a CD or USB flash drive, and that you're always using the latest version.

To install the SBS 2011 Essentials Connector on your computers running Windows, follow these steps:

1. Connect to your network, open Windows Internet Explorer, and type in the following URL: **http://servername/connect** (where *servername* is the name of your SBS 2011 Essentials server). This will display the Connector software download screen, as shown in Figure 6-2.

FIGURE 6-2 The SBS 2011 Essentials Connector software download screen.

2. Click the Download Software For Windows button, and when prompted, click Run. If you want to save a local copy of the software, you can choose to save the file and then run it later.

3. When the server has been located, you will see the Getting Started screen, as shown in Figure 6-3.

4. Click Next. The computer is checked to verify that it meets the prerequisites. Click Next again.

 Best Practices When the installation has completed, it is a good idea to perform a Windows Update check on each computer, in case there are any updates to the components that have just been installed.

5. On the page shown in Figure 6-4, enter the user name and password for the user account that belongs to this computer.

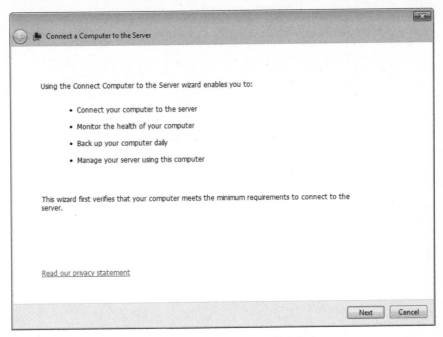

FIGURE 6-3 The Getting Started screen of the Connector installation.

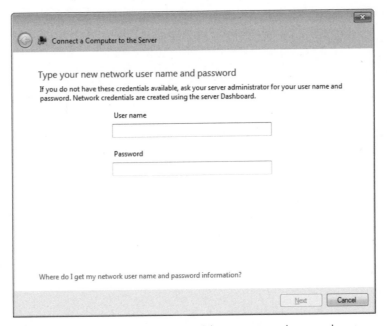

FIGURE 6-4 Entering the SBS 2011 Essentials user name and password.

6. Click Next. You will then be given the option to move all the data and settings associated with the user on the computer to the new user account, as shown in Figure 6-5.

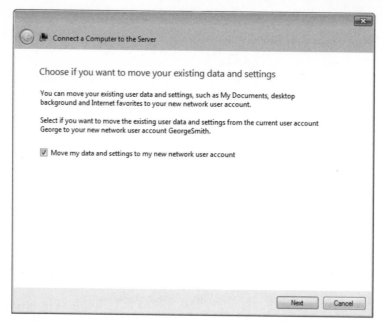

FIGURE 6-5 Choosing to move existing data and settings to the new user account.

Note The option to move existing user data and settings appears only if you are using a business edition of Windows, such as the Windows 7 Ultimate, Professional, or Enterprise edition. For all other editions, you will have to move your data and settings manually.

7. Make your selection and click Next to continue. You now are given the option to add a computer description to go along with the computer name, as shown in Figure 6-6.

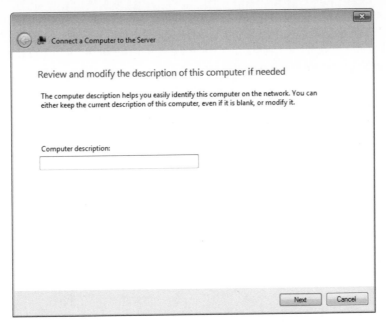

FIGURE 6-6 You can add a computer description if you want.

8. Click Next to continue. You will then be asked if you want to automatically wake up the computer to back it up. Make your selection, and click Next to continue.

> **Note** If you select the Wake This Computer For Backup option when connecting a computer to the network, the computer will automatically be woken up for backup if it is in sleep or hibernate mode. When the backup is finished, the computer will return to either sleep or hibernate mode based on its power management settings.

9. You will then be asked if you want to participate in the Windows Customer Experience Improvement Program. This is entirely optional, so make your selection and click Next to continue.

The computer is now connected to the server and is ready to be backed up (as shown in Figure 6-7). When you click the Finish button, the Dashboard will be opened by default. If you don't want to open the Dashboard, clear the Open The Dashboard To Administer Your Server check box before clicking Finish.

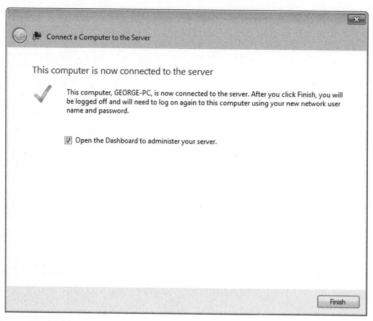

FIGURE 6-7 The computer is now connected to your SBS 2011 Essentials server.

Installing the Connector on a Mac

You can install the SBS 2011 Essentials Connector on any of your supported Mac computers in one of two ways. You can either download the Connector software and run it on each of your computers from a CD or a USB flash drive, or you can connect to SBS 2011 Essentials from each of your computers and install it that way.

Best Practices Installing the SBS 2011 Essentials Connector directly from the server ensures that you are always using the latest version of the connector software.

To install the SBS 2011 Essentials Connector on your Mac computers, follow these steps:

1. From the computer on which you want to install the Connector, ensure that you are connected to your network, open your browser, and type in the following URL: **http://servername/connect** (where *servername* is the name of your SBS 2011 Essentials server). This will bring up the Connector software download screen, as shown in Figure 6-8.

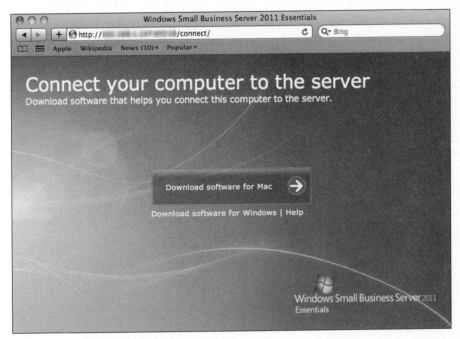

FIGURE 6-8 The SBS 2011 Essentials Connector software download screen on the Mac.

2. Click the Download Software For Mac button. This will then download the .dmg file and place it in the Downloads folder on your Mac.

3. Double-click the Connector for Mac software to begin the installation. You will need to enter your password for your Mac computer to continue.

4. When the SBS 2011 Essentials Connector software has started, you will be presented with the Introduction screen, as shown in Figure 6-9. All you have to do here is click Continue.

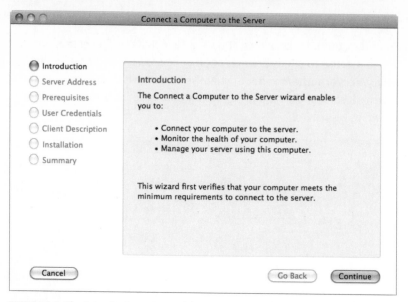

FIGURE 6-9 The Introduction screen of the Connector installation.

5. You must then enter the server name, as shown in Figure 6-10.

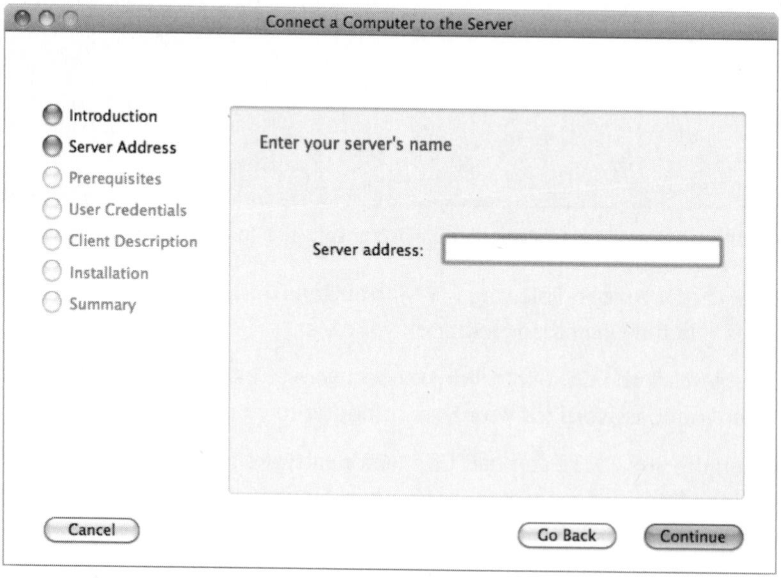

FIGURE 6-10 Entering your server name to connect.

6. Click Continue. After your Mac is checked to ensure that it meets all the requirements for connection to SBS 2011 Essentials, you will be asked to review and modify the identification of the Mac, if required, as shown in Figure 6-11. Change the identification if you want.

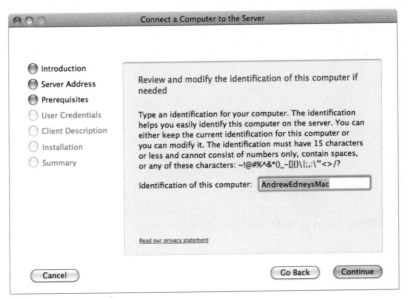

FIGURE 6-11 Reviewing and changing the computer identification details.

> **Note** You should enter a useful description for the computer, such as *AndrewEdneysMac* (especially if you have more than one computer). The current description might be perfectly adequate. The description can be up to 15 characters but cannot use only numbers or include spaces or certain special characters.

7. Click Continue. You will then be asked to enter the network user name and password (which is the user account name and password of the Mac user you created earlier), as shown in Figure 6-12.

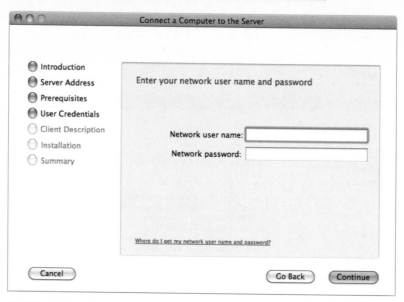

FIGURE 6-12 Entering the network user name and password.

8. Click Continue. You are now given the option to add a computer description to go along with the computer name, as shown in Figure 6-13. Add a description if you want, and click Continue when you are done.

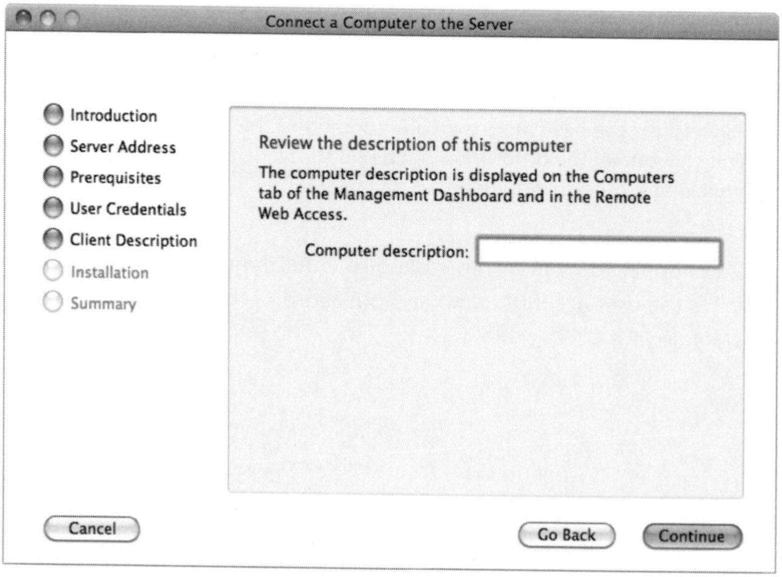

FIGURE 6-13 You can add a computer description if you want.

The installation is complete, as shown in Figure 6-14. By default, the Launchpad will automatically start when the Mac is started. If you don't want that, just clear the Automatically Start Launchpad At Startup? check box before clicking Close.

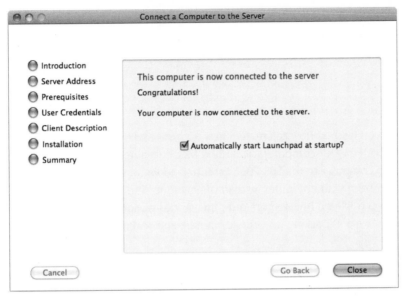

FIGURE 6-14 The Mac computer is now connected to your SBS 2011 Essentials server.

Removing the Connector from a Computer Running Windows

There could be any number of reasons why you would want to remove the SBS 2011 Essentials Connector from a computer. For example, you might no longer want to back up the computer, or you might want to connect it to another SBS 2011 Essentials server, or you might even have used all of your 25 allowed computer connections, so in order to add that 26th computer, you need to remove one that might not be as important as the new one.

You can easily remove the SBS 2011 Essentials Connector from a computer running Windows by following these steps:

1. On the computer running Windows, click the Start button and then click Control Panel.

2. In Control Panel, click Uninstall A Program from the Programs section.

3. In the list of installed programs, scroll down until you find SBS 2011 Essentials Connector. Click it once to highlight it, and then click the Uninstall button at the top of the screen.

4. You will then be asked to confirm that you really want to uninstall the SBS 2011 Essentials Connector. Click Yes, and the software will be removed.

Removing the Connector from a Mac

You can remove the SBS 2011 Essentials Connector from a Mac by following these steps:

1. From the Mac computer, open the Applications folder and locate Launchpad.

2. Drag Launchpad to the Trash.

3. Empty the Trash on your Mac to reclaim the disk space.

Summary

In this chapter, you learned how to create a user account and install the SBS 2011 Essentials Connector on each of your computers, including Mac computers. The installation enables you to join each computer to the SBS 2011 Essentials server and also to control the SBS 2011 Essentials server from your computer instead of having to sit directly at the server. In the next few chapters, you will learn how to configure the various options that are available and how to perform tasks such as backing up your computers and adding disk storage.

Part II
Using Windows Small Business Server 2011 Essentials

Chapter 7
Configuring and Maintaining Storage

Arguably the single most important function that a server provides to the rest of the network is to be a central, secure, managed file storage area. When you centralize file storage on a server, it becomes much easier to ensure the safety, integrity, recoverability, and availability of the core files of your business. Instead of having files spread across the network on individual users' computers, you have them in one place—easier to share among collaborators, easier to back up, easier to recover in the event of a disaster, and easier to secure so that only those people who should have access to a file have that access.

The downside to having all your important files in one location is the potential for a single point of failure. You need to make sure that your files are seriously protected and always available—your business depends on them. This makes it imperative that you carefully manage the underlying disks that support your file storage and that those disks be both redundant and thoroughly backed up.

Storing, securing, backing up, and making available the core files of your business is a bigger topic than we could fit into one chapter, so we've spread it out and organized it according to the various functions involved. But we can't stress this enough: All of the pieces are essential to a safe, secure, and available network. Don't shortchange any of them. We already covered the basics of planning your hardware (Chapter 2, "Planning Hardware") and your network (Chapter 3, "Planning Your Network") to ensure that your hardware and network are designed well from the beginning.

In this chapter, we'll cover the underlying disk management that makes it possible to store your files and protect against loss, corruption, or disaster. Chapter 9, "Backing Up and Restoring," covers the details of how to ensure that your server is protected by backups and how to recover individual files and folders, or entire volumes, in the event of a major failure.

Storage Terminology

Before we talk about disks and storage, it's a good idea to make sure we're using a common vocabulary. We'll break this into two sections: disk and volume terminology, and storage connection terminology.

Disk and Volume Terminology

Disks, drives, volumes, and partitions have a vocabulary all their own. Most of these you probably already know, but it's a good idea to be sure we're clear on specific terms as we'll use them in this book, so let's review some definitions:

- **Physical drive**   The actual hard disk itself, including the case, electronics, platters, and all that stuff. Not terribly important to the disk administrator.

- **Partition**   A portion of the hard disk. In many cases, this is the entire hard disk space, but it needn't be.

- **Master Boot Record (MBR)**   A technique for partitioning a hard disk. This is the default method for Windows Small Business Server 2011 Essentials. MBR-partitioned disks are limited to a maximum of four partitions per disk and a maximum size of 2 terabytes.

- **GUID Partition Table (GPT)**   A technique for partitioning a hard disk that is replacing MBR for larger hard disks and large storage arrays. Microsoft supports GPT-partitioned disks on the SBS 2011 Essentials server for all disks except the boot disk. *GPT disks on Windows clients are not supported for client backup.* GPT disks support 128 partitions and are required for disks (or arrays) larger than 2 terabytes.

- **Allocation unit**   The smallest unit of managed disk space on a hard disk or logical volume. Also called a cluster.

- **Primary partition**   A portion of the hard disk that's been marked as a potentially bootable logical drive by an operating system. SBS 2011 Essentials can support four primary partitions on an MBR hard disk and 128 primary partitions on a GPT hard disk.

- **Extended partition**   A non-bootable portion of the hard disk that can be subdivided into logical drives. There can be only a single extended partition per hard disk, but this partition can be divided into multiple logical drives. Extended partitions are deprecated in SBS 2011 Essentials and can't be directly created from the GUI.

- **Volume** A unit of disk space composed of one or more sections of one or more dynamic disks.

- **Simple volume** The dynamic equivalent of a partition. A portion of a single dynamic disk, a simple volume can be assigned either a single drive letter or no drive letter and can be attached (mounted) on zero or more mount points. In SBS 2011 Essentials, creating a simple volume actually creates a partition.

- **Extended volume** Similar to, and sometimes synonymous with, a spanned volume, an extended volume is any dynamic volume that has been extended to make it larger than its original size. When an extended volume uses portions of more than one physical disk, it is more properly referred to as a *spanned volume*.

- **Logical drive** A section or partition of a hard disk that acts as a single unit. An extended partition can be divided, for example, into multiple logical drives.

- **Logical volume** Another name for a logical drive.

- **Basic disk** A traditional disk drive that is divided into one or more partitions, with a logical drive in each primary partition. Basic disks do not support the more advanced functions of disk management, but they can be converted to dynamic disks in many cases.

- **Dynamic disk** A managed hard disk that can be used to create various volumes.

- **iSCSI (Internet Small Computer Systems Interface)** A protocol for using remote, centralized storage as if it were local. Uses either shared or dedicated TCP/IP networks. Traditionally reserved for storage area networks (SANs) with specialized (and very expensive) hardware, but now readily available with software implementations.

- **iSCSI target** The iSCSI server or provider. A free iSCSI target is available for download at *http://www.microsoft.com/downloads/en /details.aspx?FamilyID=45105d7f-8c6c-4666-a305-c8189062a0d0*.

- **iSCSI initiator** The client or requester for an iSCSI storage device. The iSCSI initiator is built in to SBS 2011 Essentials.

- **LUN (logical unit number)** The "disk" that an iSCSI target presents to an iSCSI initiator. A LUN can be any portion of the available storage on the iSCSI server.

- **RAID (redundant array of independent [formerly "inexpensive"] disks)** The use of multiple hard disks in an array to provide for larger volume size, fault tolerance, and increased performance. RAID comes in different levels, such as RAID 0, RAID 1, and RAID 5. Higher numbers don't necessarily indicate greater performance or fault tolerance, just different methods of doing the job.

- **Spanned volume**   A collection of portions of hard disks combined into a single addressable unit. A spanned volume is formatted like a single drive and can have a drive letter assigned to it, but it will span multiple physical drives. A spanned volume—occasionally referred to as an extended volume—provides no fault tolerance and increases your exposure to failure but does permit you to make more efficient use of the available hard disk space.

- **Striped volume**   Like a spanned volume, a striped volume combines multiple hard disk portions into a single entity. A striped volume uses special formatting to write to each of the portions equally in a stripe to increase performance. A striped volume provides no fault tolerance and increases your exposure to failure, but it is faster than either a spanned volume or a single drive. A stripe set is often referred to as RAID 0, although this is a misnomer because plain striping includes no redundancy.

- **Mirror volume**   A pair of dynamic volumes that contain identical data and appear to the world as a single entity. Disk mirroring can use two drives on the same hard disk controller or use separate controllers, in which case it is sometimes referred to as *duplexing*. In case of failure on the part of either drive, the other hard disk can be split off so that it continues to provide complete access to the data stored on the drive, providing a high degree of fault tolerance. This technique is called RAID 1.

- **RAID 5 volume**   Like a striped volume, this combines portions of multiple hard disks into a single entity with data written across all portions equally. However, it also writes parity information for each stripe onto a different portion, providing the ability to recover in the case of a single drive failure. A RAID 5 volume provides excellent throughput for read operations but is slower than a single disk for write operations. This speed penalty can be substantially offset by using a hardware RAID controller with a dedicated RAID processor and a large cache.

- **SLED (single large expensive disk)**   Now rarely used for servers, this strategy is the opposite of the RAID strategy. Rather than using several inexpensive hard disks and providing fault tolerance through redundancy, you buy the best hard disk you can and bet your entire network on it. If this doesn't sound like a good idea to you, you're right. It's not.

- **JBOD**   Just a bunch of disks. The hardware equivalent of a spanned volume, this has all the failings of any spanning scheme. The failure of any one disk will result in catastrophic data failure.

 Note Additional RAID levels are supported by many hardware manufacturers of RAID controllers. These include RAID 0+1, RAID 10, RAID 6, and RAID 50. For more details on the various RAID levels, see the manufacturer of your RAID controller or go to *http://en.wikipedia.org/wiki /RAID#Standard_levels*.

Storage Connection Technologies

If you're reading this chapter before you buy your server, congratulations on being a thorough person. If not, some of these decisions have already been made, but you might well find that you will have to add storage. If you do, you'll want to focus on storage solutions designed and optimized for servers—a very different set of needs from that of the typical workstation. Your choices are:

- **Integrated device electronics (IDE)**   Strictly a client solution. Inexpensive, but not appropriate on a server. Now being replaced even at the client end by SATA.

- **Serial Advanced Technology Attachment (SATA)**   A newer and faster version of IDE. Still primarily a workstation solution, but acceptable for smaller servers when combined with hardware RAID.

- **External Serial Advanced Technology Attachment (eSATA)**   A variation of SATA used for external, secondary, or backup storage.

- **Small computer system interface (SCSI)**   Perfect for servers and high-end workstations, but significantly more expensive than SATA. Has the ability to have up to 13 drives per SCSI channel. Now being phased out and replaced by SAS.

- **Serially Attached SCSI (SAS)**   Perfect for servers. This is a relatively new technology that is rapidly becoming the mainstream server storage interface. Prices are still more than for SATA.

- **Internet SCSI (iSCSI)**   Covered in the previous section, "Disk and Volume Terminology."

- **FireWire**   Hot-pluggable. Primarily a backup storage device technology, but not common on servers.

- **USB storage devices**   Only appropriate if you use USB 2.0 or USB 3.0. Good for CD and DVD drives. Hot-pluggable. The preferred choice for an SBS 2011 Essentials backup storage device. USB 3.0 is now generally available and provides improved throughput.

- **Fibre Channel**   Great if you have really large amounts of money to spend.

- **Network-attached storage (NAS)**   A good way to provide large amounts of storage that can be flexible to meet your needs. Specify Windows Storage Server–based NAS for the greatest flexibility and compatibility.

- **Storage area networks (SANs)**   Faster and more flexible than the typical NAS, but also much more expensive and difficult to configure. Hardware SANs are generally not for small business networks, but software-based SANs are becoming a viable option.

- **Solid-state disks (SSDs)**   Initially used primarily for notebook computers, these are starting to find their way into servers, especially high-density servers in data centers, where their power savings are a plus. Still too pricy for most SBS networks.

Managing Disks

During the installation of SBS 2011 Essentials, the primary hard disk is partitioned into three partitions (volumes)—a hidden 100 MB partition that is the system volume, a 60 GB partition (drive C) that holds the Windows system files, and a third partition (drive D) that has the remaining available space, as shown in Figure 7-1.

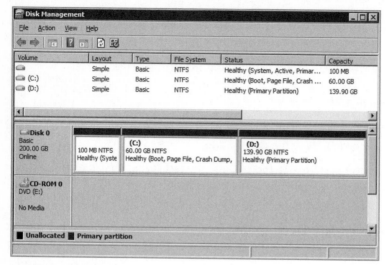

FIGURE 7-1 Windows Small Business Server 2011 Essentials creates three partitions by default.

> **Note** With SBS 2011 Essentials, it's not normally recommended to use the native Disk Management console. You should use the Dashboard whenever possible, but certain operations can only be done from the Disk Management console, such as initializing a completely new disk. In this case, we used Disk Management to clearly show how the initial installation configured our primary disk.

The Windows Small Business Server 2011 Dashboard (hereafter referred to as simply *the Dashboard*) has a slightly different view of your disks, as shown in Figure 7-2. The hidden partition is not visible. Because there is nothing you should be doing with this partition, that's perfectly acceptable and even desirable.

One thing that isn't clear from either view of this disk on our SBS 2011 Essentials server is that it is not a single physical hard disk. It is a pair of disks in a RAID 1 or *mirrored* configuration. If either of the disks in the RAID 1 array fails, it can be removed and replaced with no loss of data or downtime, because it is in a hot-swap disk cabinet.

SBS 2011 Essentials neither knows nor cares that this is a RAID configuration; the entire RAID configuration and mirroring happens at the hardware level, and then the array is presented to the operating system (Windows Server 2008 R2 Standard edition) as a 200 GB disk.

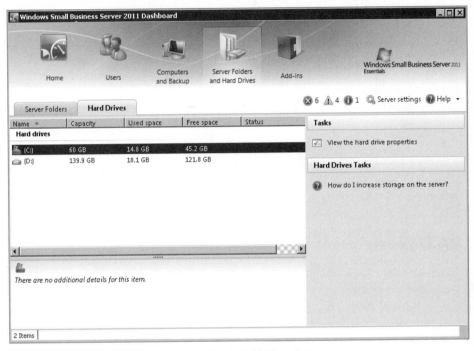

FIGURE 7-2 The Dashboard view of disks after the initial installation.

The Importance of Redundancy

SBS 2011 Essentials doesn't do any duplication or other protection of your business-critical files—that is entirely *your* responsibility, and it's a responsibility that you should take very seriously. If a hard disk fails, you will almost certainly lose at least some data, even if you're fully backed up. (We'll talk about backups in detail in Chapter 9.) You'll certainly lose time and productivity while the failed disk is replaced and the data from your most recent backup is restored. Even though the published mean time to failure (MTTF) of the modern hard disk is quite long (up to 20 years, in many cases), this is deceptive. The MTTF is calculated after taking all of the early failures entirely out of the equation. And as you can see in Figure 7-3, those early failures can be substantial.

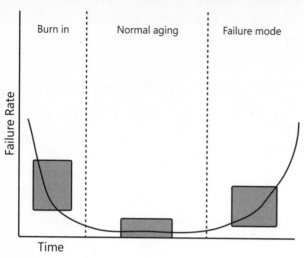

FIGURE 7-3 The typical "bathtub curve" of MTTF for hard disks.

RAID Levels

To prevent data loss in the event of a disk failure, use a version of RAID that will enable redundancy and allow you to repair the RAID array by replacing the failed disk. There are several kinds of RAID array, each with its strengths and weaknesses. There is no perfect RAID type, but all versions of RAID, with the exception of RAID 0, provide some protection against disk failure. The key RAID types for a typical SBS 2011 Essentials network are as follows.

- **RAID 0** Requires a minimum of two identical disks. The disks are striped, and data is written across the stripes. There is *no redundancy,* and the risk of data loss is actually increased compared to a single disk. There is no loss in capacity.

- **RAID 1** Requires pairs of identical disks. Data is written to both disks of a pair simultaneously, ensuring an exact duplicate of the data on each disk. The total size of the RAID 1 array of two 500 GB disks is 500 GB, a 50 percent loss in capacity.

- **RAID 5** Requires a minimum of three identical disks. The disks are striped. Data is written to the stripe, and then the parity of the data is calculated and that parity value is written to the stripe on a different disk. As the disks fill up, parity is distributed evenly across all disks in the array, and in the event of failure, the data on the failed disk can be recalculated based on the parity written on the remaining disks in the array. The total size of a RAID 5 array is one less than the number of disks in the array multiplied by the size of the disks. The amount of lost capacity in a RAID 5 array is at most 33 percent, and will decrease as the number of disks in the array increases.

- **RAID 6**   Requires a minimum of four identical disks. The disks are striped. The data is written to the stripe, and then the parity of the data is written to two different disks. Parity is distributed evenly across all disks, and in the event of failure of a disk, the data from the missing disk is reconstructed from the parity information. Even with the failure of a single disk, redundancy is maintained. A RAID 6 array protects against the failure of two disks. The amount of lost capacity in a RAID 6 array is at most 50 percent, and will decrease as the number of disks in the array increases.

- **RAID 0+1**   Requires a minimum of four identical disks. A RAID 0 array is mirrored onto an identical RAID 0 array. The RAID 0 array provides high throughput and performance, while the RAID 1 mirror provides redundancy. There is a 50 percent loss in capacity.

- **RAID 10**   Requires a minimum of four identical disks. Pairs of disks are mirrored as RAID 1 arrays, and data is distributed across multiple pairs in a RAID 0 striped array. The RAID 1 arrays provide redundancy, and the RAID 0 stripe provides for excellent performance and throughput. There is a 50 percent loss in capacity.

There are several other types of RAID array, but those listed in the previous list are the most likely to be used in a typical small business. RAID types with higher numbers are not necessarily better, just different, and all types of RAID, except for RAID 0, provide redundancy and data protection in the event of disk failure.

RAID 5

The most cost-efficient RAID array is a RAID 5 array. RAID 5 is fast for reading data on the disks, it provides good protection against a single disk failure, and you can increase the size of the array by adding one or more additional disks if your RAID controller supports dynamic array expansion. The downside, however, is that RAID 5 is slower than other types of RAID or even single disks during write operations, because the data and parity information has to be first read from the disk, calculated and compared to the data to be written, and then written to the array.

To improve the overall performance of a RAID 5, increase the number of disks in the array and use a hardware RAID controller that has a dedicated processor to do the parity calculations. Ideally, this RAID controller should also have a substantial cache memory that allows writes to be cached and written more efficiently. However, you should never enable write caching unless your controller is equipped with a battery backup of the cache, to protect against data loss in the event of a power failure.

One concern with RAID 5 is that the failure of a single disk will substantially degrade the performance of the array, and replacing a failed disk will require an additional penalty period while the array is rebuilt.

A second concern is that the failure of a second disk before the first disk has been replaced, or before the array has been rebuilt, will cause permanent data loss. Recovering the data in an array in the event of a RAID controller or motherboard failure requires having a similar RAID controller and computer available on which the array can be read.

We think RAID 5 is a good (but not great) choice for the data volumes on most SBS 2011 Essentials servers. The workload tends to be moderately read intensive, and RAID 5 provides good performance for read operations.

Real World: Hot Swap and Hot Spare

Modern RAID controllers support both *hot swap* of failed disks and *hot spare* disks. Hot swap allows you to remove a failed disk from the server without having to open up the server to remove the disk, or even shut down the server at all. Each OEM has a different arrangement, but all allow you to remove a disk from the array cabinet and replace it with an identical disk without powering down the server at all.

A hot spare disk is a disk, identical to the disks already used in the RAID array, that is mounted in the array cabinet. In the event of a disk failure, the hot spare is automatic-ally configured into the array, and the array is rebuilt to restore redundancy quickly. The failed disk can then be replaced at a more leisurely pace without worrying about lost redundancy in the meantime.

RAID 1

RAID 1 (also called *mirroring*) is an excellent choice for system volumes in an SBS 2011 Essentials server. Each disk in the RAID 1 array has a complete copy of the data, and the fail-ure of a disk does not materially degrade the overall performance of the array. RAID 1 arrays are more expensive than RAID 5 arrays because you must buy more (or larger) disks for the same amount of net space.

RAID 1 arrays do not provide a major performance improvement during reads, but they also don't have a significant performance degradation during write operations. In the event of a failure of one of the disks, all redundancy is gone, but there isn't a significant change in the overall performance. When the failed disk is replaced, there will be a performance degrada-tion during the rebuild process, but this can be managed and moved to less busy hours.

In the event of a motherboard or RAID controller failure, the RAID 1 array can be moved to another server or controller, either as an array or by breaking the array and using one of the disks alone as a single boot disk.

RAID 0+1 and RAID 10

RAID 0+1 and RAID 10 provide excellent performance for both read and write operations and good redundancy against the failure of a single disk. RAID 10 is preferred because it can withstand the failure of more than one disk, as long as the second failed disk isn't the RAID 1 pair of the first failed disk.

RAID 10 arrays provide improved performance of both reads and writes, and don't suffer significant performance penalties when there has been a single disk failure, except during the rebuild process after the disk is replaced.

The big disadvantage to RAID 10 is that a minimum of four identical disks are required, and adding disks requires at least two additional disks. This raises the initial cost of the server, and also the cost to increase the storage capacity of the server at a later date.

We think that RAID 10, or even RAID 0+1, makes an excellent choice for an SBS 2011 Essentials when the budget can afford the additional cost. The resulting improvement in performance is noticeable. RAID 10 is also strongly recommended for virtualized environments, where the load on the I/O subsystem is often substantially higher than for a non-virtualized server.

RAID 6

A reasonably cost-efficient RAID array is a RAID 6 array. RAID 6 is fast for reading data on the disks, it provides good protection against the failure of two disks, and you can increase the size of the array by adding one or more disks if your RAID controller supports dynamic array expansion. The downside, however, is that RAID 6 is slower than other types of RAID or even single disks during write operations, because the data and parity information must be first read from the disk, calculated and compared to the data to be written, and then written twice to the array.

RAID 6 provides dual redundancy, and even after a single disk failure, you have an effective RAID 5 array. Performance while there is a failed disk, however, is degraded, and will continue to be degraded until the disk has been replaced and the array rebuilt.

To improve the overall performance of a RAID 6 array, increase the number of disks in the array and use a hardware RAID controller that has a dedicated processor to do the parity calculations. Ideally, this RAID controller should also have a substantial cache memory (256 MB or larger) that allows writes to be cached and written more efficiently. However, you should never enable write caching unless your controller is equipped with a battery backup of the cache to protect against data loss in the event of a power failure.

We think RAID 6 is an excellent choice for the data volumes on most SBS 2011 Essentials servers. The workload tends to be moderately read-intensive, and RAID 6 has good performance for read operations, plus the extra redundancy of RAID 6 provides protection against the failure of more than one disk.

RAID 0

RAID 0 should not even be called RAID, because the array offers no redundancy. RAID 0 provides excellent performance and throughput for both read and write operations, but it is a bad choice for an SBS 2011 Essentials server because of the lack of redundancy.

RAID 0 actually *increases* your risk of catastrophic data loss. If *any* drive in the array fails, the array is unrecoverable, and any data on the array is lost. The more disks you add to the RAID 0 array, the greater the risk of catastrophic failure.

Real World: Dynamic Disks and Software RAID

Many modern motherboards include a built-in RAID controller. This RAID controller is a limited software and firmware RAID controller that requires operating system drivers. These controllers are not as fast or as efficient as a dedicated hardware RAID controller that has its own custom processor dedicated to managing the I/O and parity calculations of the RAID array.

Another alternative to a dedicated hardware RAID controller is the built-in software RAID that is part of the underlying Windows Server 2008 R2 operating system. This software RAID requires the disks to be reconfigured as dynamic disks, and all RAID management is done at the operating system level and uses the main CPU of the SBS 2011 Essentials server.

As a general rule, both firmware and software RAID solutions do not support hot-swap or hot-spare disks, meaning that any failure of a disk will require you to shut down the server to replace the disk. They also don't have a dedicated, battery-backed cache and so should not have write caching enabled. The overall performance of software and firmware RAID will not be as good as a dedicated hardware RAID card with a large, battery-backed cache.

We aren't big fans of either firmware or software RAID, and that's particularly true of the built-in software RAID that comes with Windows Server. Recovery in the event of a failure is complicated, especially if your boot disk is a dynamic disk. If your hardware budget is very tight, however, and your server includes a firmware RAID controller, we think this is generally a better idea than no RAID at all. But carefully monitor RAM usage, because the drivers for some brands of firmware RAID controllers have exhibited significant memory leaks over time, leading to unexplained server crashes.

Adding Disks

Adding disks (or additional RAID array volumes) is a minor nuisance in SBS 2011 Essentials. A new disk isn't visible in the Dashboard until it has been formatted. This means that you either have to open up the Disk Management console or use the Alert Viewer to format the drive, as shown in Figure 7-4. Somehow, using the Alert Viewer to do this just seems counter-intuitive to us, so we tend to use the Disk Management console.

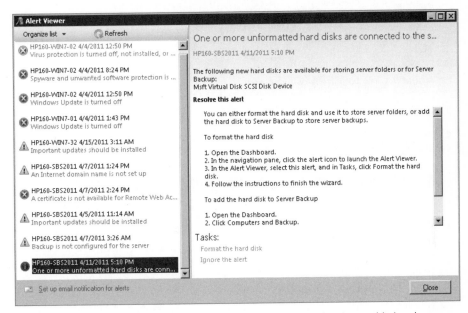

FIGURE 7-4 The Alert Viewer allows you to format a new disk that has been added to the server.

To add the new disk by using the Disk Management console, follow these steps.

1. Open the Disk Management console by typing **diskmgmt.msc** into the Search Programs And Files field on the Start menu.

2. If this is a completely new hard disk that has never been used, you'll see an initialization dialog box, as shown in Figure 7-5.

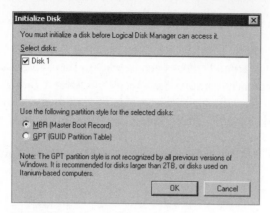

FIGURE 7-5 The Initialize Disk dialog box.

3. Unless the disk is larger than 2 terabytes, select MBR and click OK.

4. In the main Disk Management console, select the new disk and right-click and select New Simple Volume, as shown in Figure 7-6, to open the New Simple Volume Wizard.

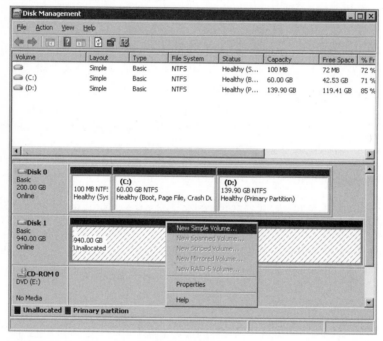

FIGURE 7-6 Creating a new simple disk volume.

5. Click Next to open the Specify Volume Size page of the New Simple Volume Wizard, as shown in Figure 7-7.

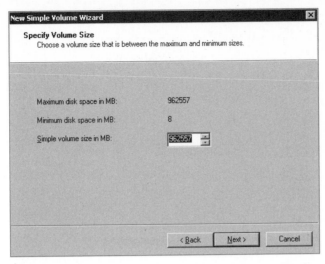

FIGURE 7-7 The Specify Volume Size page of the New Simple Volume Wizard.

6. If the disk is less than 2 terabytes in size, accept the default, which allocates the entire disk for the volume. For disks greater than 2 terabytes in size, you should specify a volume size of less than 2 terabytes to avoid issues with backups. Two terabytes is 2,097,152 MB.

7. Click Next to open the Assign Drive Letter Or Path page. Accept the defaults.

8. Click Next to open the Format Partition page, as shown in Figure 7-8.

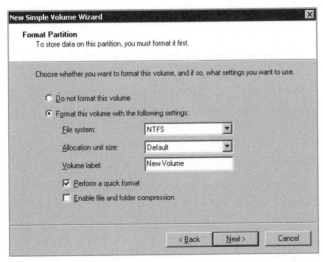

FIGURE 7-8 The Format Partition page of the New Simple Volume Wizard.

9. Enter a volume label that will make it easier to identify the new volume, and accept the rest of the defaults.

10. Click Next and then Finish to create the volume and format it.

11. Close the Disk Management console and return to the Dashboard. The new drive is now visible in the Dashboard, as shown in Figure 7-9.

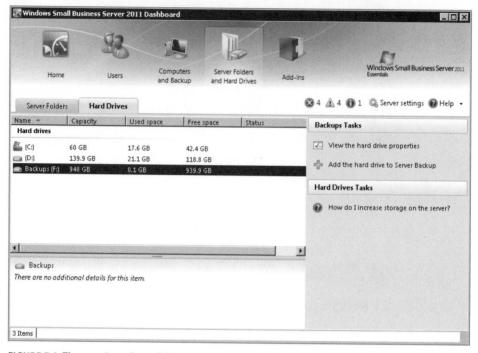

FIGURE 7-9 The new 1-terabyte disk is now visible in the Dashboard.

Additional Tasks with New Disks

After a disk has been added to SBS 2011 Essentials, you can start using it immediately, but there are really two additional tasks that should be completed:

- Add the new disk to Server Backup.
- Enable Volume Shadow Copy (VSS) on the disk.

The first task will let Server Backup know that the disk needs to be backed up, and the second task will allow you to recover previous versions of files directly from the disk without having to restore a backup first.

Adding a Disk to Server Backup

When you configure Server Backup, you can enable backup of all the disks currently recognized by SBS 2011 Essentials. But if you later add disks to the server, they will not automatically be added to Server Backup. To add a new disk to Server Backup, use the following steps:

1. Open the Dashboard if it isn't already open, and navigate to the Server Folders And Hard Drives tab.

2. Click the Hard Drives tab and select the new disk, as shown in Figure 7-10.

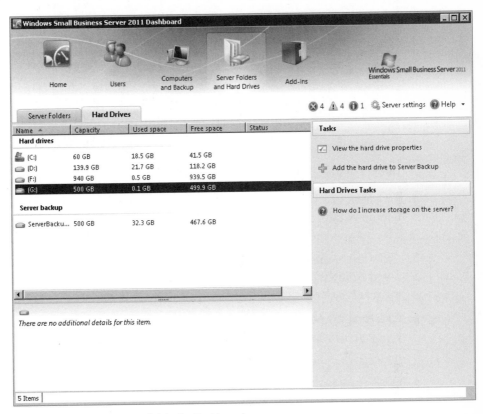

FIGURE 7-10 Select the new disk in the Dashboard.

3. Click Add The Hard Drive To Server Backup in the Tasks pane. This will open the Customize Server Backup Wizard, as shown in Figure 7-11.

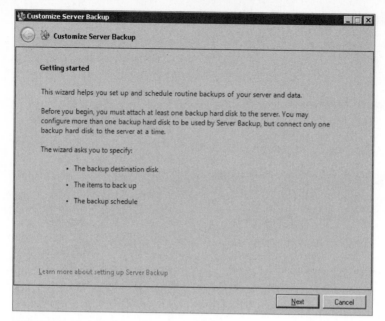

FIGURE 7-11 The Customize Server Backup Wizard.

4. Click Next to open the Select The Backup Destination page of the Customize Server Backup Wizard, as shown in Figure 7-12. If your new disk is shown as a backup destination, but you intend to use it for data and not backups, clear the drive's check box.

5. Click Next to open the Label The Destination Disks page. Your current backup destination disks are shown, each with its current label. You can change these labels or leave them as they are.

6. Click Next to open the Specify The Backup Schedule page. You can make changes to your current schedule here.

7. Click Next to open the Select Which Items To Back Up page, as shown in Figure 7-13.

8. Select the disk or disks you just added. You can select whole disks for backup (preferred) or individual files and folders. The space used for backups reflects the actual data being backed up, not the size of the original volumes.

9. Click Next to open the Confirm The Backup Settings page. If everything looks correct, click Apply Settings and the change is made. Click Close when the wizard completes.

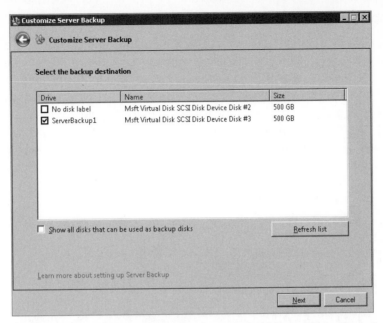

FIGURE 7-12 The Select The Backup Destination page of the Customize Server Backup Wizard.

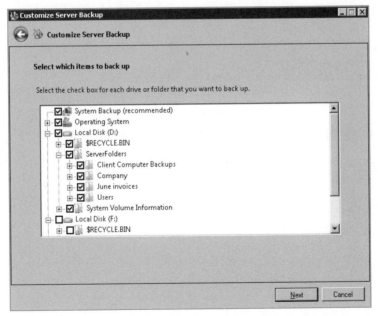

FIGURE 7-13 The Select Which Items To Back Up page of the Customize Server Backup Wizard.

Enabling Shadow Copies

Shadow copies are a feature of Windows Server that allows users to restore previous versions of files they have created on network shares without having to restore from a backup or involve the system administrator. Shadow copies use the Volume Shadow Service (VSS), which is enabled by default on the SBS 2011 Essentials server, to take a snapshot of files stored on the server twice a day, keeping track of changes to those files. When you add a new hard disk to the SBS 2011 Essentials server, it doesn't automatically enable shadow copies on that disk. In most cases, you'll probably want to add this functionality, though you shouldn't enable shadow copies on disks that are used for storing regular backups.

To enable shadow copies for a drive, follow these steps:

1. Open the Dashboard if it isn't already open, and navigate to the Server Folders And Hard Drives tab.

2. Click the Hard Drives tab and select the new disk.

3. Right-click the disk and select View The Hard Drive Properties, as shown in Figure 7-14.

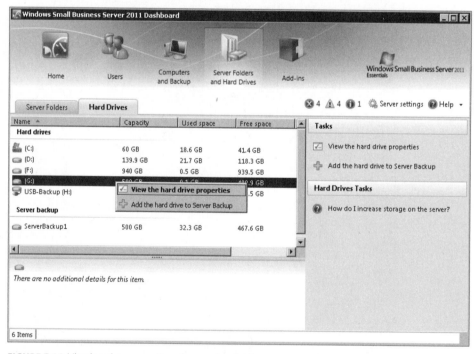

FIGURE 7-14 Viewing the properties of a new hard drive.

4. In the Properties dialog box for the drive, click the Shadow Copies tab and select Enable Shadow Copies, as shown in Figure 7-15.

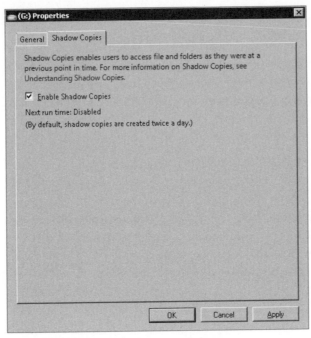

FIGURE 7-15 Enabling shadow copies for drive G.

5. Click OK and the change is made. A shadow copy will be made at the next scheduled snapshot time.

Backup Storage

The final storage topic is where to store your backups. There are several possible options for SBS 2011 Essentials, but the primary supported method is to use a removable hard disk attached to the server.

 Note If you're running SBS 2011 Essentials virtualized, directly attached removable disks aren't an option, so you'll need to use one or more virtual hard disk (VHD) files on the virtualization host server as a backup target. You can use the ability of Hyper-V to dynamically add and remove hard drives from a virtual machine to provide a removable backup target.

The available technologies for removable hard disks that are supported by SBS 2011 Essentials are USB (including USB 3), FireWire, and eSATA. You should plan on your backup target being *at least* equivalent to 1.5 times the total size of the data stored on you server, though we prefer to have at least twice that. The removable hard disk can be a single disk or multiple disks, and you can remove disks for off-site storage.

Of the available disk connection technologies, we prefer USB 3.0 over eSATA, and eSATA over USB 2.0. USB 2.0 is slow enough to be an issue if you have a very large backup. The advantage of eSATA is speed, but there can be issues with SBS 2011 Essentials not recognizing it as removable, depending on the server design. USB 3.0 is as fast or faster than eSATA and provides an excellent backup storage connection technology for SBS 2011 Essentials.

Summary

In this chapter, we covered the basics of storage and storage technologies for Windows Small Business Server 2011 Essentials, including the available RAID technologies and the day-to-day tasks of disk management. In the next chapter, we cover the details of how to use the storage on your server to provide a central network storage repository for critical business assets.

Chapter 8
Managing Shared Folders

On a business network, sharing files is the key to getting work done. However, not everything needs to be shared with everyone, which is why the use of shares is always linked with the use of permissions.

In this chapter, we look at using the Dashboard to create shared server folders on the Windows Small Business Server 2011 Essentials server and to set up access to existing shared folders. We also show you how to move folders from one drive to another.

To store digital data on your server and share it with others, you use a shared server folder. You are probably familiar with the concept of shared folders from other versions of Windows. A folder is created and permissions are assigned to it, indicating the users who have limited access, those who have full access, and those who have no access at all. In previous versions of Windows Small Business Server, setting the permissions on folders could be complicated and time consuming, and you could easily end up giving someone permissions that you didn't want a person to have.

In SBS 2011 Essentials, however, all the complexity and risk have been removed. Now it's easy to create and remove shared folders and add and remove permissions whenever you need to.

Out of the box, there are three default shared folders: Client Computer Backups (where all the backups are stored), Company, and Users. When a new user account is created, a folder for that user is automatically created and added to the Users folder.

Creating a Server Folder

All top-level server folders should be created from the Dashboard. This ensures that the folders are created correctly and with the right permissions. To create a server folder, follow these steps:

1. On the Dashboard, click the Server Folders And Hard Drives tab, as shown in Figure 8-1. This shows all of the top-level shared server folders.

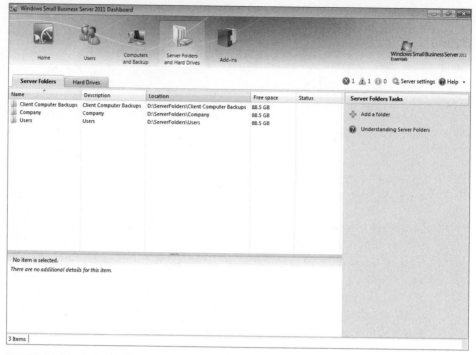

FIGURE 8-1 The Server Folders And Hard Drives tab on the Dashboard.

2. Click Add A Folder in the Server Folders Tasks list. The Add A Folder Wizard opens, as shown in Figure 8-2.

3. Enter a name and description for the new folder. You can also change the location of the shared folder if you don't want it to be in the default location. Then click Next to continue.

> **Note** A folder description is optional, but it makes sense to add one so that you can easily see what the contents might be. For example, if you wanted to have several folders of project documents, you could call the folders *Project1*, *Project2*, and so on, but in the description you could put something like *Project Delta*, *Project Gamma*, and similar.

4. Select the level of access (permissions) for each of the listed user accounts from the drop-down lists shown in Figure 8-3. The access levels are Read/Write, Read, and No Access. When you are done, click Add Folder.

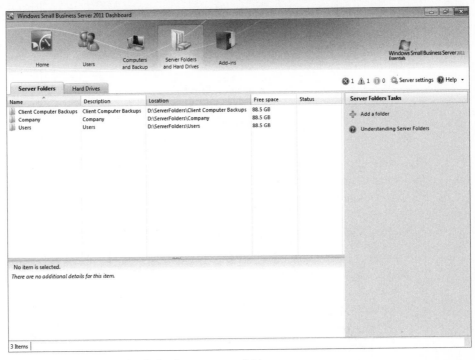

FIGURE 8-2 Entering the details for the new server folder.

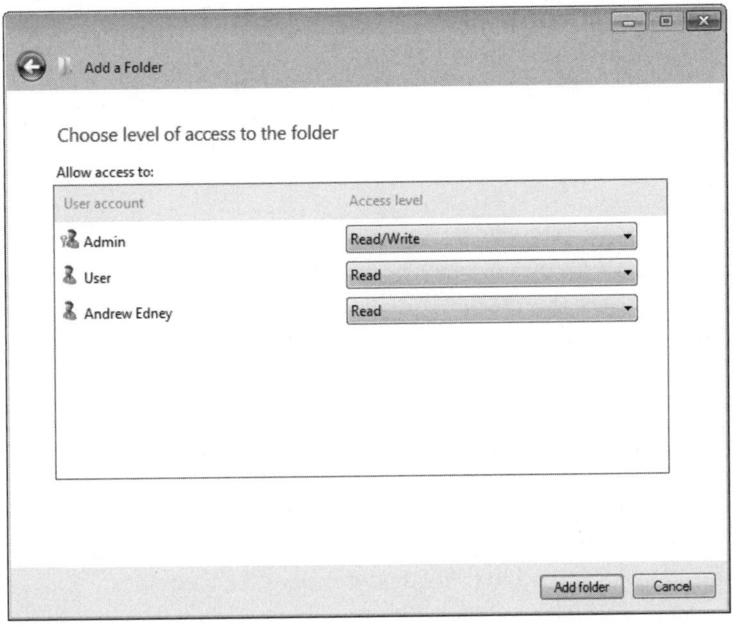

FIGURE 8-3 Selecting the access level for each user on the new server folder.

Folder Properties

The Server Folders view on the Dashboard doesn't display the size of any of the shared folders. However, it is very easy to find that information:

1. Click the Server Folders And Hard Drives tab.

2. Click the server folder you want to know more about.

3. Click View The Folder Properties on the tasks list.

The folder information is then displayed, as you can see in Figure 8-4. Here you can see the folder name, its description, and the folder size, along with a clickable link that allows you to open the folder from here.

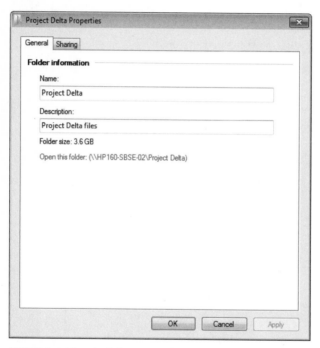

FIGURE 8-4 View the information of a server folder.

Adding Users to an Existing Server Folder

If you want to grant users access to an existing server folder, you can either view the properties of the specific user account and make your changes there, or you can add or remove multiple users on the Sharing tab of the folder properties dialog box:

1. In the folder properties dialog box, click the Sharing tab.

2. Choose the access level for each available user from the drop-down lists, as shown in Figure 8-5. When you are done, click OK.

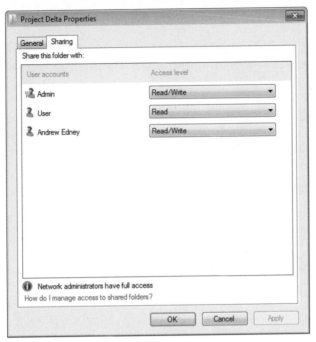

FIGURE 8-5 Changing the access levels for users on a server folder.

Real World: What Do Permissions Mean?

When you set up a folder to be shared, users can be assigned one of three levels of permissions:

- **Read** This level of permissions allows a user to see all items in the folder but not change any of them.

- **Read/Write** This allows users to read all of the files in the folder and change any of them.

- **No Access** Users who have been assigned this permissions level can see the folder but not any of the files inside it.

These settings are adequate for most uses, but if you need a more granular approach, you can use Group Policy settings, as described in Appendix B.

Moving a Shared Folder

Sometimes you need to move a shared folder, perhaps because the drive is running low on disk space.

> **Important** Make sure that no users are working on files within the folder that's being moved. Work can be lost.

To move a shared folder:

1. Open the Dashboard. Click the Server Folders And Hard Drives tab, and then click the folder you want to move.

2. Click Move The Folder in the Tasks list, and then click Next on the Getting Started page.

3. Choose a new location for the folder by clicking a drive in the New Location list, as shown in Figure 8-6.

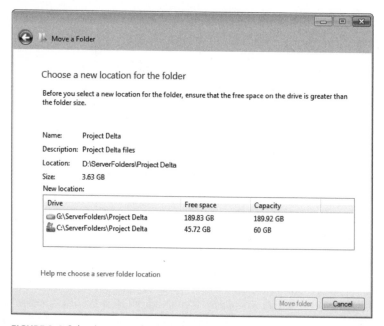

FIGURE 8-6 Selecting a new location for a server folder.

4. Click Move Folder, and then click Close.

> **Note** Move folders to internal hard drives only. A USB-connected hard drive can easily become disconnected, and then the folders stored on those drives will be inaccessible.

Unsharing a Folder

Sometimes it might be necessary to unshare a folder. This could be for any number of reasons—for example, the reason for sharing the folder might have passed (because the project has been completed).

> **Note** Make sure that no users are working on files within the folder that's being unshared. Work can be lost.

To unshare a folder:

1. On the Server Folders And Hard Drives tab on the Dashboard, right-click the folder you want to unshare.

2. In the Tasks list, click Stop Sharing The Folder. A confirmation dialog box appears, as shown in Figure 8-7.

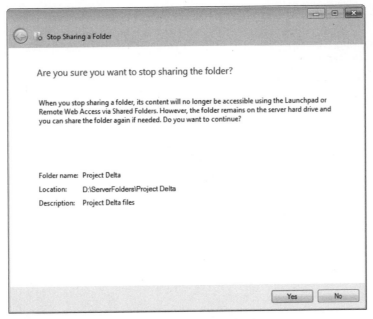

FIGURE 8-7 Confirming that you want to stop sharing a folder.

3. Confirm that you want to stop sharing the folder by clicking Yes.

4. Click Close.

The contents of the server folder are not deleted, so you can re-enable sharing at any time, or if you want to delete the folder completely you can do so. This will save you some disk space and keep things tidy.

Accessing a Server Folder

Accessing a server folder can be done in several different ways. Users can start the Launchpad and click Shared Folders, as shown in Figure 8-8. This is by far the easiest way for users to access a server folder, because the Launchpad is available to them on their computers.

FIGURE 8-8 The Shared Folders option on the Launchpad.

Users can also use Remote Web Access (RWA) if they are away from the office. For more information on RWA, see Chapter 14, "Managing Remote Access."

When the user clicks the Shared Folders option on the Launchpad, the available shared server folders are displayed, as shown in Figure 8-9. Users can access a folder by double-clicking it.

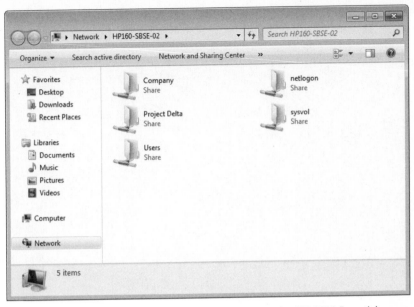

FIGURE 8-9 Viewing the available shared server folders on the SBS 2011 Essentials server.

Note Users can view every shared server folder but can open only those which they have permission to access.

Summary

In this chapter, you learned about shared server folders: how to create them, how to apply permissions, and also how to move and unshare them if you need to. In the next chapter, we discuss backing up and restoring computers.

Chapter 9
Backing Up and Restoring

Backup is one of those chores that everyone knows is necessary but that everyone hates to deal with. The backup function in Windows Small Business Server 2011 Essentials provides a simple interface for scheduling and configuring your backups.

Backing Up Client Computers

SBS 2011 Essentials automatically schedules daily backups for client computers. These backups can be modified to suit your organization.

The following events happen during the daily backups:

- Network computers are backed up one after another.
- A backup that is in progress finishes even if the end of the backup time has passed.
- Windows updates are installed and SBS 2011 Essentials restarts, if necessary.
- On Sundays, Backup Cleanup runs, deleting old backups that you have manually marked for deletion.

Changing the Backup Schedule

By default, computers on the network are backed up every day between 6:00 P.M. (18:00) and 9:00 A.M. (09:00). To change the backup schedule, open the Dashboard and follow these steps:

1. Select Computers And Backup.
2. In the Computers And Backup Tasks pane, click Additional Client Computer Backup Tasks to open the dialog box shown in Figure 9-1.

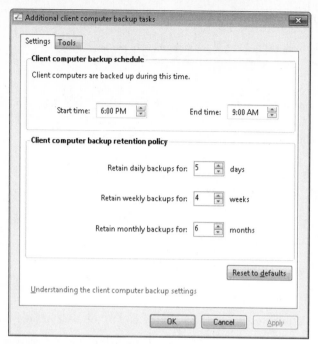

FIGURE 9-1 Configuring the backup schedule.

3. Click the Settings tab.

4. Change the settings. Click OK when you're finished.

Table 9-1 details the settings and what they mean.

TABLE 9-1 Backup Settings

Backup Setting	Default Setting	Description
Start Time	6:00 P.M. (18:00)	The time the daily backup starts. Set this to a time when computers are not in use.
End Time	9:00 A.M. (09:00)	The time when the backup must be finished.
Retain Daily Backups	5 days	The number of days that backups are retained.
Retain Weekly Backups	4 weeks	The number of weeks that the last backup of the week is retained.
Retain Monthly Backups	6 months	The number of months that the last backup of the month is retained.

Starting a Manual Backup

To perform a manual backup on a client computer, open the Dashboard and follow these steps:

1. Select Computers And Backup. Right-click the computer you want to manually back up, and select Start A Backup For The Computer from the shortcut menu.
2. In the Backup Description dialog box, provide a description for the backup, as shown in Figure 9-2.

Backup Description for HP160-WIN7-02
Type a description for this backup
Manual backup 4-24-2011
OK
Cancel

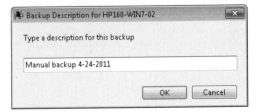

FIGURE 9-2 Providing a backup description.

3. Click OK.

The backup will start and you can view its progress on the Dashboard, as shown in Figure 9-3.

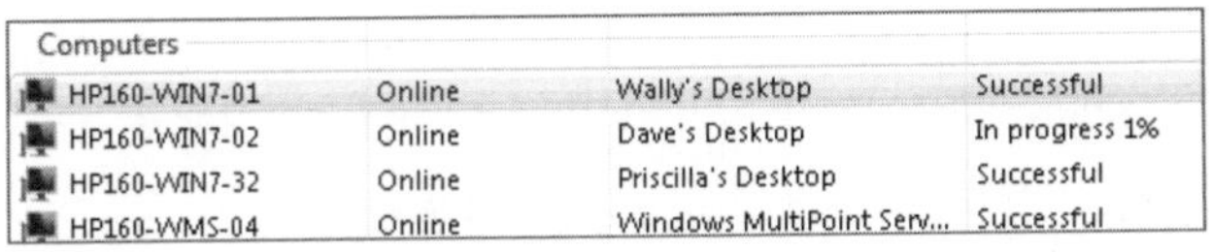

Computers
HP160-WIN7-01 Online Wally's Desktop Successful
HP160-WIN7-02 Online Dave's Desktop In progress 1%
HP160-WIN7-32 Online Priscilla's Desktop Successful
HP160-WMS-04 Online Windows MultiPoint Serv... Successful

FIGURE 9-3 The Dashboard tracks the manual backup's progress.

Modifying Backup Content

In SBS 2011 Essentials, the default backup setting is to back up the System Reserved partition and the content of hard drives. To modify these settings, open the Dashboard and follow these steps:

1. Highlight the computer to be modified, and select Customize Backup For The Computer from the shortcut menu, as shown in Figure 9-4.

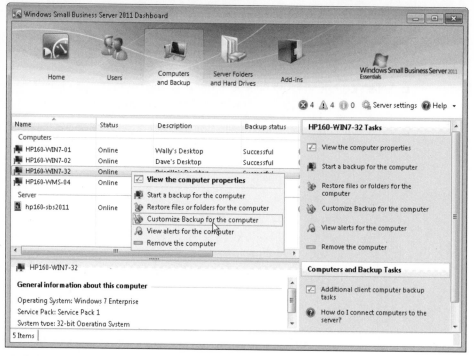

FIGURE 9-4 Customizing a backup.

2. In the Customize Backup dialog box, click Add Or Remove Backup Items.

3. In the list of checked items, click the plus sign to expand the list.

4. Clear the check boxes for any items you don't want to include in the backup. Click Next.

5. In the Confirm Items To Back Up dialog box, review the list and then click Save Changes.

Reviewing Backups

To check on backups, open the Dashboard and follow these steps:

1. Select Computers And Backup, and then highlight the computer whose backup status you want to review.

2. Right-click the computer and select View The Computer Properties from the shortcut menu.

3. Double-click one of the backups in the list to see the backup details (see Figure 9-5).

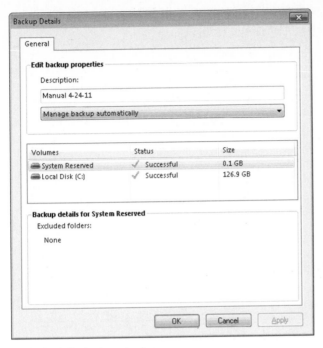

FIGURE 9-5 Reviewing a backup.

4. By default, all backups are managed automatically. Use the drop-down list in the top section of this dialog box to change the setting to Delete This Backup When Cleanup Runs or to Keep This Backup Permanently.

5. Click OK when you're finished.

Restoring Client Backups

Backups are all well and good but useless if they can't restore files. So it's imperative not only that backups be performed religiously but also that they be tested periodically to make sure that computers can be restored in the event of a disaster, large or small.

To restore files to a client computer, you need to log on to the client by using an administrative account. After you have done so, click the Dashboard on the Launchpad and follow these steps:

1. Select Computers And Backup. Right-click a computer and select Restore Files And Folders For The Computer from the shortcut menu.

2. The Choose A Backup window opens, showing all the available backups for the computer, as shown in Figure 9-6. Double-click the backup to be restored.

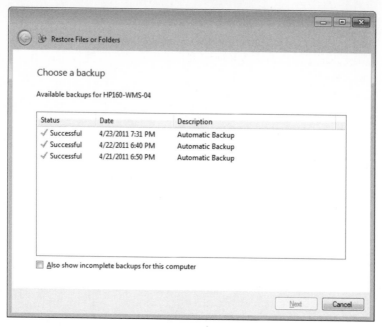

FIGURE 9-6 Selecting the backup to be restored.

3. The volume is opened. Press the Ctrl and Shift keys to select the items to be restored (see Figure 9-7), and then click Next.

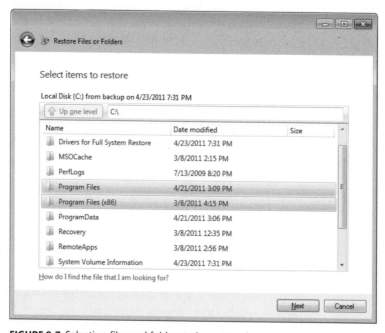

FIGURE 9-7 Selecting files and folders to be restored.

4. Select a restore location for the file, and click Next. The wizard will copy the files to the computer.

When the operation is complete, a screen like the one in Figure 9-8 appears, showing that the restore operation was successful and displaying the location of the restored data.

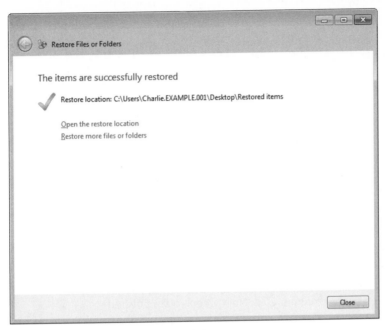

FIGURE 9-8 Message showing a successful restore.

Backing Up the Server

Server backups require a bit more configuration than client computer backups but are nevertheless quite straightforward. To configure the server backup, open the Dashboard and then follow these steps:

1. Select Computers And Backup. Right-click the server and select Configure Backup For The Server from the shortcut menu.

2. Read the information in the Getting Started window, and then click Next.

3. In Configuration Options, select Change Server Backup Settings.

4. Select the backup destination, and then click Next.

5. Enter a label description for the backup disk. Click Next.

6. On the Specify The Backup Schedule page (shown in Figure 9-9), accept the default settings or provide your own backup times. Click Next.

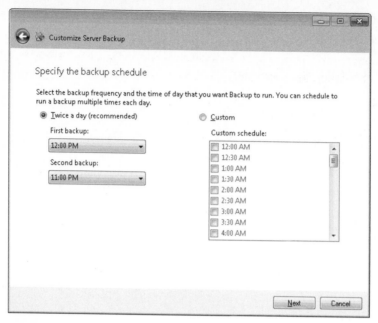

FIGURE 9-9 Specifying a server backup schedule.

7. On the Select Which Items To Back Up page (shown in Figure 9-10), you can accept the default, which is to back up everything, or you can exclude some items by clearing the check boxes by their names. Click Next when you're finished.

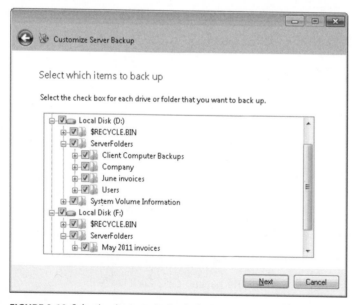

FIGURE 9-10 Selecting items to be backed up.

8. The next page asks you to confirm the settings. If they're correct, click Apply Settings. To change any of the settings, use the Back arrow to return to prior pages.

 Note Repeat these steps when you need to change the schedule, the backup destination, or the files and folders to back up.

Reviewing Server Backups

To check the details of server backups, open the Dashboard, select Computers And Backup, and then double-click the server to open the Properties dialog box. Double-click a listed backup to see the details (as shown in Figure 9-11).

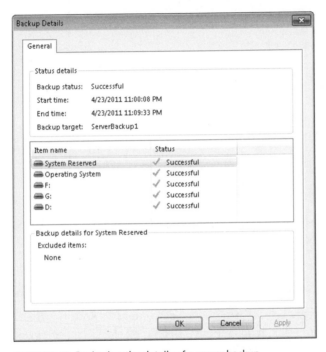

FIGURE 9-11 Reviewing the details of a server backup.

Restoring Server Backups

The ability to restore backups is essential when disaster strikes. So in addition to regular backups, you should have a regular schedule of checking the backups to make sure that they can be used for restoration.

To restore files or folders to the server, open the Dashboard, select Computers And Backup, and then follow these steps:

1. Select the server, and then click Restore Files Or Folders For The Server. The Restore Files Or Folders Wizard starts, as shown in Figure 9-12. Click Next.

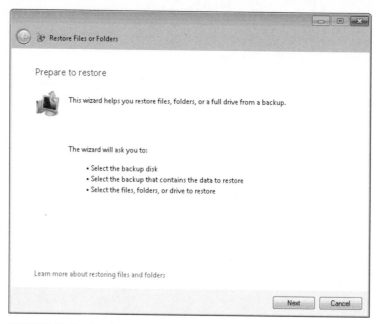

FIGURE 9-12 Starting the Restore Files Or Folders Wizard.

2. Specify the backup location. Click Next. If the location is other than the local server, you're asked to provide the location information. Click Next.

3. Choose the backup you want to restore. Click Next.

4. Select whether to restore individual files and folders or an entire disk. Click Next.

5. To restore individual items, select them on the Select Items To Restore page (see Figure 9-13). To restore an entire disk, highlight the disk on the Select The Server Drive To Restore page (see Figure 9-14). Click Next.

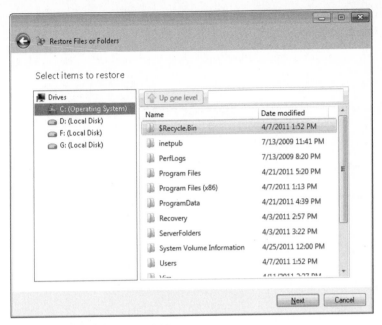

FIGURE 9-13 Selecting files or folders to restore.

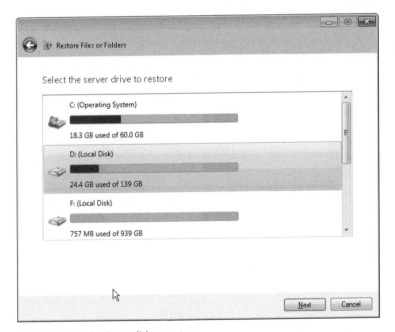

FIGURE 9-14 Selecting a disk to restore.

6. Choose where you want the files to be restored and what to do with existing files in that location. Click Next.

7. Confirm the restore information (see Figure 9-15) and click Restore Now.

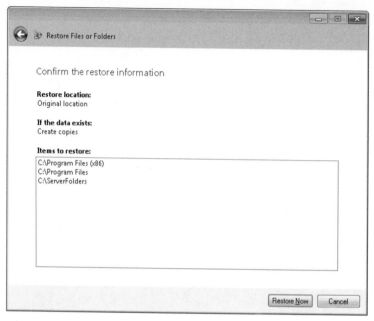

FIGURE 9-15 Confirming the restore selection.

Repairing Backups

If SBS 2011 Essentials detects a problem in your backup database, an alert will appear in the Dashboard. Right-click the computer with the alert and select View Alerts For This Computer. If the alert reports that the database of backups is corrupted, you can try to repair the database by using the Repair The Backup Database Wizard.

> **Note** Repairing the database might take several hours, depending on its size.

> **Important** Before starting the wizard, make sure that all the external hard drives used on your server are connected, turned on, and working properly.

To run the wizard, open the Dashboard, select Computers And Backup, and then follow these steps:

1. In the Computers And Backup Tasks pane, select Additional Client Computer Backup Tasks.

2. Select the Tools tab, and then click the Repair button. Carefully read all the information on the Prepare To Repair The Backup Database page. When you're ready to proceed, select the check box signifying that you understand what you've read, and click Next.

   The wizard analyzes your database and attempts to correct any errors found.

Depending on the kind of errors found, the wizard might not be able to repair some of the backups.

Using a USB Key for Restoring Backups

SBS 2011 Essentials makes it easy to create a bootable USB key from which an entire computer can be restored using an existing backup. To run the wizard, open the Dashboard, select Computers And Backup, and then follow these steps:

1. In the Computers And Backup Tasks pane, select Additional Client Computer Backup Tasks.

2. In the Computer Recovery area, click Create Key.

3. You're prompted to insert a USB key into the server. Do so and then click Next.

4. Select the USB drive to use. Select the check box to acknowledge your understanding that the USB drive will be formatted and all existing files on it deleted. Click Next.

5. The USB key will be formatted and made ready for a backup.

SBS 2011 Essentials automatically adds the necessary drivers to the USB key.

Running Windows Server Backup by Using Native Tools

The alternative to using the Customize Backup For The Server option in the Dashboard is to run the native Windows Server Backup console, shown in Figure 9-16. If you configure your SBS 2011 Essentials server's backup by using the Windows Server Backup console, you will have additional configuration choices while still fully protecting the server. To open the Windows Server Backup console, select Administrative Tools from the Start menu and then select Windows Server Backup.

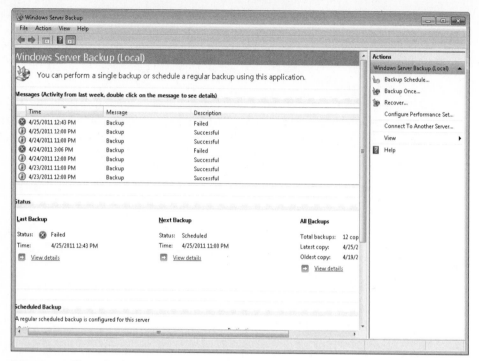

FIGURE 9-16 The native Windows Server Backup console.

Creating a Backup Schedule with Windows Server Backup

The native tools equivalent of the SBS 2011 Essentials Customize Backup Wizard is the Backup Schedule Wizard, which is launched by selecting the Backup Schedule task on the Actions menu in the Windows Server Backup console. This wizard configures the backup type, file selection, backup destination, and backup frequency.

To create a new backup schedule that backs up the entire server, open the Windows Server Backup application and then follow these steps:

1. Select Backup Schedule from the Actions menu to open the Backup Schedule Wizard, shown in Figure 9-17.

2. Click Next to continue to the Select Backup Configuration page of the Backup Schedule Wizard, as shown in Figure 9-18. Select Full Server (Recommended).

3. Click Next to continue to the Specify Backup Time page. The default is twice a day, but you can choose to have backups occur more frequently.

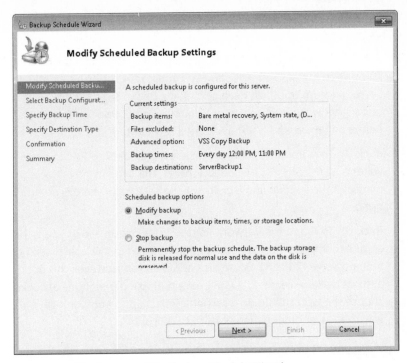

FIGURE 9-17 The first page of the Backup Schedule Wizard.

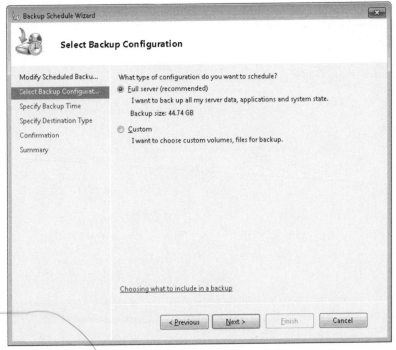

FIGURE 9-18 The Select Backup Configuration page of the Backup Schedule Wizard.

4. Click Next to continue to the Specify Destination Type page, shown in Figure 9-19. The choices are:

❑ **Back Up To A Hard Disk That Is Dedicated For Backups (Recommended)** This option is essentially the same as running the SBS 2011 Essentials Configure Server Backup. You must have a separate, dedicated hard disk, preferably external, that will only be used for Windows Server Backup. The disk is formatted before initial use and is not assigned a drive letter.

❑ **Back Up To A Volume** This option allows the backup files to share an existing volume on the SBS 2011 Essentials server. This significantly affects the performance of the volume and should only be selected if there is no other viable option.

❑ **Back Up To A Shared Network Folder** This option allows you to back up to another computer on the network that has shared disk space, such as a Windows Storage Server 2008 R2 Essentials (WSSE) server. However, this option only keeps a single backup file, so you won't have multiple generations of backups. If you choose this, you should do a secondary backup to another location to provide a way to recover older generations of backups.

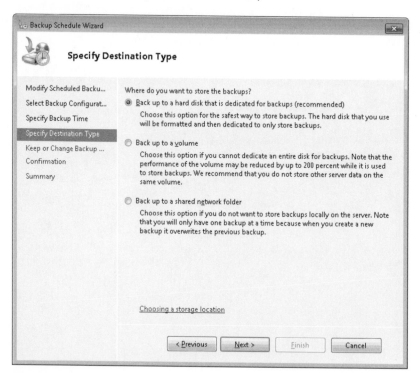

FIGURE 9-19 The Specify Destination Type page of the Backup Schedule Wizard.

5. Specify the destination type and then click Next to continue to the Select Destination Disk, Select Destination Volume, or Specify Remote Shared Folder page. The options on this page will vary slightly depending on which type you choose. For this example, we'll use Back Up To A Hard Disk That Is Dedicated For Backups (Recommended).

6. Click Next to keep or change the backup destination.

7. Click Next to view the confirmation page, and then click Finish.

8. The backup is configured. Click Close to exit the wizard.

Using the Wbadmin Command

If you're accustomed to using the command line, you can forego the GUI to back up and restore volumes and files by using *Wbadmin*. This section lists *Wbadmin* commands and their syntax. Table 9-2 lists and describes the parameters used with *Wbadmin*. For additional assistance, type **Wbadmin /?** at a command prompt.

> **Note** Not all the *Wbadmin* commands are visible from the command line. Certain commands are available only from the Windows Recovery Environment or are hidden but available for use. For the complete Command Reference, go to *http://go.microsoft.com/FWLink/?Linkid=93131*.

TABLE 9-2 *Wbadmin* **Parameters**

Parameter	Description
-addtarget	Storage location for backup. Disk is formatted before use and any existing data on it is permanently erased.
-allCritical	Automatically includes all critical volumes (volumes that contain system state data). Can be used along with the -include option.
-backupTarget	Storage location for this backup. Requires a hard disk drive letter (F:) or a Universal Naming Convention (UNC) path to a shared network folder (\\servername\sharename). If a shared network folder is specified, this backup will overwrite any existing backup in that location.
-excludeDisks	Can be used only with the -recreateDisks parameter. Must be input as a comma-delimited list of disk identifiers (as listed in the output of wbadmin get disks). Excluded disks are not partitioned or formatted. This parameter helps preserve data on disks that you do not want modified during the recovery.
-include	Comma-delimited list of volume drive letters, volume mount points, or GUID-based volume names to include in the backup.
-noInheritAcl	If specified, the computer-name folder applies access control lists (ACLs) for the user whose credentials were given when running the backup. To access the backup later, you must use these credentials or be a member of the Administrators group or the Backup Operators group on the computer with the shared folder. If -noInheritAcl is not used, the ACL permissions from the remote shared folder are applied to the <ComputerBackedUp> folder by default so that anyone with access to the remote shared folder can access the backup.

Parameter	Description
-items	Comma-delimited list of volumes, applications, and files to recover.
	If -itemtype is Volume, it can be only a single volume that is specified by providing the volume drive letter, volume mount point, or GUID-based volume name.
	If -itemtype is App, it can be only a single application. Applications that can be recovered include Microsoft SQL Server and Windows SharePoint Services. You can also use the value ADExtended to recover an installation of Active Directory.
	If -itemtype is File, it can be files or directories, but it should be part of the same volume and it should be under the same parent.
-itemtype	Type of items to recover. Must be Volume, App, or File.
-machine	Specifies the name of the computer for which you want to recover the backup. Should be used when -backupTarget is specified.
-notrestoreacl	Can be used only when recovering files. Specifies to not restore the security ACLs of the files being recovered from backup.
	By default, the security ACLs are restored (the default value is true). If this parameter is used, the default ACLs for the location to which the files are being restored are applied.
-noVerify	If specified, backups written to removable media (such as a DVD) are not verified for errors. If not specified, backups written to such media are verified for errors.
-overwrite	Valid only when recovering files. Specifies the action to take when a file that is being recovered already exists in the same location.
	Overwrite causes the recovery to overwrite the existing file with the file from the backup.
	CreateCopy causes the recovery to create a copy of the existing file so that the existing file is not modified.
	Skip causes the recovery to skip the existing file and continue with recovery of the next file.
-password	Password for the user name that is specified by the parameter -user.
-recoveryTarget	Specifies the drive to restore to. Use if this drive is different than the one that was previously backed up. Can also be used for restorations of volumes, files, or applications. If you are restoring a volume, you can specify the volume drive letter of the alternate volume. If you are restoring a file or application, you can specify an alternate backup path.
-recreateDisks	Restores a disk configuration to the state that existed when the backup was created.
-recursive	Can be used only when recovering files. Recovers the files in the folders and all files subordinate to the specified folders. By default, only files that reside directly under the specified folders are recovered.
-removetarget	Storage location specified in the existing backup schedule.

Parameter	Description
-restoreAll-Volumes	Restores all volumes from the selected backup. If this parameter is not specified, only critical volumes (volumes that contain system state data) are restored from the selected backup. Useful when you need to restore non-critical volumes during system recovery.
-schedule	Comma-delimited times of day specified as HH:MM.
-showsummary	Can be used only with *Wbadmin start systemstaterecovery*. Reports the summary of the last run of this command. This parameter cannot be accompanied by any other parameters.
-skipBad-ClusterCheck	Can be used only when recovering volumes. This skips the checking of your recovery destination disks for bad cluster information. If you are restoring to an alternate server or hardware, this switch should not be used. You can manually run the command *chkdsk /b* on your recovery disks at any time to check them for bad clusters, and then update the file system information accordingly.
-user	Specifies the name of the user with write access to the backup destination (if it is a shared network folder). The user needs to be a member of the Administrators or Backup Operators group on the computer.
-quiet	Runs the command with no prompts to the user.
-version	Specifies the version of the backup in MM/DD/YYYY-HH:MM format, as listed by *Wbadmin get versions*.
-vssFull	If specified, performs a full backup using Volume Shadow Copy Service (VSS). Each file's history is updated to reflect that it was backed up. If this parameter is not specified, *Start Backup* makes a copy backup, but the history of files being backed up is not updated. Important: Do not use this parameter when using a non-Microsoft program to back up applications.

The following sections show a few examples of *Wbadmin* for specific uses.

Wbadmin enable backup

The following subcommand enables or configures a scheduled daily backup.

```
Wbadmin enable backup
[-addtarget:{backuptargetdisk | backuptargetnetworkshare}]
[-removetarget:{backuptargetdisk | backuptargetnetworkshare}]
[-schedule:timetorunbackup]
[-include:volumestoinclude]
[-allcritical]
[-user:username]
[-password:password]
[-inheritacl:inheritacl]
[-quiet]
```

Wbadmin start backup

The following subcommand runs a backup job.

```
wbadmin start backup
[-backupTarget:{TargetVolume | TargetNetworkShare}]
[-include:VolumesToInclude]
[-allCritical]
[-vssFull]
[-noVerify]
[-user:UserName]
[-password:Password]
[-noinheritAcl]
 [-quiet]
```

Wbadmin disable backup

The following subcommand disables scheduled daily backups.

```
wbadmin disable backup
[-quiet]
```

Summary

Because backups are so essential to the running of a network, we've covered several different ways to go about getting and restoring backups. In the next chapter, we move on to monitoring the health of your network.

Part III
Enhancing, Optimizing, and Maintaining Windows Small Business Server 2011 Essentials

Chapter 10
Monitoring Network Health

In this chapter, we take a look at network health reporting and alerting within Windows Small Business Server 2011 Essentials and how to use Performance Monitor to detect and resolve problems.

Health reporting is a key feature for proactive IT management. With health monitoring, you can identify potential issues on the network and correct them before they become an issue and before your business suffers any downtime. SBS 2011 Essentials assesses not only the health of the server but also the health of the clients on the network.

Health alerts are visible from within the Dashboard, as well as from the Launchpad on the client computers. You can ignore, sort, and in some cases attempt to repair the error condition. Additionally, you can have notifications delivered via email on a recurring schedule.

Viewing Alerts from the Dashboard

The Dashboard displays alerts and notifications so that you can always see the latest health status of the network.

As you can see in Figure 10-1, there are three different icons: Critical, Warning, and Information.

FIGURE 10-1 Health monitoring within the SBS 2011 Essentials Dashboard.

To view more information about an alert, just click any of the icons to open the Alert Viewer, as shown in Figure 10-2.

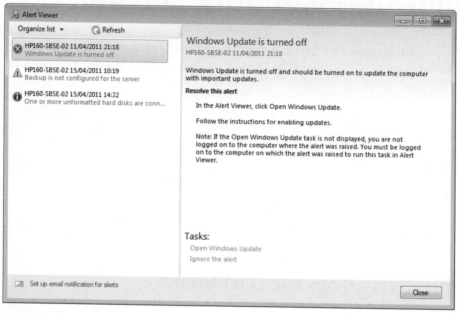

FIGURE 10-2 Accessing the Alert Viewer.

Each alert is shown in the left pane and, when you click an alert, additional information is displayed in the right pane.

This additional information is extremely useful, because it provides specifics about the issue and suggestions for resolving the problem. In versions prior to Windows Vista and Windows Server 2008, only an error code and usually just a generic error message were displayed. This meant spending precious time and resources to troubleshoot the problem, often just trying to figure out what the problem was, before finding and implementing a solution.

The Alert Viewer also displays tasks at the bottom of the right pane to assist you in resolving whatever issue has occurred. In the example in Figure 10-2, you can click the Open Windows Update task and then enable Windows Update, which would resolve the issue and remove it from the Alert Viewer.

Some of the alerts are purely informational and are automatically removed after 24 hours, such as the alert that notifies you that your server has unexpectedly restarted.

If there are a large number of alerts displayed, you can filter the alerts by computer (if you want to only see alerts for a specific computer or for the server itself) and also by alert type (for example, if you are only concerned with Critical alerts at this time). This filtering is controlled by the Organize List drop-down list within the Alert Viewer.

Ignoring Alerts

There might be a reason for ignoring an alert. In our example, you might not want to enable Windows Update, in which case you probably don't want to be constantly reminded that it is switched off.

To ignore the alert, just click the Ignore The Alert task and click Yes when prompted, as shown in Figure 10-3.

Important Think carefully before choosing to ignore the alert—you could potentially miss something very important.

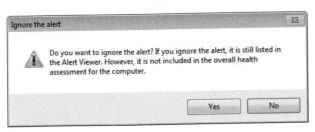

FIGURE 10-3 Choosing to ignore an alert.

If you decide at a later time that you do want the issue to be monitored as part of the overall health assessment, simply select the ignored alert and click Enable The Alert in the Tasks list.

Configuring Email Notifications

To make sure that alerts get attention more quickly, you can configure email alerts and have any notifications automatically sent to any email account.

1. Click the Set Up Email Notification For Alerts link at the bottom of the Complete These Tasks list, and then click Enable to open the page shown in Figure 10-4.

FIGURE 10-4 Configuring email for alerts.

2. Fill in the fields using the information provided by your mail service, and then click OK.

Client Computer Alerts

The Alert Viewer can also be launched from the Launchpad on client computers. The key distinction is that administrators by default have access to local alerts (on the local computer) as well as all alerts on the network, whereas regular users only have access to local alerts. This setting can be controlled through the user properties on the Dashboard to allow regular users to have access to network alerts as well as to block some administrators from network alerts.

To allow a user to view network health alerts in his or her Alert Viewer, select the User Can View Network Health Alerts check box within the user account properties.

The client computer also displays alerts (including network health alerts) in the taskbar, as shown in Figure 10-5. The user can then click the alert message to view the alert details.

FIGURE 10-5 Alert information displayed on the client computer.

Monitoring Performance

To keep a network operating at its best, you must be able to recognize bottlenecks and take action to eliminate them.

Performance Monitor includes simple tools that can help you track server loads, locate persistent errors, customize the data collected in logs, define limits for alerts and automatic actions, generate reports, and view past performance data.

- To open Performance Monitor, click Start, type **perfmon** in the Start Search box, and press Enter. Or you can select Performance Monitor from the Administrative Tools menu.

    The initial view of Performance Monitor (shown in Figure 10-6) includes a brief overview as well as a system summary.

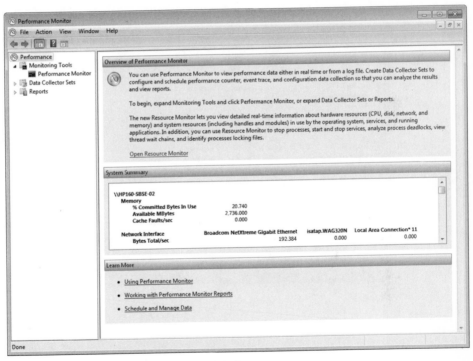

FIGURE 10-6 The initial view of Performance Monitor.

Resource Monitor Overview

Resource Monitor lets you view detailed real-time information about hardware resources (CPU, disk, network, and memory) and system resources (including handles and modules) in use by the operating system, services, and running applications. In addition, you can use

Resource Monitor to stop processes, start and stop services, analyze deadlocks, view thread wait chains, and identify processes that are locking files.

To use Resource Monitor, follow these steps:

1. Click the Open Resource Monitor link in the Overview Of Performance Monitor section to access Resource Monitor, or click Start, type **resmon** in the Start Search box, and press Enter.

   The Resource Monitor page, shown in Figure 10-7, shows four scrolling graphs for real-time monitoring of CPU, disk, network, and memory usage.

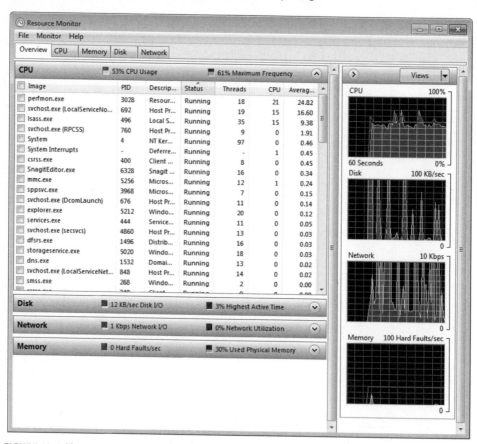

FIGURE 10-7 The Resource Monitor page.

2. The four sections next to the graphs contain details about each resource. Click a section to display the details, as shown in Figure 10-8.

Note When you click a row, the highlight remains on that row, even when the application's position changes in the display.

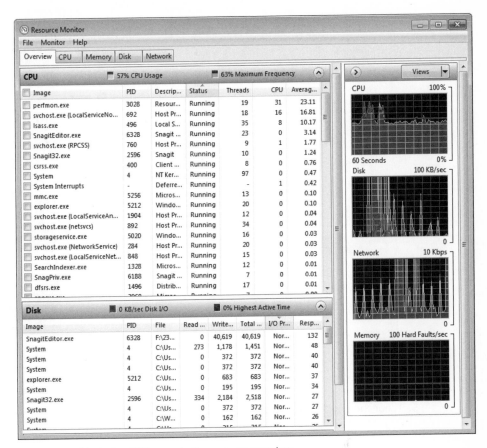

FIGURE 10-8 Displaying CPU usage in the resource overview.

3. Click a column header in the detail view to sort by ascending order. Click a second time to sort in descending order.

4. If you click the CPU tab, you can see check boxes next to the Image header. Select the images that you are interested in investigating. When you are viewing the Overview again, an orange bar opens on each section, showing what is being filtered, as shown in Figure 10-9. With filtering turned on, Resource Monitor now displays any associated modules or associated handles.

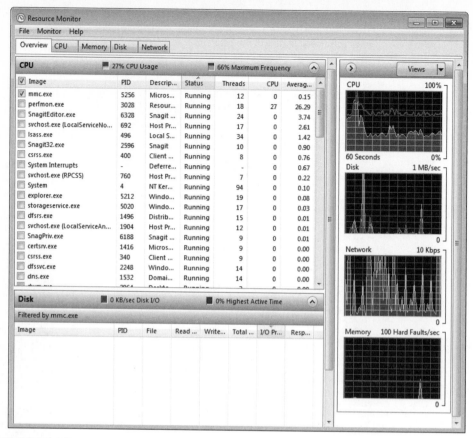

FIGURE 10-9 Resource Monitor with filtering enabled.

5. Clear the check boxes to remove filtering.

The following list defines the headers in each Resource Monitor detail view:

- CPU Details

  - **Image**   The application using the CPU.

  - **PID**   The process identification for the application instance.

  - **Description**   The name of the application.

  - **Status**   Shows whether the process is Running, Suspended, or Terminated. Right-click to change the status.

  - **Threads**   The number of active threads in this instance.

  - **CPU**   The number of currently active cycles for this instance.

  - **Average CPU**   The average CPU load over the past 60 seconds, expressed as a percentage of the total capacity of the CPU.

- Disk Details
  - ❏ **Image**   The application using the disk
  - ❏ **PID**   The process identification for the application instance
  - ❏ **File**   The file being read or written
  - ❏ **Read**   The speed (in bytes per second) at which the file was read in the past 60 seconds
  - ❏ **Write**   The speed (in bytes per second) at which the file was written in the past 60 seconds
  - ❏ **Total**   The average number of bytes per second read and written to the disk in the past 60 seconds
  - ❏ **I/O Priority**   The priority of the IO task
  - ❏ **Response Time**   The disk response time in milliseconds

- Network Details
  - ❏ **Image**   The application using the network resource.
  - ❏ **PID**   The process identification for the application instance.
  - ❏ **Address**   The network address with which the local computer is exchanging information. This can be an IP address, computer name, or fully qualified domain name.
  - ❏ **Send**   The amount of data (in bytes per second) sent in the past 60 seconds from the local computer to the network address.
  - ❏ **Receive**   The amount of data (in bytes per second) that the application received in the past 60 seconds from the network address.
  - ❏ **Total**   The total bandwidth (in bytes per second) of the data sent and received in the past 60 seconds.

- Memory Details
  - ❏ **Image**   The application using the memory resource
  - ❏ **PID**   The process identification for the application instance
  - ❏ **Hard faults/min.**   The number of hard faults caused by the application instance in the past 60 seconds

> **Note**   A hard fault (also called a *page fault*) is not an error. It happens when a page at the address referenced is no longer in physical memory and has been swapped out or placed on a hard drive. However, an application that causes a high number of hard faults will be slow to respond because it constantly has to read from a hard drive rather than from memory.

  - ❏ **Commit**   The amount of virtual memory (in kilobytes) reserved for the process
  - ❏ **Working Set (KB)**   The amount of memory (in kilobytes) currently used by the application instance

❑ **Shareable (KB)**   The amount of the working set memory (in kilobytes) that might be available for other use

❑ **Private (KB)**   The amount of the working set memory (in kilobytes) that cannot be shared

Filtering Information from Resource Monitor

Resource Monitor produces a *lot* of data, so filtering out the unessential data is necessary to avoid being overwhelmed by graphs. To designate filters, start Resource Monitor and follow these steps:

1. Select a Resource Monitor tab. In the Image column, select the check box next to the name of each process you want to monitor. As you select a process, it's moved to the top of the column.

   After you select a process for filtering, the Associated Handles and Associated Modules tables on the CPU tab contain data related to your selection.

2. Click another tab to view additional resource usage data for your selection. Tables that contain only filtered results have an orange information bar below the title bar of the table.

3. To stop filtering for a single process or service, clear its check box. To stop all filtering, clear the check box next to Image.

> **Note** If the process is not using any of the resources displayed on the current tab, the process name won't appear in the key table.

Troubleshooting Problem Applications

There can be many reasons for an application to appear nonresponsive—few of them obvious without some deeper checking. Resource Monitor allows you to view a process wait chain and to end processes that are preventing a program from functioning properly. In Resource Monitor, the entry for an unresponsive process appears in red.

> **Important** Take care when using Resource Monitor to end a process. If an open program is dependent on the process, it immediately closes and unsaved data will be lost. Ending a system process can result in system instability and can also cause data loss.

To examine a process:

1. Open Resource Monitor and click any tab. In the Image column, right-click the name of the process you want to analyze, and select Analyze Wait Chain (see Figure 10-10).

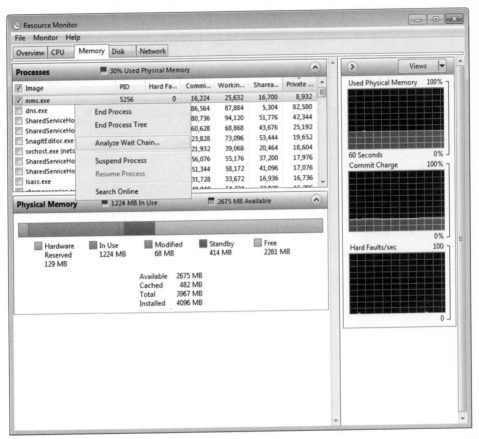

FIGURE 10-10 Checking for a process wait chain.

If the process is running normally and is not waiting for any other processes, no wait chain information is displayed.

2. If the process is waiting for another process, a tree organized by dependency on other processes is displayed. To end one or more of the processes in the tree, select the check boxes next to the process names and click End Process.

Using Performance Monitor

Performance Monitor can help you visualize what is happening on your network and on individual computers. Like Resource Monitor, it displays events in real time but can also preserve data in logs for later viewing.

Insufficient memory or processing power can cause bottlenecks that severely limit performance. Unbalanced network loads and slow disk-access times can also prevent the network from operating optimally. Bottlenecks occur when one resource interferes with another resource's functioning. For example, if one application monopolizes the system processor to the exclusion of all other operations, there is a bottleneck at the processor.

Bottlenecks can occur in Windows subsystems or at any element of the network for many reasons, including:

- Insufficient resources.

- The monopolization of a resource by a program or client.

- Failure of a program, service, or device.

- Incorrectly installed or configured software.

- Incorrect configuration of the system for the workload.

Performance Monitor includes performance counters, event trace data, and configuration information, which can be viewed separately and can also be combined into Data Collector Sets.

- **Performance counters** These are measurements of system state or activity. They can be included in the operating system or can be part of individual applications. Performance Monitor requests the current value of performance counters at specified time intervals.

- **Event trace data** This is gathered from trace providers that are part of the operating system or of applications that report events. Information from several trace providers can be collected as a trace session.

- **Configuration information** Configuration information is collected from key values in the Windows registry. Performance Monitor can document the value of a registry key at a specific time into a log file.

Adding Performance Counters

Performance counters show you the state of an application or a process in the operating system. You can display any number of counters on Performance Monitor. Simply right-click inside the Performance Monitor display and select Add Counters. This opens the Add Counters dialog box, as shown in Figure 10-11.

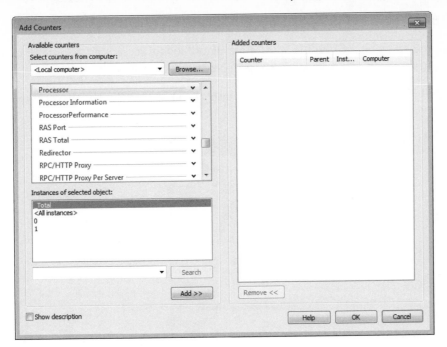

FIGURE 10-11 Viewing available counters.

To add a counter to Performance Monitor:

1. Select a computer from the drop-down list, or click Browse to find other computers.

2. Available counters are listed below the computer selection box. You can add all the counters in a group or click the arrow to display and select individual counters.

> **Note** Select the Show Description check box in the lower-left corner of the window for information on what the selected counters are actually counting.

3. When you click a group or an individual counter, the current instances display in the Instances Of Selected Object window. Select a particular instance or select All Instances. To search for a particular instance, type the process name in the drop-down box below the Instances Of Selected Object pane and click Search. If your search produces no returns, highlight another group to clear the search. The Search function is offered only if multiple instances are available.

4. Click Add to put the counter in the Added Counters list. Click OK when you're finished.

Changing the Performance Monitor Display

After you add multiple counters, the Performance Monitor screen can be difficult to decipher. To make the display more readable, follow these steps:

1. Right-click the Performance Monitor display and select Properties to open the Performance Monitor Properties dialog box, as shown in Figure 10-12.

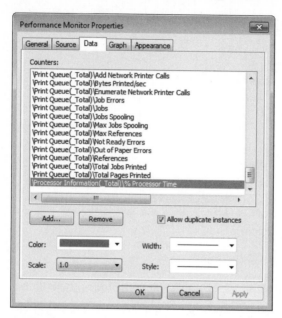

FIGURE 10-12 Changing how the Performance Monitor displays.

2. On the Data tab select how to display the counters. Change the color, width, or style of the counter lines.

3. Change other display elements on the General, Graph, and Appearance tabs.

4. Click the Source tab to change the data source from Current Activity to a specified log file.

Saving the Performance Monitor Display

The current display of Performance Monitor can be saved as an image or as a webpage.

To save the display as an image, follow these steps:

1. Right-click the Performance Monitor display and select Save Image As.

2. Select a location, and type in a name for the saved image. The image will be saved as a .gif file.

3. Click Save.

To save the Performance Monitor display as a webpage, follow these steps:

1. Right-click the Performance Monitor display and select Save Settings As.

2. Select a location, and type in a name for the saved display. The display will be saved as an .html file.

3. Click Save.

Summary

In this chapter, you learned about network health alerts and how to respond to them. You also learned about Performance Monitor and Resource Monitor and how to use them both to help monitor the system. In the next chapter, we cover managing updates.

Chapter 11
Managing Updates

Software updates (formerly called *patches*) are an unavoidable fact of life in the modern computing world. This chapter covers the basics to make the update-management process as straightforward and as easy as possible.

Why Patches Are Important

In the old days, when networks weren't connected to the Internet, when system administrators were the only people who installed software, and when users had only a green-screen terminal, deciding when to apply a patch was a fairly straightforward decision. If you were having a specific problem and you wanted a bit of overtime on the weekend, you came in and applied a patch. If no one was complaining and you didn't want to work on the weekend, you threw the tape (patches always came on tapes in those days) in a drawer and waited until you had to come in on the weekend for some other maintenance, or until users started complaining about a problem that seemed related. Or you simply never got around to it at all.

Even in the more recent past it was possible to have a considered and gradual approach to applying patches. When a vulnerability was identified, it often took months before there was any real risk to your network.

Today that approach simply won't work, as Code Red, Nimda, Slammer, and other computer worms have all too clearly demonstrated. Within hours or (at most) days of the release of a critical security update, there will almost certainly be sample exploit code posted on the Internet, telling anyone and everyone how to exploit the vulnerability. If you ignore critical security updates, you place your entire Windows Small Business Server 2011 Essentials network—and the data stored on it—at risk.

Applying software updates is only one part of a defense-in-depth strategy to protect your network, but it's a critical part. Don't neglect it.

Real World: Terminology

Microsoft uses several different terms to describe patches, each with a slightly different meaning, but the reality is that to much of the rest of the world, they're still called *patches*. We call them patches, the magazines and newspapers call them patches, even most Microsoft employees call them patches, unless they're giving a formal presentation. But Microsoft does have official terminology, and we should all be clear on what it is:

- **Critical update**   A generally available fix for a critical but non-security-related bug. A critical update has an accompanying Microsoft Knowledge Base article.

- **Security update**   A generally available fix for a security vulnerability. Security updates have an accompanying Microsoft Knowledge Base article and a security bulletin.

- **Software update**   A broad term that covers service packs, hotfixes, update rollups, security updates, feature packs, and so on. A software update has an accompanying Microsoft Knowledge Base article.

- **Service pack**   A generally available collection of fixes and feature enhancements. Service packs are cumulative and contain all currently available updates, update rollups, security updates, critical updates, and hotfixes, and they might contain fixes for problems that were found internally and have not been otherwise released. Service packs also sometimes add new features. (Windows Server 2008 R2 SP1, for example, adds dynamic memory allocation and Microsoft RemoteFX support for the Hyper-V role.)

- **Hotfix**   A narrowly available fix for a specific issue. Hotfixes are generally available only through Microsoft Product Support Services and cannot be redistributed. Hotfixes are not tested as thoroughly as updates, update rollups, or service packs.

- **Update**   A generally available fix for a specific, nonsecurity-related, noncritical problem. An update has an accompanying Microsoft Knowledge Base article.

- **Update rollup**   A generally available and tested collection of hotfixes, security updates, critical updates, and updates that are packaged together. An update rollup has an accompanying Microsoft Knowledge Base article.

For complete, up-to-date details on Microsoft update terminology, go to *http://support.microsoft.com/kb/824684*.

> ### Real World: Patch Tuesday
>
> In the not-too-distant past, patches—especially security updates—were released whenever a new vulnerability was identified and corrected. When that happened a few times a year, it wasn't a big problem, and system administrators dealt with each patch as it came out. In most cases, you could just wait until the service pack came out and deal with a whole bunch of them at once. But as security updates and critical updates started being released almost daily, it became increasingly difficult to properly test and identify all the patches that were necessary for your system. The whole process became a serious impediment to productivity and security.
>
> In direct response to many, many complaints, Microsoft moved to a monthly update release process. Unless there is a compelling and immediate need for a critical security update to be released off cycle, all security updates are released once a month, on the second Tuesday of the month. This change has greatly simplified the planning and deployment of patches.

The Patching Cycle

There are four phases in the ongoing cycle of maintaining a well-patched, up-to-date network:

- Assessment
- Identification
- Evaluation and planning
- Deployment

Each of these phases is essential to the successful management of updates on your server.

Given the relative simplicity of SBS 2011 Essentials networks, and the constrained IT budgets of most people, you can combine and simplify the overall process a bit, and probably even bypass phases on occasion. However, it's good to have an understanding of the phases and to think through the steps involved in each one, even if you're combining them. In the following sections, we'll cover each of the phases of the full patching cycle, and then provide an "SBS 2011 Essentials Version" subsection that provides a realistic description of the phase for an SBS 2011 Essentials network. Obviously, you should tailor this information to your own network's needs—the resources and requirements of an SBS network of 25 users are quite different from those of 5 users.

Assessment

The *assessment* phase of patch management is all about understanding what your environment is, where and how it's vulnerable, and what resources and procedures are in place to reduce those vulnerabilities.

When a patch is released, you can't make an informed decision about whether you need to install that patch unless you first know what software is present in your environment and what critical business assets must be protected. So the first step to an overall patch management process is to figure out what software you're running in your environment. All of it. Whether you build a spreadsheet, have a Microsoft Access database, or just keep all of your software records in a chart in Microsoft Word, you need to get your software environment audited and documented.

Identify your critical business assets. Is there confidential data that you couldn't function without? Are there critical systems that must be available at all times?

The next part of the assessment phase is to understand what security threats and vulnerabilities you currently have. According to CERT (Carnegie Mellon University's Computer Emergency Response Team), more than 90 percent of security events result from intruders taking advantage of known vulnerabilities in software where patches exist but haven't been applied.

Are you running old versions of software programs that can't be easily updated or replaced? Do you have a public-facing website that isn't behind your firewall? What are your security policies and how are they enforced?

SBS 2011 Essentials Version

If all that seems a bit much, it's really just a somewhat formal way of saying that you need to know what software is running on your network and how it is updated. It's also good to have a record of what kinds of patches have caused trouble for you in the past—when you see new patches that affect these areas, you'll probably want to do some additional testing before you send the patch out.

Identification

The *identification* phase is about finding out what software updates or patches are available, and how critical it is that they be deployed in your environment. You need to take the following actions:

- Discover the patch.
- Decide if it's relevant to your environment.
- Download the patch.
- Identify the patch's criticality.

There are many ways to discover patches, but for Microsoft products, one of the best ways is to sign up for email alerts. If you do this, Microsoft will send you notifications of security updates before they are actually released. The signup page is at *http://www.microsoft.com /technet/security/bulletin/notify.mspx*. You can tailor the notification method and detail level to suit your environment.

> **Note** This link provides alerts only for security-related patches. It does *not* send you the patches in the email message, nor does it provide alerts for regular, non-security updates.

Whatever method you use to discover patches, it's important that you have a way to trust the source of the patch information. All Microsoft security update alerts are signed with a publicly available PGP key, for example. And it shouldn't be necessary to say this, but just in case: Microsoft will never send a security update as an attachment to an email message. Never.

> **Important** Wait, maybe you missed that. Again, for emphasis: Microsoft will *never* send a security update as an attachment to an email message! Never.

After you know about a patch, you need to decide whether it's relevant to your environment, and if it is relevant, you need to obtain the patch from a known and trusted source. For a Microsoft patch, this generally means downloading it directly from Microsoft.

For the SBS 2011 Essentials server, use Microsoft Update to download the patch. Find the relevant Microsoft Knowledge Base article for the patch, and then cut and paste the link to the download page directly into your browser. Do not click the link in an email message to get your patch. Even when you have verified that the email message is really from Microsoft and is a legitimate email message, you shouldn't click the link. Get into the habit of always using cut and paste. When you use cut and paste to put a link into your browser, you greatly reduce the likelihood of a phishing attack—being unknowingly redirected to a site that looks exactly like the site you expected to go to, but that is actually a site designed to steal information from you or download spyware onto your computer.

> **Best Practices** Most email clients today have the ability to force all email messages to display as plain text. This is a good thing, because it prevents unscrupulous people from hiding the real destination of a link. The giveaway for detecting a bogus link is usually that the link is to an IP address, not the actual DNS domain name, or if it is a DNS name, it's not exactly the one you were expecting. If you make the change and read your email messages only in plain text, your messages won't be as pretty, but you'll be a lot safer.

After you've downloaded the patch and read the associated Knowledge Base article, you are in a position to determine just how critical the patch is in your environment. Is this a patch that needs to be deployed immediately, with limited testing—or even with no testing? Or are there ameliorating factors that allow the patch to be deployed as part of a regular patching schedule after full testing?

SBS 2011 Essentials Version

This is what we had to go through before the release of the R2 version of Windows Small Business Server 2003 if we didn't have some method—usually a third-party solution—to automatically download and identify patches for our environment. With the R2 release of SBS 2003, we were able to let Windows Server Update Services (WSUS) take care of the downloads and the initial analysis. But now, with SBS 2011 Essentials, a preconfigured WSUS is no longer available. This means that you either must install WSUS, or a third-party patch management tool, on the SBS 2011 Essentials network, or have all your computers directly update from Microsoft Update.

Evaluation and Planning

The *evaluation and planning* phase of patch management flows naturally out of the identification phase, and in many ways is an extension of it. In this phase, you determine how to respond to the software update you've downloaded. Is it critical, or even necessary? How should it be deployed? And to whom? Should interim countermeasures be employed that will minimize your exposure to the vulnerability? What priority does the patch have?

The initial determination of need, suitability, and priority is made during the identification phase, but in the evaluation and planning phase, you should take a closer look at the patch. What priority is the patch? If it affects a critical business asset and there's no easy or appropriate countermeasure other than the patch, it will have a higher priority for testing and deployment than if there's a simple countermeasure that you can implement until the patch can be deployed. If it targets critical business assets, it's going to have a higher priority than if the only computers that are affected are several old Windows 2000 computers that aren't running any critical business applications. (But you got rid of those old Windows 2000 computers, right?)

After you've identified the priority of the patch, you need to plan the actual deployment. Which computers need to have the patch deployed to them? Are there any constraints or issues that interfere with the deployment? Who needs to be notified, and what steps need to be taken so that the deployment minimizes the disruption to the environment? If this is an emergency release, will it go through a staged deployment, or is every affected computer going to have the patch deployed as soon as possible?

SBS 2011 Essentials Version

In any SBS 2011 Essentials network larger than a few clients, you should have a couple of clients that are designated as expendable. In all but emergency-patch situations, these computers will be the first to install a new update.

Unfortunately, Microsoft Update doesn't support having a special group of client computers that are treated differently from other clients. The workaround we've found is to have one or two users go directly to Microsoft Update every Patch Tuesday and update their computers. This gets the update onto their computers more quickly than any other method and allows some testing time before any automatic deployment can happen. If you use this method, choose a user who has a fairly typical computer and, most important, who is willing to take on this role. Also, make sure that you carefully review the "Caveats" section of the security bulletin for the update. This section details known issues and interactions that you should be aware of.

Deployment

The *deployment* phase of patch management is in many ways the easiest phase. You've done all your preparatory work; now all you need to do is the actual deployment.

First and foremost, communicate. Let everyone who will be affected know that you will be deploying a patch and what application or area of the operating system it affects. If you know that the deployment will cause changes in behavior, tell your users before the deployment. You'll have far fewer support calls if you've warned people that a certain behavior is expected than if you surprise them.

SBS 2011 Essentials Version

If users have open files and SBS 2011 Essentials automatically deploys an update that requires a reboot, they could potentially lose work. Sending a reminder email message to your users on Patch Tuesday is a good idea.

Repeat

After you've deployed a patch, the process starts over again. It really is a continuous process—or it should be. At a minimum, verify that the patch has been successfully deployed to the affected computers. Update your software map and database so that you know which computers have had the patch applied. Because our assumption is that every patch is on every computer, we only keep track of the exceptions. When a patch cycle is complete, we make a note of any issues, confirm that deployment has been successful, and get ready for the next round.

Windows Server Update Services

SBS 2011 Essentials does not include Windows Server Update Services (WSUS). You have two choices—you can add a patch management solution to your SBS 2011 Essentials network (either WSUS or a third-party solution), or you can configure the update settings for the SBS 2011 Essentials server and all of the clients. In small networks, it's probably simple enough to manually configure each of the computers on the network. We think having client computers configured for automatic updates from Microsoft Update makes the most sense, and we wish that the Connector application would set this automatically when you join a client computer to the SBS 2011 Essentials network. But it doesn't, so you should ensure that all client computers are automatically updating.

Configuring Update Settings on the Server

The default software update setting for SBS 2011 Essentials is to install updates automatically. This is probably the best setting for client computers—especially for users who connect to the network remotely. However, this is not the ideal setting for a server. Automatically downloading and installing updates can lead to a problem when an update requires a reboot. An unscheduled reboot at an inconvenient time can cause data loss and unexpected downtime.

Changing the Update Settings

To change the setting for updates, open Control Panel and follow these steps:

1. Click System And Security and then Windows Update.

2. On the Windows Update page (shown in Figure 11-1), click Change Settings.

3. Under Important Updates, select Download Updates But Let Me Choose Whether To Install Them.

4. Click OK.

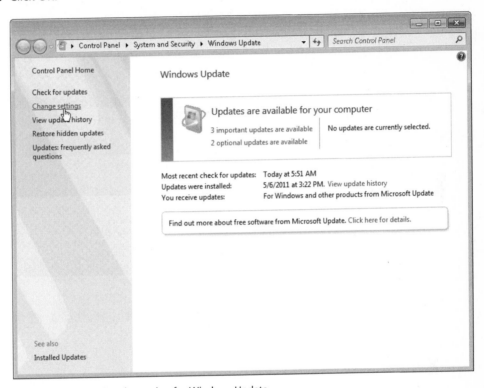

FIGURE 11-1 Changing the setting for Windows Update.

Installing Updates

As you can see in Figure 11-1, updates that have been downloaded but not installed are indicated in the Updates Are Available For Your Computer section. Click the link to view the updates. To install an update, follow these steps:

1. Select the check box next to the name of the update to be installed. As you select updates, the information on the right describes the update and its function. It also tells you if a reboot is necessary.

2. Click OK. The Windows Update screen now shows the number of updates selected and the size of the files to be downloaded (see Figure 11-2).

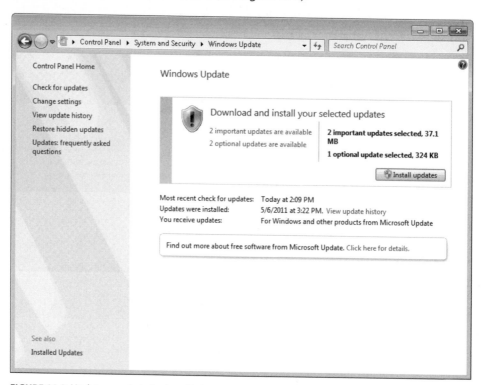

FIGURE 11-2 Updates ready to be installed.

3. Click Install Updates.

Excluding Updates

If you have chosen to have all updates downloaded but not installed automatically, you will inevitably have some updates that you don't want to install. If you just ignore an unwanted update, SBS 2011 Essentials will nag you until you either install the update or hide it.

To hide an update, right-click the update and select Hide Update, as shown in Figure 11-3.

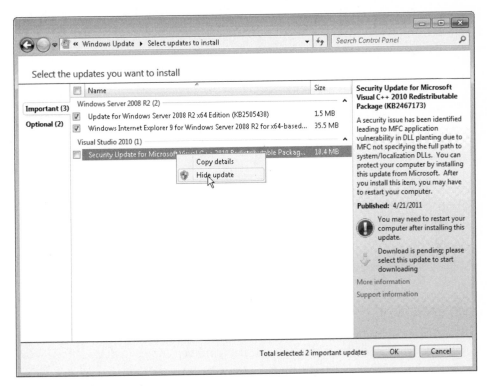

FIGURE 11-3 Hiding an update.

If you later decide to install the update, you can open Windows Update and click the Restore Hidden Updates link to redisplay it.

Checking the Update History

To review your update history, open Windows Update and select View Update History. Scroll the list to find a particular update. Right-click to view the details of the update, as shown in Figure 11-4.

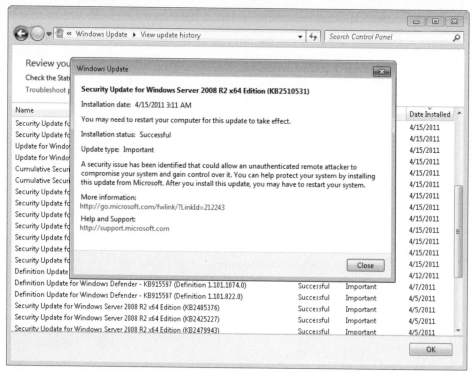

FIGURE 11-4 Checking the details of an installed update.

Removing an Update

Updates are an important element of computer security, so you shouldn't uninstall an update unless you're sure that the update is causing a problem. Some updates—those related to a security area of the operating system—cannot be removed.

Real World: Finding a Solution

A problem that occurs after an update is installed might be coincidental to the update and actually might be caused by something else. Before removing the update, check for another possible solution. Open Control Panel and follow these steps:

1. Select System And Security and then Action Center.

2. Click Maintenance.

3. Under Check For Solutions To Problem Reports, click Check For Solutions.

Windows will check for a solution and report if one is found. Note that some problems and solutions are available only when you're signed in with an administrator account.

To uninstall an update, follow these steps:

1. Open Control Panel, select Programs, and then in the Programs And Features group, click View Installed Updates.

2. Right-click the update you want to uninstall, and select Uninstall.

3. In the Uninstall An Update dialog box (shown in Figure 11-5), click Yes.

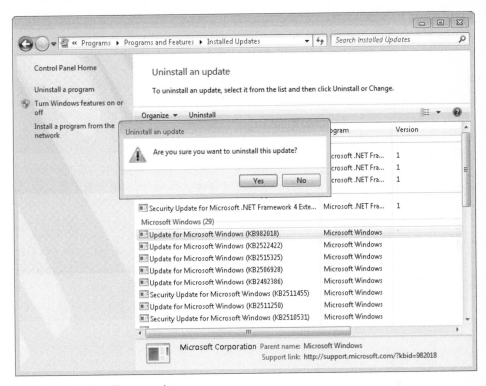

FIGURE 11-5 Uninstalling an update.

Depending on the nature of the update, you might be prompted for administrative credentials.

Third-Party Solutions

SBS 2011 Essentials does a good job of managing the various patches for Microsoft products on your network. However, it does have some limitations.

Microsoft Update will only manage the updates of Microsoft products, and it doesn't give you the fine-grained control that some SBS networks might need. If your needs go beyond the basics of Microsoft Update, you should consider using either a product such as Windows Intune (a Microsoft product) or a third-party product. Windows Intune is a good product and is well-suited to larger SBS networks, but it does move your update management and deployment from your own network to a managed, fee-based, cloud subscription service. Windows Intune includes software licensing for updating your client computers to Windows 7 Enterprise.

An alternative to the Microsoft patch-management solutions, one that we've used and like a lot, is Shavlik NetChk Protect (*http://www.shavlik.com/netchk-protect.aspx*). This is a full-featured, powerful product that gives you the ability to create multiple patch groups, control the download and deployment actions and schedules for each group differently, and even patch computers that aren't part of your SBS 2011 Essentials domain but that are connected to your network. It supports patching of popular products that are not from Microsoft that you might have on your network, such as WinZip, Firefox, Apple QuickTime, and Adobe Acrobat.

Summary

In this chapter, we covered both the process of patch management and the mechanics of applying SBS 2011 Essentials updates.

In the next chapter, we cover the sharing of printers from the SBS 2011 Essentials server. Sharing printers is something that virtually all SBS 2011 Essentials networks do, but that many networks have problems with. Printer problems are a major source of help desk trouble calls.

Chapter 12
Installing and Sharing Printers

As much as everyone would like to have a paperless office, it appears that we'll all be much grayer (or balder, or both) before that completely comes to pass. Since 2000, the quantities of waste in the office paper-recycling bin have levelled off and in some places they have actually begun to shrink—slightly. However, paper remains at the center of many business operations.

The cost of basic printers has declined dramatically, and companies are investing in sophisticated high-speed printers that allow users to handle jobs that once required an outside print shop. These printers are expensive both to buy and to use. Therefore, printer sharing remains an important function of enterprise networks. Setting up multiple users to share printers reduces cost and can improve printing output. You can direct routine work to low-cost-per-page printers, schedule long print jobs for off hours, and limit access to high-end printers.

In other words, there's not much you can do to keep people from printing out the occasional grocery list or soccer schedule, but you can prevent them from doing it on the full-color laser printer with toner cartridges that cost as much as a new printer.

Printer Terminology

Although the term *printer* is usually used to refer to both the physical device and its software interface, strictly speaking a printer is a device that does the actual printing, and a *logical printer* is the software interface (printer driver) for the printer. You can have one logical printer associated with a single printer, or you can have several logical printers associated with a single printer. In the latter arrangement, the logical printers can be configured at different priority levels so that one logical printer handles normal printing and another handles print jobs that should be printed during off-peak hours. For a printer that supports both PostScript (PS) and printer control language (PCL), having two logical printers allows users to choose which type of printing to do.

A single logical printer can also be associated with multiple physical printers in a printer pool, as long as all the printers work with the same driver. Printer pools distribute the printing load more evenly, increasing performance. Because the physical printers in the pools are interchangeable, printer pools also make it possible for an administrator to add or remove physical printers without affecting the users' configurations.

Real World: Understanding Print Servers

Print servers are computers (or sometimes network appliances) that manage the communications between printers and the client computers that generate the print jobs.

Generally, there are two approaches to print servers. The Microsoft approach is to use a computer running Windows as an "intelligent" print server that handles communication between the printers and the client computers (reducing strain on the clients) and maintains a common print queue for all clients. Microsoft print servers also make it easy to find printers on the network by name (NetBIOS, DNS, or Active Directory directory service) and install the appropriate printer drivers.

In contrast, other operating systems, such as Linux, and printers with built-in network interfaces, use a relatively "dumb" print server called the Line Printer Daemon (LPD), which acts strictly as an interface between the network and the printer. Each client maintains its own printer queue and performs all preprint processing, increasing the amount of time the computer is partially or completely unavailable for other tasks.

These two approaches aren't in opposition to each other and, in fact, the best way to connect a printer to a Windows print server is via a network connection to a printer, which usually runs the LPD service. The Windows print server connects to the printer by using the traditional Line Printer Remote (LPR) service (the client-side equivalent of LPD) or via the higher-performance standard TCP/IP printer port, and shares the printer on the network. The Windows print server holds the printer queue and sends each print job to the LPD, which passes the job to the printer.

Selecting Printers

Choosing the right printers for an organization is a lot like choosing the right car. There are certain practical matters to look at, such as up-front cost, cost of consumables (gas, ink, or toner), and suitability to the task at hand (for example, hauling lumber or printing brochures).

Color laser printers have become affordable for most businesses, but the cost of color toner remains very high. However, if you have a property sales office and need to print hundreds of high-quality color photos daily, a color laser printer is not an extravagance. A printer that will produce beautiful color at a rate of 20 or more pages per minute can be had for a very modest price.

On the other hand, if you need a lot of black-and-white pages and only occasional color, a black-and-white laser printer plus a color inkjet printer might be the most economical option. Color ink cartridges for inkjet printers are expensive, but they last a long time if used infrequently. And inkjet printers themselves are so low in cost that they're practically disposable (as reprehensible as that is from an environmental point of view).

Look for printers with built-in network interfaces because they print faster, require less processing power on the print server, and can be flexibly located anywhere that there's a network cable. Printers with a USB connection can be used if print volumes are low (or for backup printers), but steer clear of printers using parallel port connections—they can drastically slow a print server.

Real World: Other Ways That Printers Are Like Cars

In our office, we have three printers:

- A standard, small-business-size, black-and-white laser printer (the sensible sedan)
- A multifunction color inkjet copier/scanner/printer/fax (the efficient hybrid)
- A very fast color laser printer the size of a small file cabinet (the impractical but cool sports car)

Printers are undoubtedly essential to your business, but there's no reason you can't have some fun at the same time.

Planning Printer Placement

In a very small office, there's no need to spend time planning printer deployment. The printers go wherever there's room for them. However, in a larger organization, you'll need to establish printer-naming and location-naming conventions, evaluate whether to upgrade or migrate existing print servers, and prepare for print server failures.

Naming Printers

An effective printer-naming convention is important so that users can easily identify printers on the network. When creating a printer-naming convention, consider the following:

- The *printer name* can be any length up to 220 characters, which is long enough for any scheme you devise. Of course, the name should also be as short as possible without sacrificing clarity.

- The *share name* is the name that all clients see when they browse for a printer, use the Add Printer Wizard, or use the *Net Use* command. The share name can be up to 80 characters long, but again it should be shorter for readability. Some older applications cannot print to printers with fully qualified printer share names (the computer name and printer share name combined) that exceed 31 characters, or to print servers where the default printer's share name exceeds 31 characters. Clients using operating systems other than Windows might also have trouble with names longer than 31 characters or names containing spaces or other special characters. But whether you have to deal with such applications or not, shorter is generally better.

Naming Printer Locations

In small organizations, finding printers is easy—just stand up and look around or ask the person sitting next to you. This doesn't work as well in larger organizations, where printers have varying capabilities and might be widely scattered. Under these circumstances, users need to be able to browse or search for printers based on the criteria they want, including printer features and printer location.

Location names are similar in form to domain names and use the *name/name/name...* syntax. They start with the most general location name and become progressively more specific. Each name part can have a maximum of 32 characters and can contain any characters except the forward slash (/), which Windows reserves as a delimiter.

Keep the naming convention simple and easy to understand. Users are usually interested in the answer to only one question: "Where's my printout?"

Design/ArtStudio/HPOfficeJetE809 is one example of a clear location name, as is Marketing /DirectMail/RicohProofing.

Installing Printers

Before a Windows print server can share a printer on the network, it must first connect to the printer and install the necessary drivers. The following sections walk you through adding printers that are attached directly to the print server via a USB or parallel port interface, as well as connecting to printers with built-in network adapters.

Real World: Local vs. Network Printers

In the consumer world, most printers are directly connected to a computer with a parallel port, USB port, or IEEE 1394 port. This solution—simple to use and to understand—is perfectly adequate and appropriate for individual users, or even most very small offices. But it has some significant disadvantages when compared to a network-attached printer. Direct connection limits where the printer can be physically located because it must be within a few feet of the computer that supports it. And it can seriously slow the work of the individual whose computer acts as the print server. Printer input/output is not very efficient, especially when using the traditional parallel printer port.

A network-attached printer, on the other hand, can be located virtually anywhere. If you're using a standard Ethernet connection to connect to the printer, you'll need a network port nearby, but if you use a wireless print server, even that requirement is eliminated. As a bonus, network printing doesn't have an adverse effect on the server that supports it—you can manage all your print queues directly from the server, thereby simplifying management.

If your printers don't have a network interface, you can use one of the widely available stand-alone print server appliances, either wireless or Ethernet. Windows Small Business Server 2011 Essentials treats these appliances as if they were standard network printers, but you don't have to buy a printer with a network card included—the print server appliance has a port or ports to connect to the printer as well as a network interface.

An exception to the "all printers are network printers" rule is for the user who needs a locally attached printer for reasons of privacy or other factors.

Adding a Network Printer

When you add a new printer to your network, you need only plug it in and turn it on, and the printer will find and use a TCP/IP address. However, you also should make sure that the printer keeps that same address so that SBS 2011 Essentials will always be able to find it. To make the printer available to everyone on the network, you'll need to find the IP address that is assigned to the printer.

- If the printer has a web interface, as shown in Figure 12-1, you can get the IP address there.

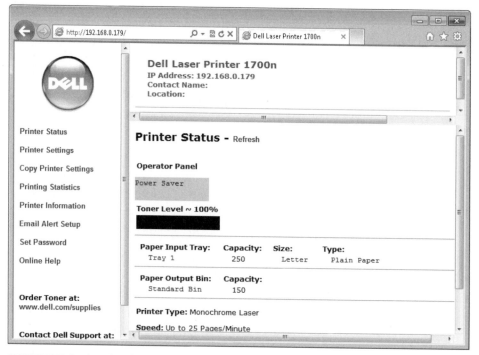

FIGURE 12-1 A printer's web interface showing its IP address.

- A printer's test page will also show its IP address.

To install and share a printer, follow these steps:

1. Make the physical connection between the printer and a network jack using a network cable.

2. Turn the printer on. (If the printer is already on, turn it off and then on again.)

3. Select Devices And Printers from the Start menu. Select Add A Printer.

4. On the first page of the Add Printer Wizard, select Add A Local Or Network Printer As An Administrator (shown in Figure 12-2).

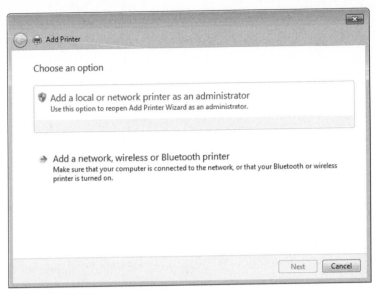

FIGURE 12-2 Choosing the Add Printer option.

5. On the next page, under What Kind Of Printer Do You Want To Install?, select Add A Local Printer.

6. On the Choose A Printer Port page, select Create A New Port, and select Standard TCP/IP Port from the drop-down list. Click Next.

7. On the Type A Printer Hostname Or IP Address page, type the IP address you noted earlier. The port name is automatically filled in (see Figure 12-3). Click Next.

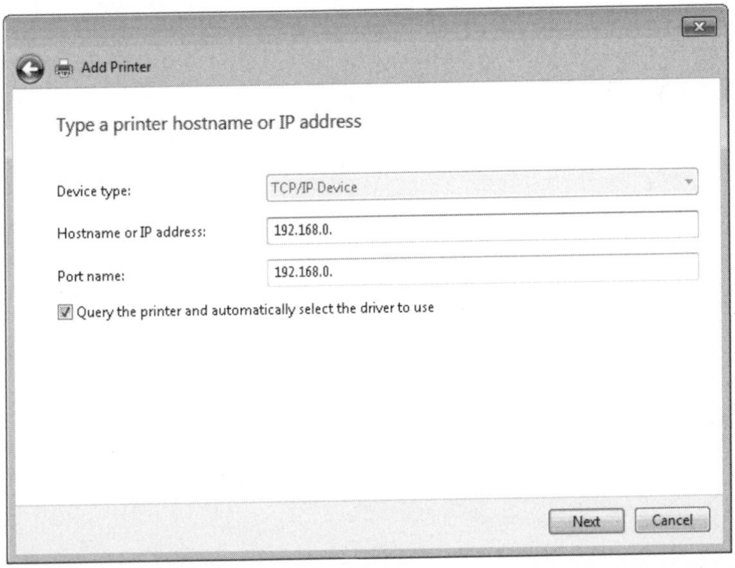

FIGURE 12-3 Entering the printer IP address.

Note To query the printer and automatically select the driver to use, leave the check box selected. If SBS 2011 Essentials already has built-in drivers for the printer, you won't need to provide additional ones.

8. SBS 2011 Essentials contacts the printer and displays the Install The Printer Driver page. Choose the manufacturer's name from the list on the left and the printer model from the list on the right. If your printer isn't on the list, select Windows Update to refresh the list. Click Next.

Note An (MS) designation next to the printer name indicates that the driver is part of SBS 2011 Essentials. If your printer needs multiple drivers (such as PostScript in addition to PCL), click Have Disk and point to the location of the drivers.

9. On the Type A Printer Name page, accept or revise the printer name. Click Next.

10. On the Printer Sharing page, accept or revise the share name. Add a location and comments if you want. Click Next.

11. The successful installation is announced (as shown in Figure 12-4). Print a test page to confirm that all is well. Click Finish.

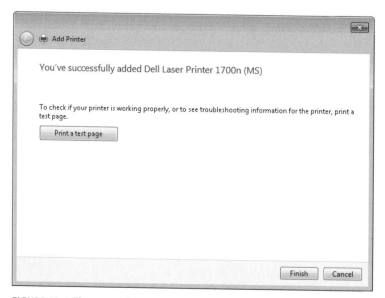

FIGURE 12-4 The successful installation is reported.

Sharing the Network Printer

To share a newly installed printer with users, open Devices And Printers from the Start menu and follow these steps:

1. Right-click the printer and select Printer Properties from the shortcut menu.

2. Select the Sharing tab, as shown in Figure 12-5.

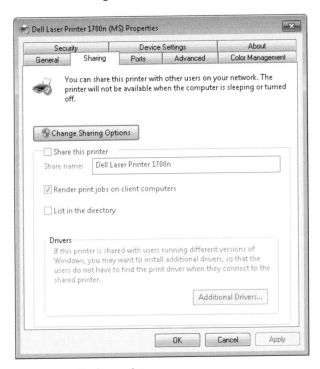

FIGURE 12-5 Sharing a printer.

3. Click Change Sharing Options.

4. Click Share This Printer and select the check boxes for Render Print Jobs On Client Computers and List In The Directory.

5. Click OK when you are finished.

Sharing Locally Connected Printers

If you're using a USB or IEEE 1394 (FireWire) connection to a printer, as soon as you plug the printer into the server, Windows automatically detects, installs, and shares the printer on the network.

Sharing a Printer Connected to a Computer Running Windows Vista

From the computer running Windows Vista, click Start and then follow these steps:

1. Select Control Panel and then click Printers or Hardware And Sound\Printers.

2. Right-click the printer you want to share, and select Properties.

3. On the Sharing tab, click Change Sharing Options.

4. Click Share This Printer and select the check boxes for Render Print Jobs On Client Computers and List In The Directory.

5. Click the General tab. In the Location text box, type a description of the printer's location. Add any notes in the Comment section. Click Apply.

6. Click Print Test Page to verify that the printer is correctly attached.

Sharing a Printer Connected to a Computer Running Windows XP

From the computer running Windows XP, click Start and then follow these steps:

1. Select Control Panel and then click Printers And Faxes.

2. In the task pane, click Add A Printer to start the Add A Printer Wizard. Follow the instructions to complete the wizard.

3. In the details pane, right-click the printer and select Properties.

4. On the Sharing tab, click Share This Printer, and then click List In The Directory. Verify that Render Print Jobs On Client Computers is selected.

5. Click the General tab. In the Location area, type the physical location of the printer.

6. Click Apply.

Sharing a Printer Connected to a Computer Running Windows 7

From the computer running Windows 7, click Start and then follow these steps:

1. Click Control Panel and then click Devices And Printers.

2. Right-click the printer you want to share and select Properties.

3. On the Sharing tab, click Change Sharing Options.

4. Click Share This Printer, and select the check box for Render Print Jobs On Client Computers.

5. Click the General tab. In the Location text box, type a description of the printer's location. Add any notes in the Comment section. Click Apply.

Adding Client Drivers for Shared Printers

Before a shared printer can be used by clients using operating systems other than Windows 7, Windows Vista, or Windows XP, you must add the drivers for the printer to SBS 2011 Essentials. This isn't automatic when you are initially sharing a printer, so you'll need to add the necessary client drivers after the shared printer is created.

To install drivers for clients of different architectures, follow these steps:

1. Open Devices And Printers from the Start menu.

2. Right-click the printer and select Printer Properties from the shortcut menu.

3. Click the Sharing tab, and then click the Additional Drivers button.

4. In the Additional Drivers dialog box, shown in Figure 12-6, select the check boxes next to the client drivers to be installed, and then click OK. To install an additional client driver, you must have access to the installation file for the driver version either locally or via the network.

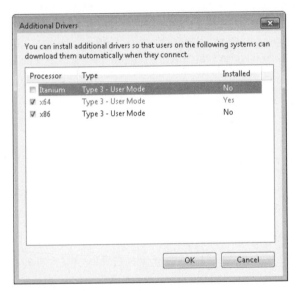

FIGURE 12-6 Installing additional printer drivers.

5. SBS 2011 Essentials will prompt you for the location of the drivers. Click OK through the next dialog boxes to install the drivers.

Setting Security Options

Security options come into play when you have a range of printers that are separate but not at all equal. For example, you might not want everyone to print to the five-dollar-per-page, dye-sublimation printer purchased for the art staff. At a more down-to-earth level, security settings can preserve printer properties or printing priorities from unauthorized changes.

To set permissions on a printer, right-click the printer, choose Printer Properties, and then use the Security tab to assign permissions to users. Click Advanced to exert finer control over permissions or to enable auditing. You can view the results of the audit settings in the security log.

A printer has three levels of permissions: Print, Manage This Printer, and Manage Documents. These are defined as follows:

- **Print**   Users with Print permission can connect to the printer; print documents; and pause, restart, or delete their own documents from the print queue.

- **Manage Documents**   Users with Manage Documents permission have Print permission along with the ability to change the settings for all documents in the print queue and to pause, restart, and delete any user's documents from the print queue. The creator/owner of a document has the Manage Documents permission level by default.

- **Manage This Printer**   Users with Manage This Printer permission have Manage Documents and Print permissions along with the ability to modify printer properties, delete printers, change printer permissions, and take ownership of printers.

Determining Printer Availability

To set up a printer so that it is available only during certain times—perhaps to discourage after-hours printing—complete the following steps:

1. Select Devices And Printers from the Start menu.

2. Right-click the printer you want to modify, and select Printer Properties from the shortcut menu.

3. Click the Advanced tab, and then click Available From.

4. Select the earliest and latest times the printer is to be available to users, and then click OK.

Group Priorities and Printer Availability

Changing printer availability as just described changes the printer use times for everyone and makes no further restrictions. With a few additional steps, you can set up a printer so that print jobs submitted by some users print before jobs submitted by other users; for example, you can give priority to managers or groups with tight deadlines. You can also reserve a printer for exclusive use by certain groups during certain times; for example, you can reserve a printer outside of normal business hours so that the groups you specify can print large, high-priority print jobs.

To control availability or group priority, create two or more logical printers for a single physical printer, give each logical printer a different priority and/or make it available at different times, and give different users permission to print to each logical printer.

Creating a Logical Printer

To create a logical printer, follow these steps:

1. Select Devices And Printers from the Start menu.

2. Select Add A Printer.

3. On the first page of the Add Printer Wizard, select Add A Local Or Network Printer As An Administrator.

4. On the next page, select Add A Local Printer.

5. On the Choose A Printer Port page, click Use An Existing Port, select the port that the physical printer is on, as shown in Figure 12-7, and then click Next.

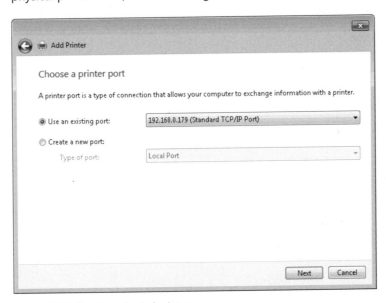

FIGURE 12-7 Creating a logical printer.

6. On the Install The Printer Driver page, choose the manufacturer's name from the list on the left and the printer model from the list on the right. Click Next.

7. Choose the version of the driver you want to use, and click Next.

8. Give the printer a name that describes its function or who uses it. Click Next.

9. In the Printer Sharing dialog box, provide the location and additional comments if you want. Click Finish.

Configuring Usage of a Logical Printer

After you have added a logical printer, you next configure how it is used and by whom. Open Control Panel and follow these steps:

1. Under Hardware, select View Printers And Devices.

2. Right-click the logical printer and select Printer Properties.

3. Click the Security tab, and assign permissions to the users who will have special access to this printer.

4. Click the Advanced tab (shown in Figure 12-8). If the logical printer is to be available only at certain times, select Available From and set the times.

5. To change the priority of the users who use this logical printer, type a number in the Priority list box. The priority range goes from 1, which is the lowest priority, to 99, which is the highest priority.

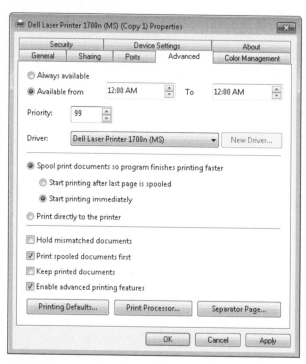

FIGURE 12-8 Advanced printer settings.

6. Click OK, and repeat the process for all other logical printers you created.

Setting Up a Printer Pool

A printer pool consists of multiple printers sharing a single driver and appears as a single printer to users. The advantage of using a printer pool is that clients don't need to look for an available printer; they simply print to the single logical printer on the print server, which then sends the print job to the first available printer. Administration of the printers is also simplified because all printers in the printer pool are consolidated under one driver. If you modify the properties for the single logical printer, all physical printers in the printer pool use the same settings.

To set up a printer pool, complete the following steps:

1. Open Printers And Devices from the Start menu.

2. Right-click the first printer to be part of the pool, and select Printer Properties.

3. Click the Ports tab.

4. Select the Enable Printer Pooling check box.

5. To add printers to the printer pool, select the ports to which the additional printers are connected.

 Note Printers in a printer pool should be located together so that users need not search for their print jobs.

 Important All printers in a printer pool must be able to use the same printer driver. If they are not identical printer models, you can sometimes achieve this by careful selection of a printer driver that will support an acceptable level of functionality for several different but related printers.

Configuring Print Spooling

Print spooling, or storing a print job on disk before printing, affects the actual printing speed as well as how clients perceive printing performance. You can change the way print spooling works to correct printing problems or to hold printed documents in the printer queue for repeated printing. To change the spool settings for a printer, access the Advanced tab of the printer's Printer Properties dialog box.

The following list describes the print spool settings on the Advanced tab:

- **Spool Print Documents So Program Finishes Printing Faster**   Spools the print documents to the print server, freeing the client to perform other tasks more quickly.

- **Start Printing After Last Page Is Spooled**   Ensures that the entire document is available to the printer when printing begins. This step might correct some printing problems, and it also helps high-priority documents print before low-priority documents.

- **Start Printing Immediately**   Select this option to reduce the time it takes to print a document.

- **Print Directly To The Printer**   Turns off spooling, causing a performance hit on the server (though it might fix some printing problems).

- **Hold Mismatched Documents**   Holds documents in the queue that don't match the current printer settings (for example, documents that require legal-size paper when letter paper is currently in the printer). Other documents in the print queue are unaffected by held documents.

- **Print Spooled Documents First**   Prints the highest-priority document that is already spooled, ahead of higher-priority documents that are still spooling. This step speeds overall printer throughput by keeping the printer from waiting for documents.

- **Keep Printed Documents**   Keeps a copy of print jobs in the printer queue in case users need to print the document again. In this circumstance, the user can resubmit the document directly from the queue rather than printing from his or her application a second time.

- **Enable Advanced Printing Features**   Enables metafile spooling and printer options such as page order, booklet printing, and pages per sheet (if available on the printer). Disable this when you're experiencing printer problems.

Using the Fax Service

As long as you have an email address and a scanner, you have no need for a fax machine or a fax modem. Ninety percent of faxes are documents generated by a computer and can therefore be sent by email. Other types of documents can be easily scanned, saved as files, and sent by email.

If you must send documents to recipients with fax numbers but no access to email, you can use an Internet-based fax service for a small monthly fee. SBS 2011 Essentials offers a way to send, receive, and manage faxes, and this section describes how to use those fax tools.

Adding a Fax Modem

To start and configure the fax service, you must first install a fax modem. Attach the fax modem to the computer and to the phone line, and then follow these steps:

1. Open Control Panel and select Phone And Modem Options.

2. Provide the location information requested, as shown in Figure 12-9. Click OK to open the Phone And Modem dialog box.

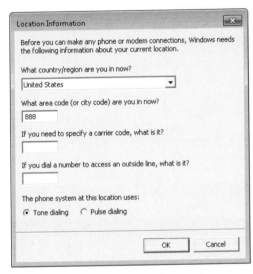

FIGURE 12-9 Providing location information.

3. In the Phone And Modem dialog box, click the Modems tab and then click Add to start the Add Hardware Wizard.

4. Follow the instructions on the Install New Modem page. Windows will automatically detect the modem you have attached unless you select the Don't Detect My Modem check box. Click Next.

5. If Windows does not detect your modem, select the type of modem from the Install New Modem dialog box (shown in Figure 12-10). Click Next.

6. Select the port for the modem. Click Next.

7. Windows installs the modem and notifies you of the successful installation. Click Finish.

To finish the setup, select Windows Fax And Scan from the Programs list on the Start menu. Configure the Windows Fax And Scan application (shown in Figure 12-11) to send and receive faxes.

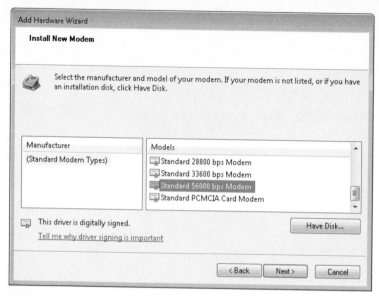

FIGURE 12-10 Designating the type of modem to install.

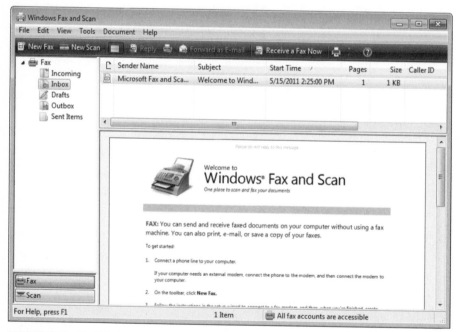

FIGURE 12-11 The Windows Fax and Scan application.

Summary

Printing is an essential service on any network. Aside from complete network failure, few things will generate as much unrest as the inability to print documents. In this chapter, we've covered the fundamentals of printer and fax administration, along with sufficient information on planning to keep your printing operations viable into the future.

Chapter 13
Extending Your Network with a Second Server

Windows Small Business Server 2011 Essentials is a single server that provides the core functionality for your Windows Small Business Server (SBS) network, and for many small businesses, that's all the server you'll need or want. But if you need a second server, there are excellent options to choose from.

In this chapter, we help you choose which solution to use, depending on the business reason for that server, and cover the process of installing and configuring that second server.

Choosing the Version of Windows

Several choices are possible for the operating system of a second server in your SBS 2011 Essentials network, and making an informed choice will save you money and ensure that you have a server that meets your needs. There are three primary reasons for having a second server, each leading to a different choice for the preferred version of Windows Server to install. The three basic choices are:

- **Line-of-business application server**   Used to run a dedicated line-of-business (LOB) application. Many such applications depend on an underlying database such as Microsoft SQL Server.

- **Virtualization Server**   Used to enable session, application, or hardware virtualization. A typical use is to enable Remote Desktop Services and RemoteApps or to run multiple Windows Servers virtualized on a single physical host server.

- **Branch Office Server**   Used to provide necessary services and authentication at a remote branch office. Typically configured as an Active Directory Domain Services controller (DC). For a typical branch office server, an inexpensive solution running Windows Server 2008 R2 Foundation (*http://www.microsoft.com/windowsserver2008/en/us /foundation.aspx*) is usually a good choice. Windows Server 2008 R2 Foundation is only available from hardware OEMs and is not covered in this chapter.

Line-of-Business Application Servers

An LOB server hosts a business-critical application based around a core database. LOB servers often require substantially more resources than other servers. The Windows Small Business Server 2011 Premium Add-on is designed around the needs of an LOB server and includes a full copy of Windows Server 2008 R2 Standard and a copy of Microsoft SQL Server 2008 R2 for Small Business. No additional Windows Server client access licenses (CALs) are required for connection to the server, but SQL Server CALs are required for each user or device that connects to SQL Server.

If your LOB application already includes an embedded database or uses a database other than SQL Server, the Premium Add-on is usually not the most cost-effective solution, because it is priced to cover both the copy of Windows Server and the copy of SQL Server that are included. In this scenario, Windows Server 2008 R2 Foundation or Windows Server 2008 R2 Standard is a more cost-effective solution.

Windows Server 2008 R2 Foundation is an excellent and cost-effective solution for businesses with fewer than 15 users, as long as virtualization isn't required. It is only available through OEMs on selected equipment. A Windows Server 2008 R2 Foundation server is limited to a single CPU socket and 8 GB of RAM and can't be a virtualization host or guest.

Windows Server 2008 R2 Standard supports a maximum of 4 CPU sockets and 32 GB of RAM. It supports Hyper-V virtualization and includes the right to run one copy of Windows Server as the virtualization host and a second copy as a virtual machine, as long as the virtualization host runs only the Hyper-V role.

Virtualization Servers

Virtualization is an important workload for the second server in many small businesses. Virtualization can be:

- *Hardware virtualization,* where multiple virtual machines run on a single physical host computer.

- *Presentation virtualization,* where multiple users connect to a single Remote Desktop (RD) Session Host and each user has a separate session in which applications run independent of other users on the host.

- *Application virtualization,* where multiple versions of an application are installed on a single instance of Windows and are segregated to prevent version incompatibilities.

Whatever kinds of virtualization you use on your SBS 2011 Essentials network, you'll need a second server to support it. You *cannot* use the main SBS 2011 Essentials server as a virtualization host server, though you can virtualize the server as a guest, if you're using hardware virtualization.

If your business needs include an LOB application that requires SQL Server, then the obvious choice for a virtualization server is the Premium Add-on. This includes "1+1" licensing for the copy of Windows Server 2008 R2 Standard, allowing you to use one license for the physical server, and a second license for another copy of Windows Server 2008 R2. You can also install the primary SBS 2011 Essentials server virtualized.

If your primary virtualization is presentation virtualization, and you don't require SQL Server, then there are two possible choices: Windows Server 2008 R2 Standard and Windows MultiPoint Server 2011. Both can be used as a RD Session Host, but they have a slightly different emphases. For several years we've been running a second server whose sole role is that of a terminal server (the earlier name for an RD Session Host). That server was initially a Windows Server 2008 server running the Terminal Services role with TS RemoteApps role service installed. But as soon as Windows Server 2008 R2 released, we migrated the second server to it.

Choosing regular Windows Server 2008 R2 as your RD Session Host is fine and gives you all the features and behavior of a standard Windows Server installation. You'll use the native tools and have all the native roles and features available. You should install, at a minimum, the RD Session Host, RD Licensing, and RemoteApp role services. See "Installing and Managing a Second Server" later in this chapter for details on how to install Windows Server 2008 R2 and enable the necessary roles and role services.

Real World: Requirements

The requirements for an RD Session Host (terminal server) or Windows MultiPoint Server depend on the number of users and the type of applications they run. Because each user will be executing his or her programs on the server itself, you need to determine exactly how your users work and what their real requirements are. Microsoft publishes a detailed white paper on capacity planning for an RD Session Host (which you can see at *http://www.microsoft.com/downloads/en/confirmation.aspx?displaylang= en&FamilyID=ca837962-4128-4680-b1c0-ad0985939063*) that has far more details than we can cover here and yet still manages to hedge its recommendations. And rightly so—capacity planning is subject to an enormous number of variables. So take the following as merely basic guidelines, and carefully consider how your environment affects these numbers.

Important Numbers in this sidebar are not intended to be definitive but are a reflection of the authors' experience in real-world usage. System administrators and consultants should refer to the "Remote Desktop Session Host Capacity Planning in Windows Server 2008 R2" white paper referenced above before making final recommendations.

RAM

Each session on the RD Session Host for a typical knowledge worker using Microsoft Office 2010—including Microsoft Word, Microsoft Outlook, Microsoft Excel, and Microsoft PowerPoint—consumes roughly 70 MB per session. If the available memory per user drops below this point, excessive paging can occur, causing an unacceptable user experience. Thus, a server or virtual machine running Windows Server 2008 R2 with 4 GB of RAM will easily support all the users you can have in an SBS 2011 Essentials environment (512 MB for the server, plus 25×70 MB per user equals 2.2 GB).

CPU

Predicting exactly how much CPU power will be required per user is difficult because each user has a different mix of applications and expectations. A physical server with a single quad-core processor running Windows Server 2008 R2, with sufficient RAM present to avoid paging, can realistically host somewhere between 100 and 150 users—in other words, much more than an SBS 2011 Essentials network has to worry about. Even when that server is a virtual machine, the numbers are quite similar if the CPU supports Second Level Address Translation (SLAT). Without SLAT, the maximum number of users drops to roughly 50-70 users for a four-processor virtual machine—still more than enough to handle any SBS 2011 Essentials environment.

One factor that affects the number of users per CPU core is the color depth used for each Remote Desktop Services (RDS) session. Limiting the maximum color depth to 16 bpp significantly improves the capacity of the RD Session Host server. However, if your RD Session Host is supporting no more than the 25 users allowed by SBS 2011 Essentials, enabling Desktop Composition (Windows Aero) and 32-bit color should not be an issue.

Network

A typical SBS network with 1–gigabit-per-second (Gbps) networking has more than sufficient network bandwidth to support as many Remote Desktop clients as necessary. If your network is limited to older 100–megabits-per-second (Mbps) networking, you might end up with network bandwidth issues if your RDS users run graphics-intensive applications, even on an SBS 2011 Essentials network. Remote users can tailor their Remote Desktop Protocol (RDP) settings to limit bandwidth use over slow connections.

RemoteApps

The maximum number of RemoteApp users that a specific server can support is actually slightly fewer than if the users were running full sessions with the same application mix, but the difference is small and is caused by higher CPU usage for RemoteApp scenarios.

An interesting new choice for a second server is Windows MultiPoint Server 2011 (WMS 2011). This product combines the functionality of a terminal server or RD Session Host with support for USB or direct video card–connected user stations, along with additional user monitoring and management tools. If you primarily intend to use your second server as a terminal server and RemoteApp server, then WMS 2011 can be a cost-effective solution that integrates well into a SBS 2011 Essentials network. The hardware cost to add users to a WMS 2011 server is significantly less than any other solution.

Application Virtualization

Application virtualization (App-V) enables you to distribute and use multiple versions of the same application without causing version collision. This allows you to avoid incompatibilities when a new version of an application is released, and to deploy it alongside the existing version of the application.

Unfortunately, App-V requires volume licensing, and setting App-V up on an SBS 2011 Essentials network is fairly complicated. We think that most SBS networks would be better served to simply set up virtual machines, either locally on a user's computer using Windows Virtual PC or on the network, using Hyper-V, and dedicate the virtual machine to run a specific version of the application.

Installing and Managing a Second Server

There are no special requirements for installing the Premium Add-on or Windows MultiPoint Server as a second server that differ from installing any other version of Windows Server 2008 R2. The minimum requirements and steps remain the same. The official minimum requirements are shown in Table 13-1, along with our commentary on those requirements and suggested real-world minimums.

TABLE 13-1 Minimum System Requirements for a Second Server

Hardware	Requirements	Comments
Processor	1.4 GHz, single-core	2 GHz or greater is more realistic, and at least two cores.
RAM	512 MB	1 gigabyte (GB) of RAM is a more realistic minimum; 2 GB is recommended. For Server Core, 1 GB of RAM is normally sufficient for typical infrastructure workloads.
Disk	32 GB	No less than 60 GB of hard disk space on the system drive, please. And if your server has more than 16 GB of RAM, increase the minimum to at least 50 GB.

Hardware	Requirements	Comments
Optical drive	DVD-ROM	If no optical drive is available, a bootable USB flash drive can be used for installation. For details on creating a bootable USB drive, go to *http://msmvps.com/blogs/russel/archive/2010/03/03/making-a-bootable-usb-disk-stickdrive-pendrive-flashdrive.aspx*.
Video	800 × 600	1024 × 768 is a more realistic minimum. Some screens will be difficult to use at a resolution below 1024 × 768.
Other	Keyboard and mouse	
Network	Not required	Who are they kidding? A supported network card is required for joining a domain or almost anything you'll want to do with Windows Server 2008 R2.

Installation and configuration of Windows Server 2008 R2 has changed significantly from the process we're all more or less familiar with from Windows Server 2003. There are far fewer steps required to actually begin the installation, with hardly any input required from the user. You don't even need to enter a Product ID (PID). Eventually, you'll have to enter the PID before you can activate the server, but a lot of steps that used to be required before the installation process would begin have now been moved to the initial configuration stage.

Installation and Initial Configuration

Installing Windows Server 2008 R2 from standard distribution media onto a clean server with no operating system on it requires just seven screens at the very beginning, and the rest of the installation will complete without further interruption. You don't need to enter any network information, computer name, domain name, or other information except the actual PID associated with the installation (and you can skip that) and the language to install.

Use the following steps to install Windows Server 2008 R2 onto a bare server using standard DVD media:

1. Turn on the server, and immediately insert the Windows Server 2008 R2 installation media. If the primary hard disk doesn't have a bootable operating system on it, you'll go directly into the Windows Server 2008 R2 installation process. If the disk has a bootable operating system on it, you might be prompted with Press Any Key To Boot From CD Or DVD. If you are prompted, press a key.

2. When the initial Install Windows page appears, as shown in Figure 13-1, select the language and other regional settings to use for this installation.

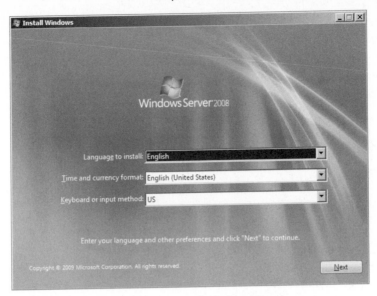

FIGURE 13-1 The initial page of the Install Windows Wizard.

3. Click Next to continue to the page shown in Figure 13-2. From there, you can choose to repair a corrupted Windows Server 2008 R2 installation or get additional information before installing.

FIGURE 13-2 The Install Now page of the Install Windows Wizard.

4. Click Install Now to continue to the Type Your Product Key For Activation page of the Install Windows Wizard, as shown in Figure 13-3.

 Note If you're installing a volume license version of Windows Server 2008 R2, you won't see this screen.

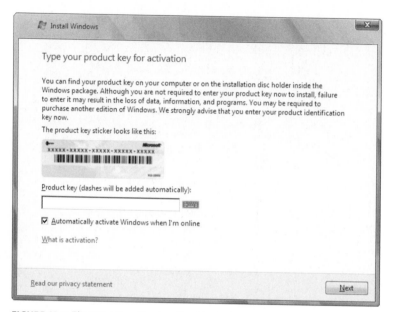

FIGURE 13-3 The Type Your Product Key For Activation page of the Install Windows Wizard.

5. Type a product key for this installation of Windows Server 2008 R2. (You can skip entering the PID on this screen, but you'll need to specify the PID later before you can activate the server.)

6. Leave the Automatically Activate Windows When I'm Online check box selected unless you need to control when activation occurs.

7. Click Next to continue to the Select The Operating System You Want To Install page of the Install Windows Wizard, as shown in Figure 13-4. If you're installing an edition that allows you to enter a product key, you'll only see a list of editions that match the product key you entered.

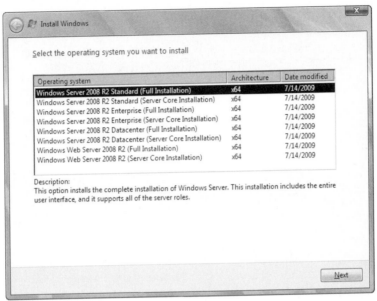

FIGURE 13-4 The Select The Operating System You Want To Install page of the Install Windows Wizard.

8. Select either a full installation or a server core installation for the edition of Windows Server 2008 R2 that you have a license for. This selection is irrevocable—you can't change an installation at a later time from full to server core, or from server core to full. In most SBS 2011 Essentials environments, a full installation is the preferred choice.

9. Click Next to continue to the Please Read The License Terms page. Select I Accept The License Terms. You don't have a choice—if you don't accept them, the installation terminates.

10. Click Next to continue to the Which Type Of Installation Do You Want page, and select Custom (Advanced) to move on to the Where Do You Want To Install Windows page shown in Figure 13-5.

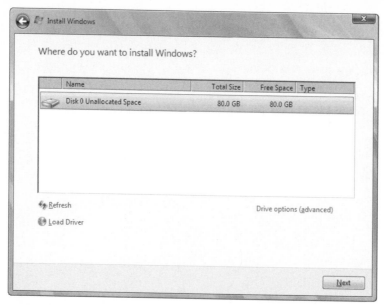

FIGURE 13-5 The Where Do You Want To Install Windows page of the Install Windows Wizard.

11. The first disk on your computer will be highlighted. You can select any disk shown, or if the disk on which you want to install isn't displayed, you can load any required driver at this point by clicking Load Driver. Clicking Drive Options (Advanced) will give you additional options to repartition or format the selected drive.

12. When you've selected the drive to install on, click Next and the installation will begin. You won't be prompted again until the installation completes and you're prompted for a password for the Administrator account.

> **Note** If you need to open a command window during the installation process, just press Shift+F10. After doing so, you can manually run Diskpart.exe or any other tool available at this point in the process to manually load a driver or fine-tune partitioning.

When the installation completes, Windows Server 2008 R2 will restart and proceed to the logon screen. You'll need to enter a new password for the Administrator account, and then log on to the new server. When you log on, if you're installing Windows Server 2008 R2 and not Windows MultiPoint Server 2011, you'll see the Initial Configuration Tasks (ICT) Wizard, shown in Figure 13-6, which makes the initial setup of your new server easy.

Note For installations of Windows MultiPoint Server, many of the initial steps are completely automated by the installation process and you'll have fewer things to configure.

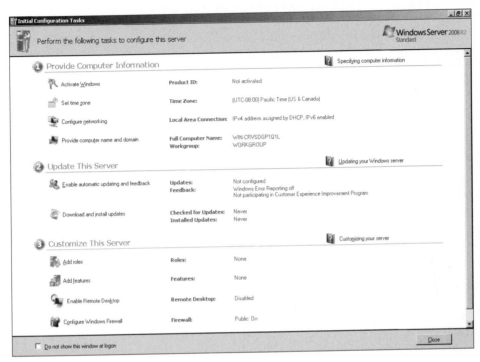

FIGURE 13-6 The Initial Configuration Tasks Wizard.

After the second server installation completes, there are still quite a few tasks to perform. The basic requirements haven't changed—they've just been shifted to after, instead of during, the install. For a Windows MultiPoint Server installation, these steps are covered later in the chapter, but if you're using the Premium Add-on, you'll need to perform the following tasks on a fresh server installation:

- Assign the initial Administrator account password. (Done.)
- Install any hardware drivers required. (Optional, only as required.)
- Set the time zone.
- Configure the networking. (Not usually required for SBS 2011 Essentials networks.)
- Assign a name to the server.
- Join the server to the SBS domain.
- Configure automatic updates and automatic feedback settings.
- Check for updates and install them.

The first of those tasks, assigning the Administrator account password, is required before you can log on for the first time, so we've already covered that.

There are additional tasks on the Initial Configuration Tasks (ICT) Wizard that you will probably want to perform as part of your initial setup:

- Activate Windows. (Required sometime in the first 30 days after installation if you didn't enable automatic activation.)
- Add server roles.
- Add server features.
- Enable Remote Desktop.
- Configure Windows Firewall. (Probably not required. The defaults are good for most scenarios.)

Exactly which roles and features you'll need to install varies depending on what the server will be used for. We'll enable Remote Desktop Session Host to show how this is done.

Installing Hardware Drivers

There's a missing piece in the ICT Wizard—there is no direct way to add hardware drivers for any hardware on the server that isn't recognized. Microsoft makes every effort to get as many drivers as possible on the installation DVD, but the reality is that new hardware continues to be released, and the drivers provided with the software are limited to what was available when Windows Server 2008 R2 shipped. So some hardware might require drivers that aren't on the DVD. If these are drivers for hard disk controllers, you always have the option of adding them during the installation, but for other hardware you need to wait until Windows Server 2008 R2 is installed.

After the installation completes and you've logged on, you can install additional drivers as required. We think it's a good idea to do this as the first step before configuring any settings in the ICT. This is especially important if your network card isn't recognized, because you'll need connectivity to the SBS network to complete the rest of the ICT.

Setting the Time Zone

During the initial installation, Windows picks a time zone (probably not the one you're in unless you live on the west coast of North America) and will also set the current date and time based on your computer's BIOS. To set the date and time, as well as the current time zone, click the link on the ICT Wizard to open the Date And Time dialog box shown in Figure 13-7. After you've set your server's clock and time zone, click Apply and then click OK to return to the ICT Wizard.

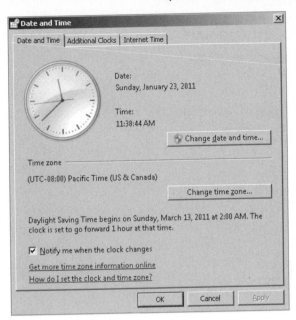

FIGURE 13-7 The Date And Time dialog box.

Real World: Additional Clocks

Windows Server 2008 R2 lets you configure two additional clocks in the Date And Time dialog box. If you configure additional clocks, the times in those time zones will be visible when you point to the clock.

If you regularly work with folks in another time zone, you eventually get used to the time difference and don't need additional clocks on your server. And, after all, you shouldn't be sitting at the server console in most cases anyway. But we still find it handy, and because we work with folks in Europe and Australia fairly often, we turn on two additional clocks: one set to Greenwich Mean Time (GMT), and the other set to GMT+10 hours, for Sydney, Australia. This ensures that when we call at a totally unreasonable hour, we have absolutely no excuse.

Setting the Computer Name and Domain

After you have your networking configured, you're ready to give the computer a name and join it to the SBS domain. The Windows Server 2008 R2 setup process automatically assigns a random and meaningless name to a new server. Although this name is certainly unique on the network, it's not a useful final name, so you'll want to change it.

Real World: Naming Computers

It's a good idea to use a computer name that is both DNS compatible and NetBIOS compatible so that all types of clients see the same name for your computer. (And yes, we're going to have to live with NetBIOS for a while longer—too many applications, including Microsoft applications, simply don't work properly without it.) To do this, keep the name to 15 characters or fewer and don't use asterisks or periods. To obtain the best application compatibility, use dashes instead of spaces and underscores.

Beyond that, you should use a naming convention that has some internal consistency. We've seen all sorts of naming conventions, from the literary obscurities of computers named after romantic poets or science-fiction characters, to Norse or Greek gods, to colors (with the server fronts all painted to match the color name of the server). But honestly, we like names that actually help identify functionality, location, address, hardware, domain, or some combination of these. So our EXAMPLE network here includes computers with the following names:

- hp160-sbse2011 (The computer is running as a virtual machine on a Hewlett-Packard DL160SE G6, and it's the main SBS 2011 Essentials server.)

- hp160-wms-04 (This one is running as a virtual machine in our Example network, it's running Windows MultiPoint Server 2011, and it has a fixed IP address of 192.168.0.4.)

- xmpl-rds-05 (This is running as a virtual machine in our Example network, it has the Remote Desktop Services role enabled, and it has a fixed IP address of 192.168.0.5.)

- hp160-win7-01 (This one is running on that same Hewlett-Packard DL160SE G6, it's a Windows 7 virtual machine, and it's the first one we created.)

- hp160-v32-03 (This is running on that same Hewlett-Packard DL160SE G6, it's a 32-bit Windows Vista virtual machine, and it's the third one we created.)

We know it's a boring way to name things, but we think it's a lot easier to understand than trying to remember that Zeus is the main SBS server and Athena is the second server running SQL Server.

You can save a reboot if you change the computer name and domain at the same time. Both require a reboot that will prevent other tasks from being completed, but fortunately they can be paired. To set the name and domain, follow these steps:

1. Click Provide Computer Name And Domain in the ICT Wizard to open the System Properties dialog box shown in Figure 13-8.

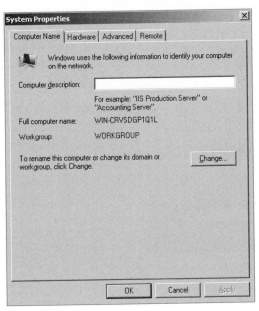

FIGURE 13-8 The System Properties dialog box.

2. You can enter a description for this computer if you want, but the description is hardly ever visible and thus not terribly useful.

3. Click Change to open the Computer Name/Domain Changes dialog box shown in Figure 13-9.

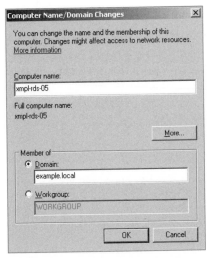

FIGURE 13-9 The Computer Name/Domain Changes dialog box.

4. Type a computer name consistent with your naming convention, and then click Domain to type the SBS domain name.

> **Note** You can use either the NetBIOS version of the domain name (EXAMPLE, in this example) or the DNS version (example.local).

5. Click OK. You are prompted for credentials to perform the change, as shown in Figure 13-10. These credentials should be those for the administrator account you chose for the SBS domain.

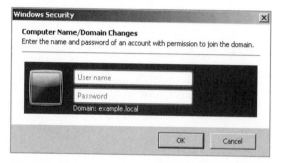

FIGURE 13-10 You must provide administrative credentials for the SBS domain.

> **Note** If the second server doesn't show the Windows Security dialog box for joining the domain, but reports that it is unable to find the domain controller, you might need to manually set the DNS server entry on the second server. Open the Network Connections dialog box (ncpa.cpl) and change the Internet Protocol Version 4 (TCP/IPv4) DNS properties to specify the IP address of the main SBS 2011 Essentials server as the primary DNS server.

6. Click OK. If there aren't any problems, you'll get a Welcome message like that shown in Figure 13-11.

FIGURE 13-11 The Welcome message lets you know that you're now joined to the domain.

7. Click OK to acknowledge the Welcome message. You'll be warned that you need to restart the server before the changes take full effect. Click OK, and then click Close. Then click Restart Now.

> **Important** It's tempting at this point to try to delay the reboot to see if you can squeeze a few more things in before having to wait for the server to shut down and restart. And we understand the temptation—we're big fans of minimizing the number of reboots required and doing as many things as we can when we know we're going to have to reboot. But this is the one time we think you shouldn't do it. You need to get that new name and security in place before anything else happens.

8. After the server has rebooted, log on with an SBS account—not the local administrator account—to complete the configuration of the server.

Enabling Updates and Feedback

The next group of settings on the ICT Wizard is used to set how updates are handled and what feedback is sent to Microsoft. The first setting in this section of the ICT Wizard is to actually configure the settings. You can make choices in three general areas when you click Enable Automatic Updating And Feedback on the ICT Wizard:

- Windows and Microsoft Update settings
- Windows Error Reporting settings
- Customer Experience Improvement Program settings

To configure these settings, follow these steps:

1. In the main Initial Configuration Tasks Wizard page, click Enable Automatic Updating And Feedback to open the dialog box shown in Figure 13-12.

2. Unless you really want your server to be automatically downloading and installing updates with no warning, and automatically rebooting (again without warning), do not select Enable Windows Automatic Updating And Feedback.

3. Click Manually Configure Settings to open the dialog box shown in Figure 13-13.

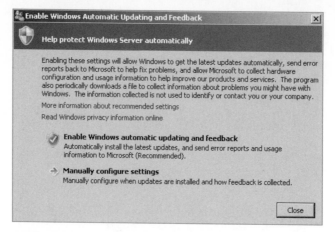

FIGURE 13-12 The Enable Windows Automatic Updating And Feedback dialog box.

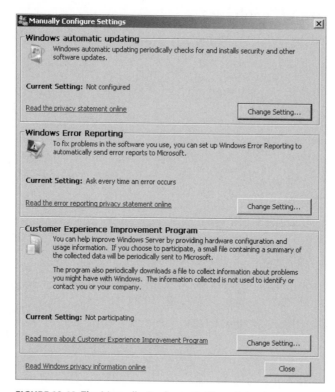

FIGURE 13-13 The Manually Configure Settings dialog box.

4. Click Change Setting in the Windows Automatic Updating section to open the Choose How Windows Can Install Updates page, shown in Figure 13-14.

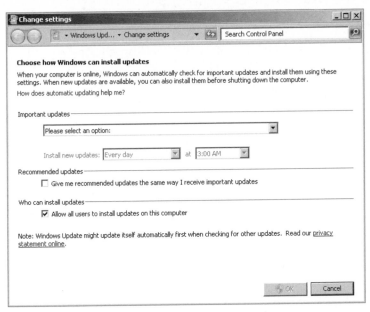

FIGURE 13-14 The Choose How Windows Can Install Updates page of the Change Settings Wizard.

5. Select Download Updates But Let Me Choose Whether To Install Them from the Important Updates drop-down list. This will automatically download all important updates to the server, but will not install them until you choose to do the install.

6. Clear the Allow All Users To Install Updates On This Computer check box, and then click OK to return to the Manually Configure Settings dialog box.

7. Click Change Setting in the Windows Error Reporting section to open the Windows Error Reporting Configuration dialog box shown in Figure 13-15.

8. Select how you want error reports handled. We think that automatically sending at least summary reports, and preferably detailed reports, is good for all of us. After you've made your selection, click OK to return to the Manually Configure Settings dialog box.

9. Click Change Setting in the Customer Experience Improvement Program section to open the Customer Experience Improvement Program Configuration dialog box shown in Figure 13-16.

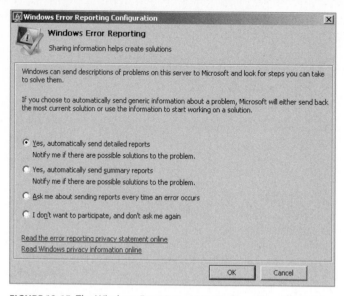

FIGURE 13-15 The Windows Error Reporting Configuration dialog box.

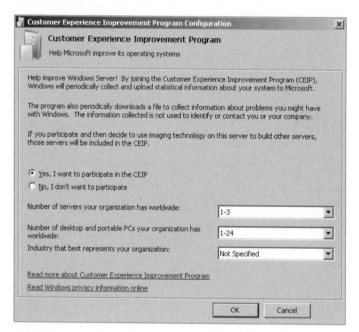

FIGURE 13-16 The Customer Experience Improvement Program Configuration dialog box.

10. The default is to not automatically participate in the Customer Experience Improvement Program (CEIP). When you choose to participate, no personal or organizationally identifiable information is sent to Microsoft. None. But they do gather information about your hardware and the server roles installed on the server, and if you include details about your organization's servers, workstations, and industry, that information is linked to the collected data. Personally, we choose to send it, but we can understand those who would rather not.

11. Make your selections, click OK, and then click Close to return to the ICT Wizard.

Getting Updates

The final option in the middle section of the ICT Wizard is to go online and download updates right now. Just click Download And Install Updates to launch Windows Update, as shown in Figure 13-17. The general rule is that you should install all important and critical updates at this point. Select the updates you want to install now and click Install Updates.

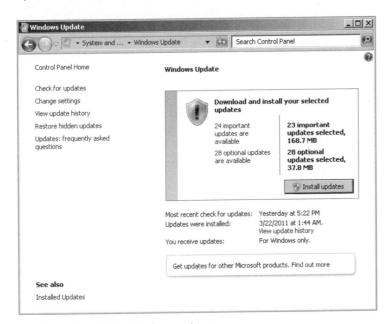

FIGURE 13-17 Installing Windows updates.

After the updates have been installed, you'll almost certainly have to reboot before going any further. When you've rebooted, log back on to the server and continue with the ICT Wizard.

Adding and Removing Roles, Role Services, and Features

The final section of the ICT Wizard is used to add roles and features to the server, enable remote access, and configure Windows Firewall. We can finally get down to actually setting the server up to do some real work. All the rest has just been getting ready.

Whether you use the ICT Wizard to add roles, role services, and features, or do the steps from within Server Manager, the process and steps are the same. To add the Remote Desktop Services (RDS) role, along with the RD Session Host and RD Licensing role services, use the following steps:

1. Click Add Roles in the Customize This Server section of the ICT Wizard to launch the Add Roles Wizard, as shown in Figure 13-18.

 Note If you need to add a role after you're done with the ICT Wizard, open Server Manager, select Roles in the left pane, and then select Add Roles from the Action menu.

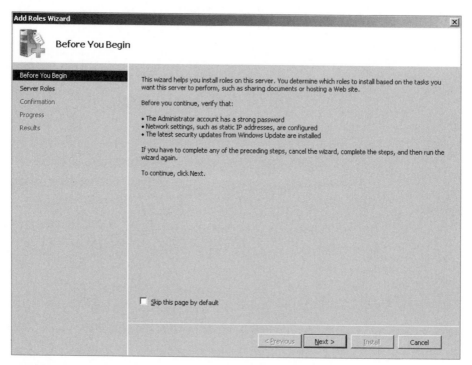

FIGURE 13-18 The Before You Begin page of the Add Roles Wizard.

2. The Before You Begin page of the Add Roles Wizard contains some general information and recommended configuration settings. After you've seen this once and have read it, you can select the Skip This Page By Default check box. Once is quite enough.

3. Click Next to continue to the Select Server Roles page. Select Remote Desktop Services, as shown in Figure 13-19.

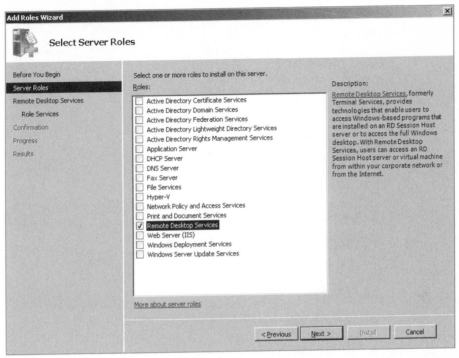

FIGURE 13-19 The Select Server Roles page of the Add Roles Wizard.

4. Click Next to move on to the Remote Desktop Services page. Read the brief Introduction To Remote Desktop Services, and if you want more information on Remote Desktop Services roles and role services, click the Overview Of Remote Desktop Services link.

5. Click Next to continue to the Select Role Services page, as shown in Figure 13-20. Select at least the Remote Desktop Session Host and Remote Desktop Licensing role services.

Important You must assign a licensing mode and specify an RD Licensing server for your RD Session Host within 120 days of enabling Remote Desktop Services. You could install this and configure it at any time during the 120 days, but there's no real value in waiting. And if you forget, and hit the 120-day limit, the server will refuse all Remote Desktop sessions until you've configured RD Licensing.

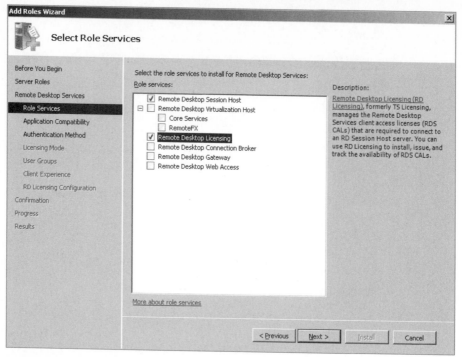

FIGURE 13-20 The Select Role Services page of the Add Roles Wizard.

6. Click Next to move to the Uninstall And Reinstall Applications For Compatibility page of the Add Roles Wizard. This doesn't really apply to a brand-new server, but is a good reminder that applications that have already been installed should be uninstalled and reinstalled so that they are properly multiuser aware.

7. Click Next to continue to the Specify Authentication Method For Remote Desktop Session Host page, shown in Figure 13-21. There are two choices for authentication:

❑ **Require Network Level Authentication** Choose this if all your clients will be domain joined and running at least Windows XP SP3, Windows Vista SP1, or Windows 7. This option is more secure and should be used when possible.

❑ **Do Not Require Network Level Authentication** Choose this option if you have clients that can't be upgraded to at least Windows XP SP3 or are not joined to the SBS 2011 Essentials domain (such as Windows 7 Home Premium clients). Clients will still require at least RDP 6 to use RemoteApps.

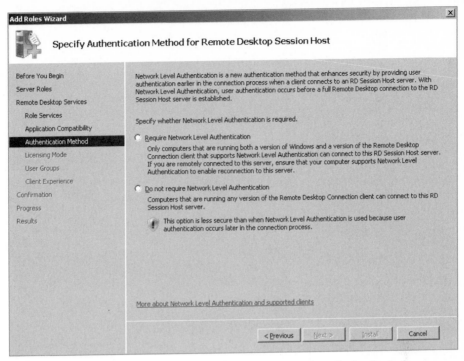

FIGURE 13-21 Setting the authentication level for the Remote Desktop Session Host.

8. Click Next to proceed to the Specify Licensing Mode page, shown in Figure 13-22. Here you can choose between per-device or per-user licensing, or you can delay the decision. The licensing choices are:

  ❏ **Per Device**   Each device that connects to the RDS server must have a Remote Desktop Device Client Access License (RDS Device CAL). If you have multiple users sharing a few computers, as would be common for a retail establishment with point-of-sale terminals, this is the preferred CAL.

  ❏ **Per User**   Each user that connects to the RDS server must have an RDS User CAL. If the user has multiple devices, such as a desktop computer, a laptop, and a smart phone, the user only needs a single CAL. This option makes the most sense where each user has his or her own computer, and some users have more than one, including users who connect from their home computers.

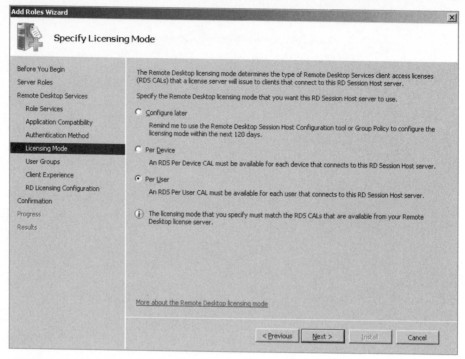

FIGURE 13-22 The Specify Licensing Mode page of the Add Roles Wizard.

9. Select your licensing mode and then click Next to continue to the Select User Groups Allowed Access To This RD Session Host Server page, as shown in Figure 13-23.

10. Click Add to open the Select Users, Computers, Or Groups dialog box shown in Figure 13-24. For most SBS 2011 Essentials scenarios, type **Domain Users** in the Enter The Object Names To Select box, as shown, and then click Check Names.

> **Note** If you have a special group of users who are allowed to use the RD Session Host, type the group name here instead of *Domain Users*.

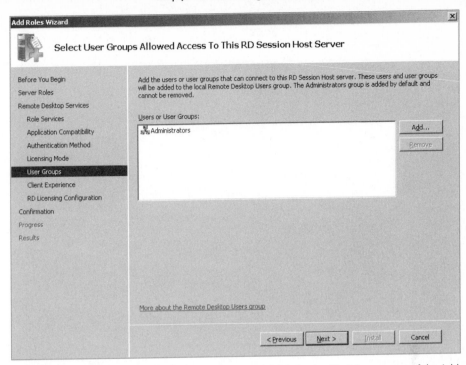

FIGURE 13-23   Select User Groups Allowed Access To This RD Session Host Server page of the Add Roles Wizard.

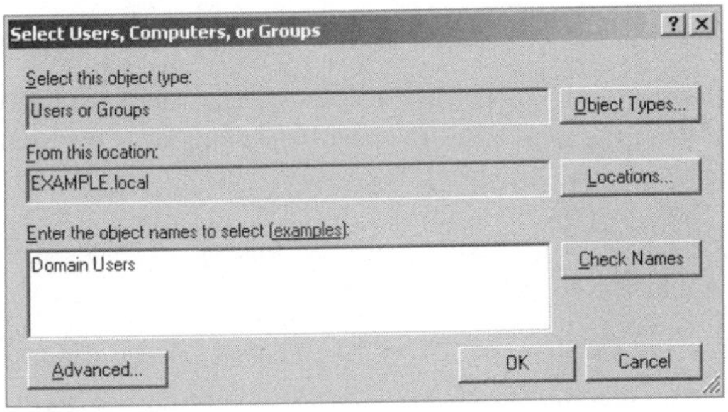

FIGURE 13-24   The Select Users, Computers, Or Groups dialog box.

11. Click OK to return to the Add Roles Wizard, and then click Next to proceed to the Configure Client Experience page shown in Figure 13-25.

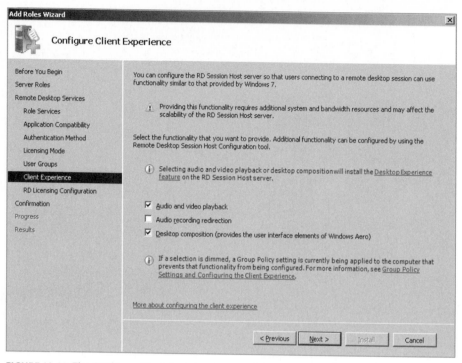

FIGURE 13-25 The Configure Client Experience page of the Add Roles Wizard.

12. For most SBS 2011 Essentials environments, select at least Audio And Video Playback and Desktop Composition (Provides The User Interface Elements Of Windows Aero). This will give your users a richer user experience.

13. Click Next to move to the Configure Discovery Scope For RD Licensing page. You should not configure a scope here.

14. Click Next and then Install to begin enabling the RDS role. When the Installation Results page appears, as shown in Figure 13-26, you'll see that a reboot is required.

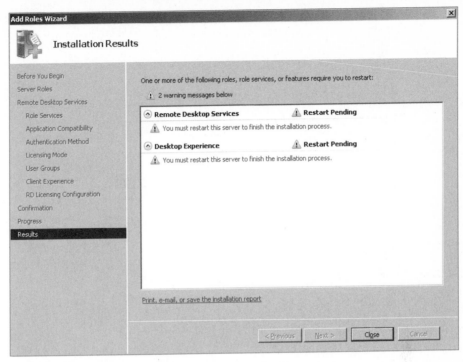

FIGURE 13-26 The Installation Results page. Another reboot is required.

15. Click Close and then click Yes to reboot the server. After the server has rebooted, log back on with the same account you used to add the role so that the installation can finish.

16. On the Installation Results page, shown in Figure 13-27, click the Configure License Settings On An RD Session Host Server link to open the Remote Desktop Services help screen on RD Licensing if you want detailed information about configuring licensing. Or skip ahead to the next section where we cover assigning a licensing server.

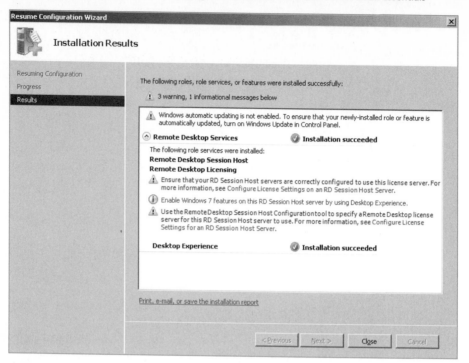

FIGURE 13-27 The Installation Results page after rebooting and logging back on to the server.

17. Click Close to complete the installation.

Adding other roles or features follows essentially similar steps to those used to add the RDS role. The specific options and pages offered vary depending on the requirements for the particular role or feature.

Native Tools

Unlike the configuration of the main SBS 2011 Essentials server, all configuration on a second server requires use of the native Windows Server tools unless your second server is WMS 2011. WMS 2011 has a special Dashboard based on the one in SBS 2011 Essentials, so we'll cover that separately later in this chapter.

The primary native tool used to manage Windows Server 2008 R2 is Server Manager, as shown in Figure 13-28.

The Server Manager console provides a single management console that integrates all the management functions for the server. To show how to use Server Manager and the native tools that are part of it, we'll cover two functions for our second server—configuring the licensing server, and creating a RemoteApp that can be deployed to client computers.

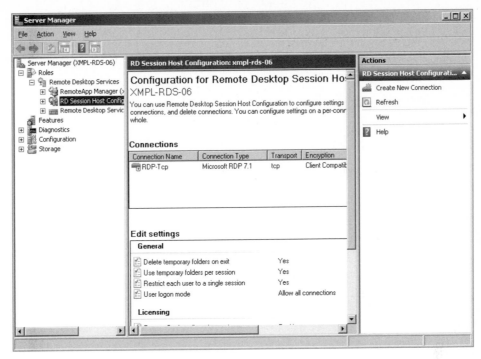

FIGURE 13-28 The Server Manager console.

Configuring the Licensing Servers for Remote Desktop

The one step we couldn't complete when we installed the Remote Desktop Services role was to assign the licensing server for it. To do that now, use the following steps:

1. Open the Server Manager if it isn't already open.

2. Expand Roles in the left pane, and then expand Remote Desktop Services, as shown earlier in Figure 13-28.

3. Select RD Session Host Configuration in the left pane, and then double-click Remote Desktop License Servers in the Licensing section of the Edit Settings pane to open the Properties dialog box for RD Session Host Configuration.

4. The warning message shown in Figure 13-29 appears. Read the warning and then click Close to acknowledge it.

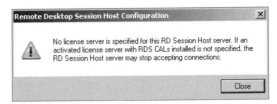

FIGURE 13-29 The warning that no license server has yet been specified.

5. On the Licensing tab of the Properties dialog box, select Per User or Per Device, as appropriate.

6. Click Add to open the Add License Server dialog box shown in Figure 13-30. Select the [Local] entry and click Add.

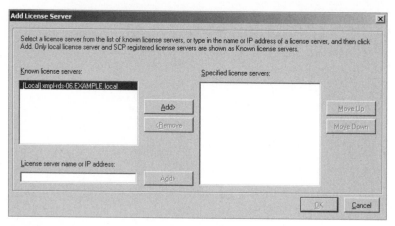

FIGURE 13-30 Select the [Local] server as the specified license server.

7. Click OK to close the Add License Server dialog box and return to Server Manager.

Before you can use the license server, you need to activate it. Unfortunately, activating the license server can't be done from inside Server Manager, so you'll need to use the RD Licensing Manager console. Use the following steps to activate the license server:

1. Open the RD Licensing Manager by clicking Remote Desktop Services in the Administrative Tools menu and selecting Remote Desktop Licensing Manager.

2. In the RD Licensing Manager console, as shown in Figure 13-31, select the server in the left pane.

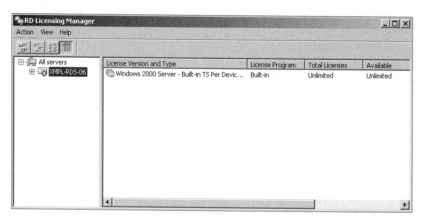

FIGURE 13-31 The RD Licensing Manager console.

3. Select Activate Server from the Action menu to open the Activate Server Wizard. Click Next to proceed to the Connection Method page shown in Figure 13-32.

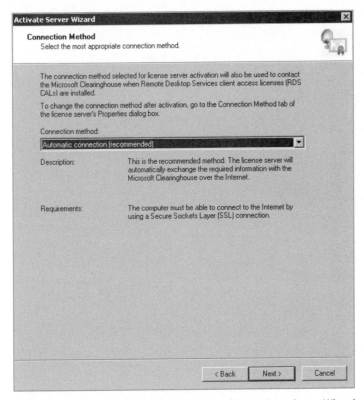

FIGURE 13-32 The Connection Method page of the Activate Server Wizard.

4. Select a connection method from the drop-down list. The choices are Automatic Connection (Recommended), Web Browser, or Telephone. Choose Automatic Connection, which does require an Internet connection from the server you are activating.

5. Click Next to continue to the first Company Information page, as shown in Figure 13-33. Fill in all the fields on this page—they are required.

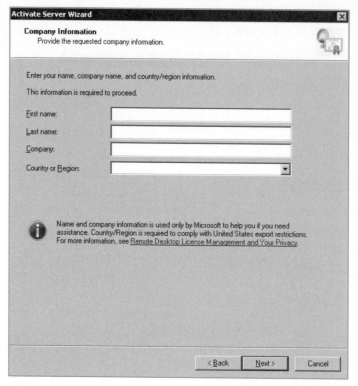

FIGURE 13-33 The required fields on the first Company Information page of the Activate Server Wizard.

6. Click Next to move on to the second page of company information. All information on this page is optional—fill it in only if you want to. Click Next, and if your connection is good, your server will activate and you'll be presented with the completion page. You can continue to add CALs by selecting the Start Install Licenses Wizard Now check box.

7. Click Next until you get to the License Program page of the Activate Server Wizard, as shown in Figure 13-34.

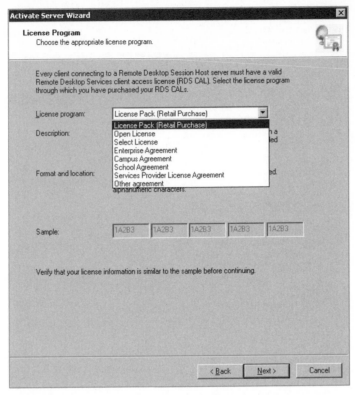

FIGURE 13-34 Choose the type of RDS CALs you've purchased.

8. Select the type of license you're entering from the License Program drop-down list.

9. Click Next and fill in the license code. Click Next again, and the activation will complete.

Note Additional steps are required for either the web browser or telephone methods. If you need to reactivate your server and reinstall licenses, you'll be required to use the telephone method.

Enabling RemoteApps

When a client runs an application by using RemoteApps, the application is presented on the local computer but is actually running on the RD Session Host. This allows you, the administrator, to centralize key applications on a terminal server while giving users the look and feel of running everything locally on their own computers. To demonstrate this, the following steps show how to enable Calculator as a RemoteApp program and create an .msi file to deploy it:

1. Open Server Manager, if it isn't already open, and navigate to the RemoteApp Manager, as shown in Figure 13-35.

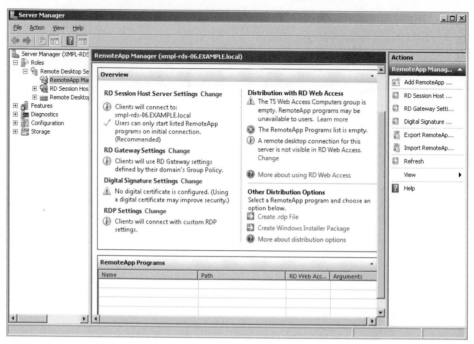

FIGURE 13-35 The RemoteApp Manager in Server Manager.

2. Click Add RemoteApp Program in the Actions pane to open the RemoteApp Wizard.

3. Click Next to continue to the Choose Programs To Add To The RemoteApp Programs List page shown in Figure 13-36. Select Calculator in the Name window, as shown.

4. Click Next and then Finish to add Calculator as a RemoteApp program.

5. Select Calculator in the RemoteApp Programs pane, and then click Create Windows Installer Package in the Actions pane to open the RemoteApp Wizard.

6. Click Next to move on to the Specify Package Settings page shown in Figure 13-37.

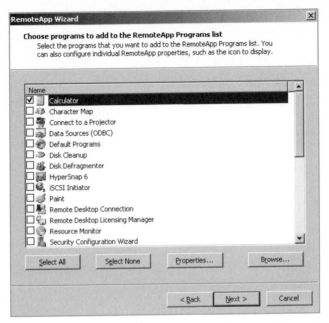

FIGURE 13-36 The Choose Programs To Add To The RemoteApp Programs List page of the RemoteApp Wizard.

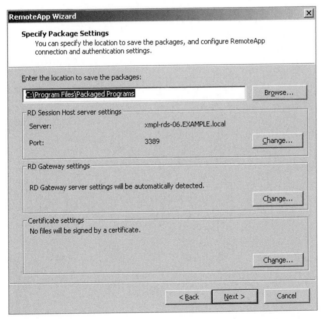

FIGURE 13-37 The Specify Package Settings page of the RemoteApp Wizard.

7. Click Next to proceed to the Configure Distribution Package page shown in Figure 13-38. Select Desktop and also specify a Start menu folder. (The default value of Remote Programs is fine for most situations.)

FIGURE 13-38 The Configure Distribution Package page of the RemoteApp Wizard.

8. Click Next and then Finish. When the Packaged Programs folder opens in Windows Explorer, click Share With and then Advanced Sharing to open the Packaged Programs Properties dialog box shown in Figure 13-39.

9. Click Advanced Sharing to open the Advanced Sharing dialog box shown in Figure 13-40. Select Share This Folder, type a name for the share, and click OK.

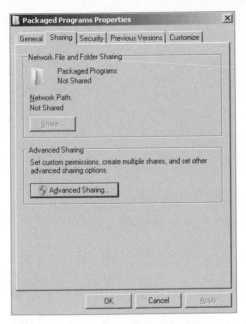

FIGURE 13-39 The Packaged Programs Properties dialog box.

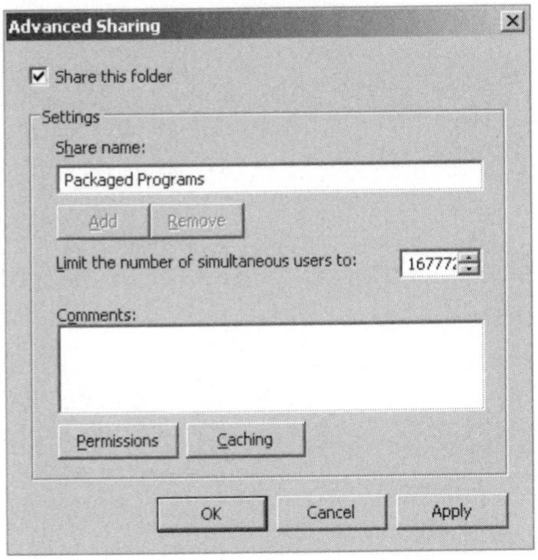

FIGURE 13-40 The Advanced Sharing dialog box.

10. Click Close to close the Properties dialog box and return to Windows Explorer.

Now you can install the program from any computer on the network. Figure 13-41 shows Calculator running as a RemoteApp on a Windows 7 client.

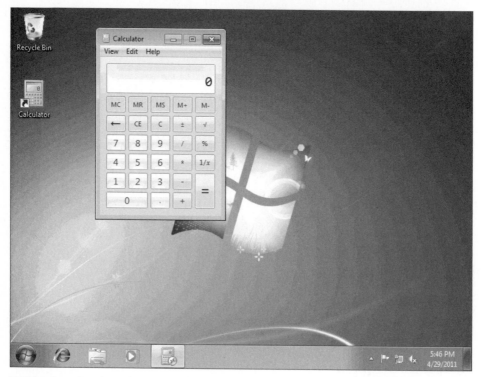

FIGURE 13-41 Running Calculator as a RemoteApp.

Now running Calculator as a RemoteApp is obviously a trivial example, but you can do this with any application that you install on the RD Session Host.

Installing and Managing Windows MultiPoint Server 2011

All the things you can do with RD Session Host as a second server can also be done using Windows MultiPoint Server 2011 as your second server, plus you can add stations to the server with a USB device or by adding a monitor to the video card and a USB hub for the keyboard and mouse. This drastically lowers the hardware cost to deploy additional worksta- tions. In addition, you can use any computer running at least Windows XP SP3, or any thin client that supports RDS 6.0, to connect to WMS just as you can with an RD Session Host.

Installing Windows MultiPoint Server 2011

The installation of WMS 2011 starts out the same as the installation of Windows Server 2008 R2, but rather than using the complicated Initial Configuration Tasks Wizard we covered earlier in the chapter, you only need to provide a name for the WMS 2011 server and select the configuration options you want, as shown in Figure 13-42, and you're done.

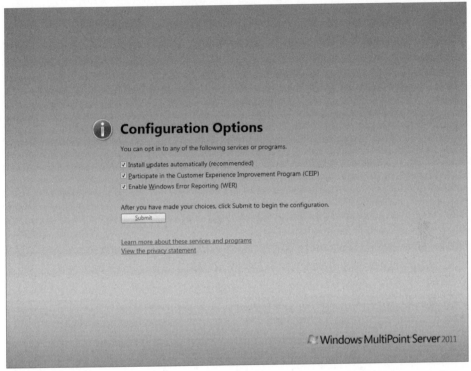

FIGURE 13-42 The Configuration Options screen for Windows MultiPoint Server 2011.

Well, almost done. You still need to join the server to the SBS 2011 Essentials domain and install applications on the server. But those are standard tasks for any computer in your network, and you can join your WMS 2011 server by using the same Connector application discussed in Chapter 6, "Adding User Accounts." Unlike running a Windows Server 2008 R2 server as your second server, with WMS 2011 as your second server, SBS 2011 Essentials treats it just like any other client workstation on the network.

Managing Windows MultiPoint Server 2011

The main management interface for WMS 2011 is the MultiPoint Manager shown in Figure 13-43. The MultiPoint Manager has the same look and feel as the Dashboard used by SBS 2011 Essentials.

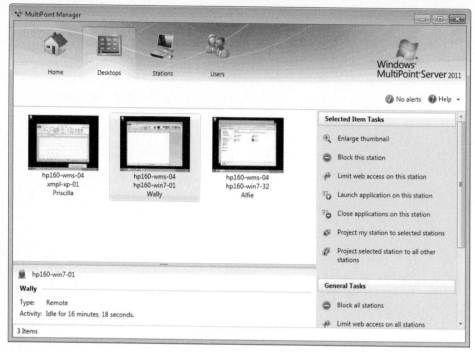

FIGURE 13-43 The MultiPoint Manager console.

As you can see from the figure, the MultiPoint Manager gives you a lot of flexibility and power to manage the sessions of the users connecting to it. Not only can you see what is happening on their sessions, you can block web access, lock out the station entirely, or launch applications on the user's desktop. Plus you have the option of projecting any workstation's desktop to one or all of the other sessions connected to WMS 2011. You can't do that with regular Windows Server 2008 R2 and RD Session Host. For more information on Windows Multipoint Server 2011, go to *http://www.microsoft.com/multipoint/*.

Summary

In this chapter, we've covered how to decide what kind of second server to add to your Windows Small Business Server 2011 Essentials network. We've also covered *how* to add that second server and shown you some of the native tools you'll need to work with when using Windows Server 2008 R2 as your second server. Finally, we covered using Windows MultiPoint Server 2011 as an alternative second server in situations that don't require SQL Server.

In the next chapter, we'll cover how to configure and use Remote Web Access to provide remote users with easy and safe access to your SBS 2011 Essentials network resources.

Chapter 14
Managing Remote Access

For several centuries, work consisted of going to a place of business, doing a job, and then going home. In the last century or so, workers at home might be reachable by phone, but most things they needed to do required them to return to the workplace. Then computers and pagers and cell phones came along, and workers were expected to be reachable virtually around the clock, no matter where they were. But that electronic leash didn't come with a corresponding ability to access the resources to resolve the problem or deal with the issue. All too often, responding to that electronic leash meant going in to work—just as it had before such technological wonders.

Windows Small Business Server 2011 Essentials, however, gives you new and improved tools so that you can access critical resources from wherever you are, without having to leave home (or the beach).

The two ways to access a network's resources are Remote Web Access (RWA) and virtual private networks (VPNs). RWA is the replacement for the Remote Web Workplace (RWW) of previous versions of Windows Small Business Server (SBS), and it adds important new functionality.

 Important VPNs are not as secure as RWA connections and are not recommended for SBS networks.

When RWW was introduced in Windows Small Business Server 2003, it was a revolutionary new way to enable remote access to network resources in a secure and convenient way that was the source of not a little envy from enterprise networks that had nothing equivalent.

In SBS 2011 Essentials, RWW has been replaced by RWA, which offers improved functionality as compared to RWW and is shared with other products, such as Windows Small Business Server 2011 Standard and Windows Home Server 2011. The basic premise of RWA is to provide a secure way for remote users to access the resources of SBS networks. Users connect to an RWA home page, shown in Figure 14-1, and from there they can:

- Connect to their desktop in the office (Professional, Enterprise, and Ultimate versions).
- Upload and download files to the folder shares on the SBS server.
- Connect to additional help or features as available.

Administrative users have additional options available, including the ability to connect to the SBS server or other servers on the network.

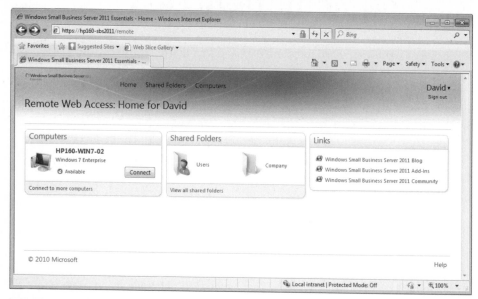

FIGURE 14-1 The home page for standard users.

Starting Remote Web Access

To start and configure Remote Web Access, start the SBS 2011 Essentials Dashboard and follow these steps:

1. Click Server Settings to open the dialog box shown in Figure 14-2.

2. Click Turn On to start the RWA Wizard.

3. Read the Getting Started page. If you want to set up your router manually, select the check box to skip router setup.

> **Note** If your router has UPnP enabled, SBS 2011 Essentials will configure the router automatically. If you're not using UPnP, you need to forward ports 80 and 443 to the SBS 2011 Essentials server before completing the wizard.

4. The RWA Wizard will proceed to verify your domain name and connect to the router, as shown in Figure 14-3.

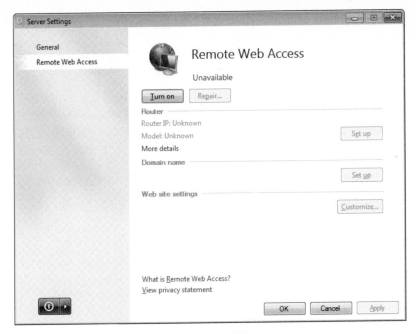

FIGURE 14-2 The Server Settings dialog box for RWA.

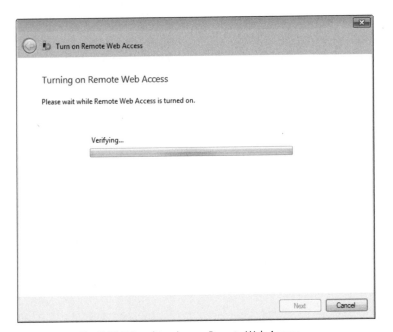

FIGURE 14-3 The RWA Wizard turning on Remote Web Access.

Configuring the RWA Computer List

In SBS 2011 Essentials, a user sees only the computers that he or she is allowed to connect to. The list is created when you join the computer to the SBS network.

After computers are set up, however, you can easily change this list. We change it by configuring the computers that a user account is assigned to. To change the list of computers that a user can connect to from RWA, open the SBS 2011 Essentials Dashboard and then use the following steps:

1. Click Users in the navigation bar, and highlight the name of the user.

2. Select View The Account Properties in the Tasks pane to open the Properties dialog box for the user.

3. Select the Computer Access tab (see Figure 14-4).

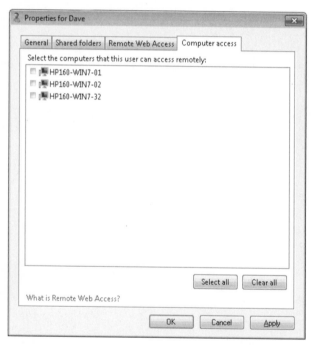

FIGURE 14-4 The Properties dialog box for user Dave Arguy.

4. Select the computers that you want the user to be able to access.

5. Click OK to close the Properties dialog box for the user and return to the SBS 2011 Essentials Dashboard.

Enabling or Disabling a User for RWA

You can enable or disable the access of individual users to RWA. Access is the default setting when you add a user. If you want only a subset of your users to be able to log in to RWA, you can disable the access of those you want to exclude.

Follow these steps to enable or disable a user from Remote Web Access.

1. Open the SBS 2011 Essentials Dashboard if it isn't already open.

2. Click Users in the navigation bar, and then right-click the user account to be changed.

3. Select View Account Properties, and then click the Remote Web Access tab, as shown in Figure 14-5.

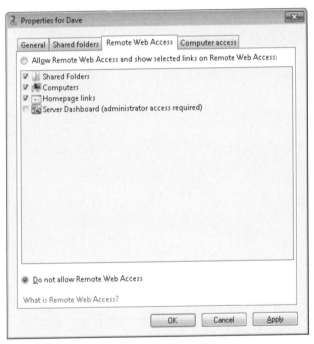

FIGURE 14-5 The Remote Web Access page of a user account's Properties dialog box.

4. Select Allow Remote Web Access or Do Not Allow Remote Web Access.

5. Click OK when you're finished.

Configuring User Settings

By default, standard users are allowed access to shared folders and links to SBS-related websites. You can define other settings for any additional folders and computers that a user is allowed to access.

Adding Shared Folders

To change the folders that a user can see, follow these steps:

1. Open the SBS 2011 Essentials Dashboard. Select Server Folders And Hard Drives.

2. Click Add A Folder to open the dialog box shown in Figure 14-6.

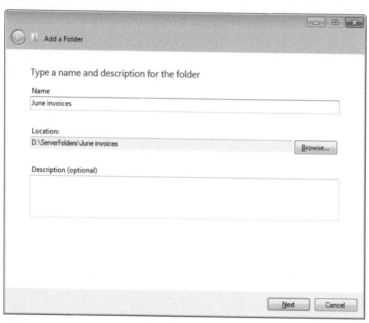

FIGURE 14-6 Adding a shared folder.

3. Provide a name for the folder and it will be created at the location shown.

4. Add a description if you want, and click Next.

5. On the next page, you can set the level of access by user. By default, standard users have Read access and administrators have Read/Write access. Click Add Folder.

   The next page prompts you to open the Backup Configuration Wizard to be sure that the folder is selected for backup.

6. Click Close when you're finished.

Note For full details on setting up backups, see Chapter 9, "Backing Up and Restoring."

Real World: Two-Factor Authentication and RWA

Remote Web Access is a secure way to connect to your SBS 2011 Essentials network. It uses IPsec tunneling, and it uses the authentication of Microsoft's Active Directory directory service (user name and password) to grant access to the resources of the SBS network. That being said, if your SBS 2011 Essentials network contains sensitive information and you're subject to regulatory requirements for data protection, you should consider two-factor authentication (TFA) on RWA, especially for any accounts that are either network administrators or have special access to sensitive data.

Authentication is the process of ensuring that the individual who requests access to a resource is, in fact, the individual he or she is claiming to be. There are four basic kinds of authentication: "what you know," "who you are," "what you have," and "where you are." TFA requires that any user requesting remote access to the resources of your SBS network use two methods to uniquely identify himself or herself. The first method is to provide the user name and password of the user, and the second is some other factor. The real beauty of TFA is that even if one of your factors is compromised, it's useless without the second factor.

The basic user name and password is a what-you-know factor, and it's the most commonly used form of authentication. When combined with a sort of loose where-you-are factor—that is, at the console of your own PC—and when passwords or passphrases are sufficiently complex, it's a good method of authentication.

Who-you-are authentication is usually some form of biometric analysis—fingerprint readers, retina scanners, and even visual recognition software all are forms of who-you-are authentication. We're not big fans of the most common of these, fingerprint readers. They're rather easily defeated from what we've seen to date.

What-you-have authentication is usually something like a smart card or a one-time password generator. Microsoft's corporate network uses smart cards for its TFA, but we think one-time passwords are a lot easier to deal with and deploy in a small business. One-time passwords don't require deploying smart card readers for everyone, and the overall costs are significantly less as a result.

Finally, where-you-are authentication uses your physical location as a proof of who you are. An example is the variable authentication process that some banks are implementing. It starts with the IP address and machine name from which you're connecting to your bank. The bank knows that the IP address is typical for you and only asks a standard set of verification questions. But if you were to connect from a public wireless access point while you're on vacation, the bank would immediately be more cautious about who you are claiming to be, and the secondary verification process is more detailed. This kind of variable authentication process is expensive to implement and outside the scope of most small businesses.

We use TFA for remote access to our SBS 2011 Essentials network. We've implemented Scorpion Software's AuthAnvil (*http://www.scorpionsoft.com*). The AuthAnvil RWA agent (formerly known as RWWGuard) extends the standard RWA logon page to require a one-time password.

What we really like about AuthAnvil is that it's almost completely transparent. It looks and feels just like SBS, except for the one additional field for our one-time password. And with the AuthAnvil SoftToken running on our phones, we no longer even have to carry around AuthAnvil key fob passcode generators.

Customizing the Logon Page

To customize the looks of the RWA logon page, open the SBS 2011 Essentials Dashboard and follow these steps:

1. Click Server Settings, as shown in Figure 14-7.

2. On the Server Settings page, select Remote Web Access and then click Customize.

3. Select the Logon Page tab.

4. Select a new logon picture or logo. You can also change the website title (see Figure 14-8).

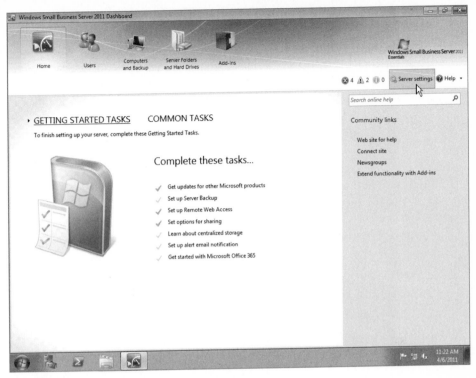

FIGURE 14-7 Configuring Remote Web Access links.

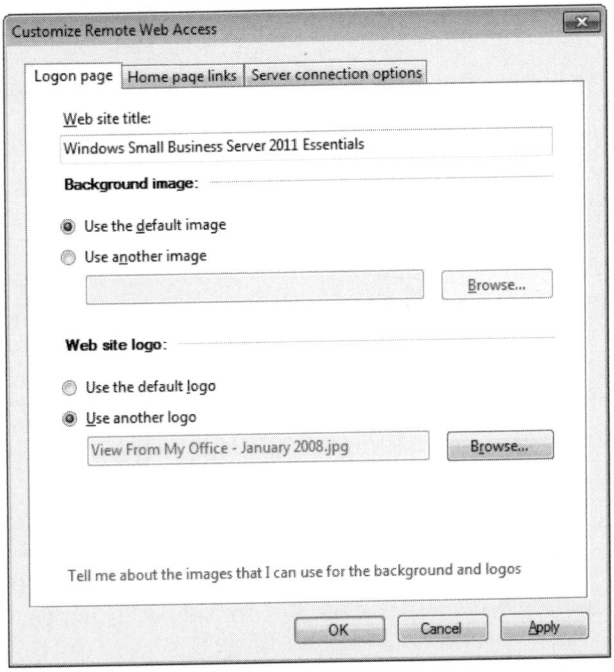

FIGURE 14-8 Changing the logon page for RWA.

5. When you've completed your changes to the RWA website properties, click OK to exit and apply the changes. Just to give you an idea of what's easily possible, we added a background image from a photo taken from the office to our example domain's RWA logon page, as shown in Figure 14-9.

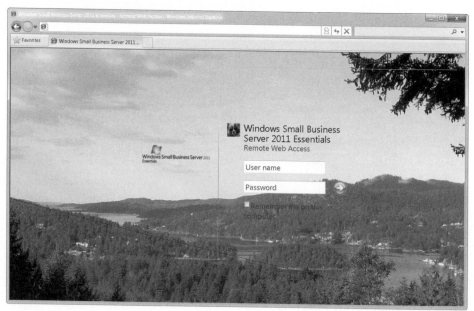

FIGURE 14-9 The customized RWA logon page.

Customizing Links on the RWA Home Page

When users log on to Remote Web Access, their home page shows not only the computers and shared folders they can access but also a section of links. Several links are included by default, but you can add links that are needed by your organization and remove irrelevant or outdated ones.

To add or delete a home page link, open the SBS 2011 Essentials Dashboard and follow these steps:

1. Click Server Settings.

2. On the Server Settings page, select Remote Web Access and then click Home Page Links.

3. To add a link, provide a name and web address, as shown in Figure 14-10.

   You can select an existing link and then click Move Up or Move Down to change the list order, or click Remove to eliminate a link. You can add or rearrange as many links as you need.

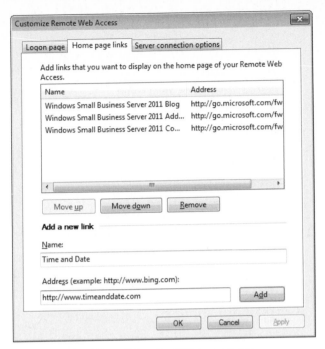

FIGURE 14-10 Adding a link to the RWA home page.

4. Click Add and then OK.

Summary

Connectivity is a huge topic, but in this chapter we focused on remote connectivity. Remote Web Access is an excellent tool for users who travel, work from home, or just need to connect remotely for any reason. Starting with the next chapter, we cover more advanced tools, including those used for troubleshooting the network.

Part IV

Advanced Tasks and Windows Small Business Server 2011 Essentials

Chapter 15
Troubleshooting

Trouble on your Windows Small Business Server 2011 Essentials network can take many forms, from sluggish response to total, catastrophic failure. We already covered sluggish response in Chapter 10, "Monitoring Network Health," and we'll talk about dealing with disaster recovery in the next chapter, so that leaves the great middle ground for this chapter.

In this chapter, we cover basic troubleshooting, in a general way, along with some topics specific to SBS 2011 Essentials. The primary problem areas we'll cover are:

- Installation
- Connectivity
- Remote access
- Sharing and file availability

There are other areas that cause users and administrators problems, such as printing, but for those other areas, we've tried to integrate basic troubleshooting into the main body of the chapter.

Troubleshooting 101

Before we jump into specifics, it's useful to step back and look at the process of troubleshooting and how it's done. This could easily be an entire book, so obviously we're going to focus here on a high-level view of the process, not on specific examples. The basic steps are:

- Eliminate distractions
- Identify variables
- Narrow the scope
- Identify one change
- Evaluate the result

As you work to troubleshoot a problem, you'll need to follow these steps to find the cause and correct it.

Eliminate Distractions

As system administrators, we spend a lot of our time working on multiple projects and tasks, essentially simultaneously. This multitasking is the normal lot of most system administrators, and for most projects, it's not an issue. However, when you're troubleshooting a problem, you need to narrow your focus and *only* deal with the problem you are troubleshooting. This is important, but contrary to how most system administrators work on their day-to-day tasks. For me, that means:

- Close Microsoft Outlook.
- Close Microsoft Word.
- Close the script or scripts I'm currently working on.
- Close Windows Live Messenger, or set it to Busy.
- Turn off my phone.
- Close Windows Mail.
- Close Windows Internet Explorer.
- Close anything else I'm working on.

Your set of distractions will be slightly different, but whatever they are, recognize that you can't effectively troubleshoot a problem if you have multiple distractions keeping you from focusing completely on the problem you're trying to troubleshoot.

Distractions are also an issue as you try to identify exactly what the problem is. Before you can troubleshoot a problem, you need to clearly and unequivocally identify what the actual problem is. Often the problem is presented to you in one of two ways: either the simple "email is broken, when will it be fixed?", or an overly complex listing of all the things the user was doing and expected to be able to do, with no clear identification of what the actual problem is. You can't fix a problem if you haven't clearly identified what it is.

For problems beyond the simplistic, identifying the actual problem is often the single most difficult and important step in correcting it. This is especially true if you want to find the real root cause of the problem and not just provide a short-term fix.

Identify Variables

After you've identified the actual problem you're trying to troubleshoot, you need to identify the variables that affect the problem. If it's a networking problem,

- Is it continuous or intermittent?
- Is it worse at night, or at lunch time?

- Is it essentially the same all the time?

- Is the problem isolated to one computer, or one group of computers?

- Do all computers have the problem?

Identifying the variables will help you to identify what you need to do to narrow the scope of the problem and focus on what changes you should be making.

Narrow the Scope

Identifying the variables of a problem often helps you narrow down the scope of the problem. If the problem is initially identified as "no Internet access," and you identify that it only happens on one group of computers and primarily only during busy periods, you already know a great deal about the problem and how to go about fixing it. You've narrowed the scope of the problem to the subset of computers that have the problem, and you've narrowed the type of problem to one that is triggered by heavy load.

Narrowing the scope is a key step as you're trying to identify *where* a problem is. If a user reports that they are unable to connect to the Internet, the problem could be almost anywhere, and it could be a DNS issue, physical network hardware problems, an operating system configuration problem, and so on—far too many variables and far too broad a scope to even begin to fix it. But if you can narrow the problem down, then you can start to identify a change and evaluate whether it has corrected the problem.

Identify One Change

If there is one troubleshooting mistake we see more than any other, it's a failure to observe the basic rule to *only change one variable at a time*. Then evaluate the result, and if it didn't resolve the problem, return to your original configuration. Don't make the mistake of *serial changes*. We see this all the time. The person troubleshooting will carefully identify the actual problem, eliminate the distractions, identify the variables, narrow the scope of the problem, and change one thing. When that doesn't work, the troubleshooter will change another variable, *without setting the first variable back to its original state*. When that doesn't solve the problem, the person changes another variable, and then another, and so on. Pretty soon no one has any idea what the original problem was or what steps have been taken already. And it's impossible to know whether any change you make that fails might have worked in your original environment. If multiple people are working on a problem, the complications are exponentially worse. Keep a log of all changes, including who made them, why they made them, when they made them, and what the result was. Even if there's only one person working on a problem, the log will provide valuable information for this and future troubleshooting tasks.

Evaluate the Result

After you've made a change in the hopes of correcting the problem, you need to actually *evaluate* that change before you do anything else. Did the change fix the problem? Great. Lock it in and document what you found and what you changed. If, however, it didn't fix the problem, you need to evaluate whether it could be part of a solution. Some problems require a multipart solution, though these are far less common than a single-issue problem.

When you suspect that you might have a problem that requires multiple changes to correct, you need to be careful not to fall into the trap of serial changes. Be clear about what you're changing and why, and then carefully evaluate each result. If the result isn't moving you in the correct direction, roll back to the last known point and start again.

Whenever you're troubleshooting a problem and evaluating a potential fix, remember what the failure scenario is, and make sure you evaluate the fix appropriately. If your failures only happen during morning logon time, and you put in a change that you hope will fix it, you can't really evaluate the result until the next morning logon time. This seems obvious, and it should be, but we've all too often seen changes made and then never properly evaluated again. This is especially likely when you're dealing with an intermittent problem.

Installation

The SBS 2011 Essentials installation is a highly automated installation that is quite reliable, but there are some areas that can cause issues. The known issues are:

- Hard disk too small or not recognized.
- Network card not found.
- Migration failures.

Hard Disk Issues

SBS 2011 Essentials requires a hard disk of at least 200 GB for the primary hard disk, and if it can't find that hard disk during initial installation, the installation will fail. The most common cause of this is that the drivers for the primary disk aren't included in Windows Server 2008 R2, and therefore the disk isn't visible to the installer. Before the installation can proceed, you need to add the missing drivers.

To add drivers during the installation, click the Load Drivers button on the All Files And Folders On Your Primary Hard Drive Will Be Deleted page of the Installing Windows Wizard to browse for the drivers, as shown in Figure 15-1.

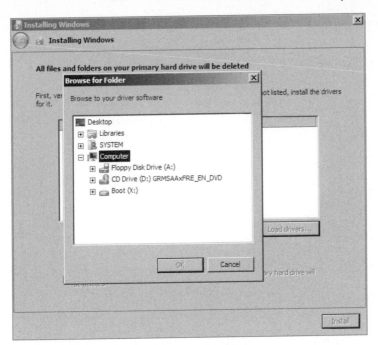

FIGURE 15-1 Adding storage drivers during installation.

Drivers that are in the \DRIVERS folder of a removable USB memory stick or floppy disk will be automatically recognized and loaded.

Network Card Not Found

Another installation problem that can prevent a successful installation is the failure to recognize that there is a network card on the SBS 2011 Essentials server. If SBS 2011 Essentials doesn't have a driver for your network card, the installation will fail during the SBS portion of the installation, as shown in Figure 15-2. The installation will not proceed without a network card being detected. Click the Install Network Drivers button to open Device Manager and install the drivers if they don't require a specialized installation program.

If your network drivers must be installed with a special installation program, you can open a command window by pressing Shift+F10, as shown in Figure 15-3. This will allow you to run the installation program for the drivers. After the drivers are loaded, you might need to restart the server and allow them to be detected and automatically configured.

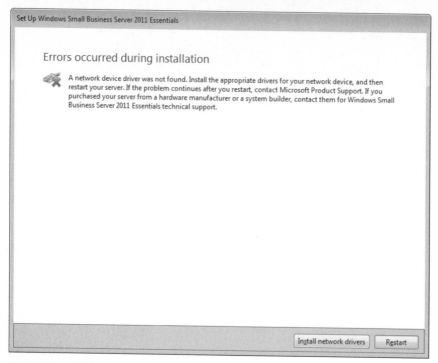

FIGURE 15-2 SBS 2011 Essentials must detect a network card to complete installation.

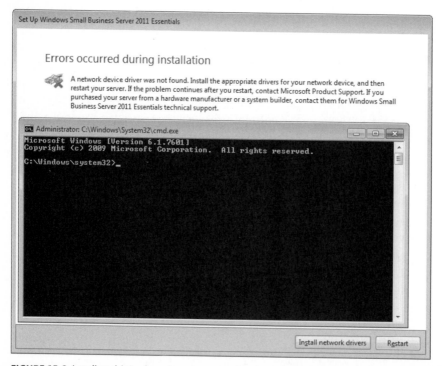

FIGURE 15-3 Loading drivers by using a command prompt during SBS 2011 Essentials installation.

Migration Failures

Most SBS 2011 Essentials installations are new installations, where an existing Windows Small Business Server server has not been installed. But when you are moving to SBS 2011 Essentials from an existing Windows Server environment, you'll want to retain your existing users and configuration. This requires a migration, not a new installation. We cover migration from an existing Windows Small Business Server 2003 R2 network to SBS 2011 Essentials in Appendix A. This a complex process, and it's easy to miss a step during the migration, leading to a failure. Keep careful notes at all stages of the process, and write down *any* error messages you encounter. Don't attempt to bypass errors, but work to identify and correct the underlying causes before proceeding to the next step of the migration.

Before you attempt any migration, make sure that you have a full and complete backup of your existing server, and that you've verified that you can restore files and folders from that backup. A migration is a one-way street, and you can't turn around in the middle of it. If there is a failure, your only recourse is to restore your backup and start over.

Before proceeding with a migration to SBS 2011 Essentials, read Appendix A and the relevant Microsoft migration documentation thoroughly. Make sure that you have all the required tools and information available before you begin.

Most migration failures fall into two broad categories—operator error and Active Directory directory services configuration errors. The SBS Best Practice Analyzer (BPA), along with the other tools shown in Table 15-1, can be used to identify Active Directory or other network issues in the source SBS 2003 network.

TABLE 15-1 Network Diagnostic Tools

Tool	Description
Netdiag.exe	Helps isolate networking and connectivity issues
Dcdiag.exe	Analyzes the state of domain controllers in a forest or enterprise, and reports issues to assist you in troubleshooting
Repadmin.exe	Assists you in diagnosing replication issues between domain controllers

Failures due to operator error are harder to troubleshoot. As you can see from the length and complexity of Appendix A, there are a lot of steps involved and it is easy to miss a step or make a mistake during the process. Create a checklist before you start that includes every major step of the process. Write down what you should expect to see at each stage of the process, and then while you work, document the condition and the process. This makes it much easier to identify a mistake before you have gone too far to simply correct it. After you go past a stage in the migration process, you might well have no option but to start over if there were unrecognized issues at that stage and you didn't stop to correct them.

Connectivity

Connectivity errors are a common problem on most networks. They can be caused by a wide variety of problems, from hardware malfunction to software configuration errors to malware. The first step for troubleshooting connectivity issues is to narrow the scope of the problem.

Local vs. Global

The starting point for troubleshooting a connectivity issue is determining whether it is a local issue or a network-wide problem. If one computer is having a problem, but all others are working as expected, then you know the issue is local to that computer or to the physical network connections to that computer.

If the problem is local to a single client computer, it's fairly obvious that the problem is local. But if the single computer having a problem is the SBS 2011 Essentials server, it often appears as a much more general problem. A failed network card on the server is a very local problem to that server, but it is a global problem because it affects every computer on the network.

It's usually useful to look at the scope of a problem, at least initially, from the perspective of the client computers on the network. If all or many of the client computers are experiencing the problem, then your initial assessment of the scope of the issue is that it's global. If only one client computer is experiencing the issue, the problem is local.

When a problem appears to be global, your next step is to see if it's caused by something on or connecting to the SBS 2011 Essentials server or the Internet gateway device (router). From there you can start to narrow down the specifics of the problem. Some possibilities include:

- Client computers can't connect to the Internet but can ping the router.
- Client computers can ping the SBS 2011 Essentials server but can't connect to the Internet.
- Some client computers can connect to the Internet and open files shared on the SBS 2011 Essentials server, but others can't.
- Some clients can connect to shares on the SBS 2011 Essentials server, but others can't. No clients can connect to the Internet.

Each of the scenarios listed is a sign of a global problem, and if you've done enough work to actually be able to describe the issue in the terms shown, you're already most of the way to solving it. Let's take a quick look at each in turn, and see how being able to clearly describe the problem has already put us most of the way toward resolving it.

Client Computers Can't Connect to the Internet but Can Ping the Router

If all the client computers can ping the router, we already know that the router is up and responding, and that the internal physical wiring and switches are in good working order. We're left with two possible problems, and our next steps will make it easy to distinguish between the two.

The first possibility is a failure of the network connection between the router and the Internet as a whole. A quick change to try is to power off the router, wait 10 seconds, and then power it back on again. Wait a half minute or so, and then see if the problem is corrected.

If not, log on to the router and verify that the router has an external IP address (router status page) and that it can ping a known external computer by IP address. A good IP address to use as a ping target is one of the DNS servers of your Internet service provider (ISP).

If connectivity from the router to the Internet as a whole fails, the problem is either external to your network or is a failure of the wide area network (WAN) side of your router. The starting point for resolution at this point is almost always a call to your ISP's help desk.

If connectivity from your router to the Internet is good, but clients still can't connect to webpages on the Internet, the problem is almost certainly name resolution. Verify that the DNS Server service is running on the SBS 2011 Essentials server, and that clients can connect to the server.

Client Computers Can Ping the SBS 2011 Essentials Server but Can't Connect to the Internet

Now we know a bit more than we did for the previous issue. We know that there is physical connectivity to the SBS server. The next step is to determine whether we can ping the router. If we can, then we're back to two possibilities—a WAN-side problem with the router or a DNS issue with the SBS 2011 Essentials server. Use a DNS tool to verify name resolution first, and then if that's OK, you've narrowed down the problem to the WAN side of the router. Reboot the router, and reboot the cable or DSL modem if it is separate from the router. If there's still a problem, it's time to call your ISP. The issue might still end up being on your premises, but your ISP needs to help you narrow it further.

Some Client Computers Can Connect to the Internet and Open Files Shared on the SBS 2011 Essentials Server, but Others Can't

You can quickly narrow this problem down by checking the IP address of one of the computers that can't connect to the SBS 2011 Essentials server. If the address begins with "169.254", then you know that the computer didn't receive a Dynamic Host Configuration Protocol (DHCP) address from the router. The next step is to determine whether the problem is a physical network issue (such as a bad network switch or a cabling issue affecting some clients but not all) or a software issue (the DHCP server on the router is not providing IP addresses).

Some Clients Can Connect to Shares on the SBS 2011 Essentials Server, but Others Can't. No Clients Can Connect to the Internet

We're one step closer than above, and we're almost certainly looking at a router problem. Those computers that can connect to the server are still working with their old DHCP addresses, but the ones that can't have most likely been rebooted since the router went out or lost their IP addresses for some other reason and can't get a new one.

Tools

There are a wide variety of tools available to system administrators for diagnosing network problems. These can be software or hardware, from the simplest (ping) to the highly sophisticated (a Fluke network analyzer). Most of us in SBS-sized networks learn to use the basic (and mostly free) tools and save the expensive stuff for large enterprise networks that can afford them. Not that we don't lust after some of the cool toys, but the reality of budgets inevitably intrudes. The three tools we use most often are:

- **ping**   Ping sends Internet Control Message Protocol (ICMP) echo request packets from a source computer to a target. If the target receives the ping, it should echo the packet back to the source computer. *Ping* is a low-level protocol and the most basic connectivity test. You can ping by IP address or by host name. If you ping by host name, a DNS server must be available to resolve the name to an IP address.

- **nslookup**   In its simplest form, *nslookup* queries a DNS server for the IP address associated with a name. This can also be used to get the name associated with an IP address or get details about the various kinds of DNS records associated with a name. You can use the default DNS server associated with your client or specify a particular DNS server.

- **net commands**   The *net* commands (*net use, net share, net view,* and so on) are useful for verifying and troubleshooting server message block (SMB) networking, which includes drive maps and printer sharing.

 Note For syntax for these and most other command-line tools, use the */?* switch to the command.

There are lots and lots of other tools, and each administrator develops his or her own set of comfortable tools to use. The three we've listed are really basic tools, but we find that well over 90 percent of the issues we have to troubleshoot never require more than these three.

Remote Access

Remote access issues fall into three basic categories—certificates, name resolution, and router or software configuration. All three are directly manipulated by the SBS 2011 Essentials Repair Remote Web Access Wizard shown in Figure 15-4.

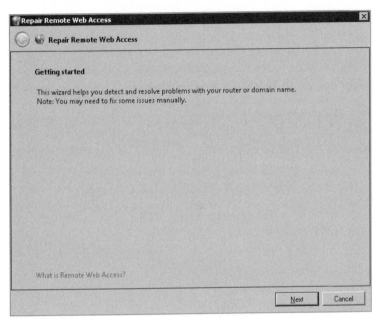

FIGURE 15-4 Use the Repair Remote Web Access Wizard to repair problems with remote access.

You should run the Repair Remote Web Access Wizard whenever you experience RWA issues. It won't fix them all, but it does an excellent job of repairing most issues and provides links to Microsoft TechNet topics to provide additional information about repairing other problems you might encounter.

Sharing and File Availability

The final area of troubleshooting is file sharing and availability. We lump these together because they often overlap. If a file is located on a network share and the cable to the server gets unplugged, the file is still being shared, it just isn't available. But to the user, it appears as a sharing problem, because he or she can't connect to the shared folder on the server. If a user doesn't have *permission* to access a file, the file is still shared, but the file isn't available to the user.

When troubleshooting sharing and availability problems, always start by verifying network connectivity between the file source and the user or computer needing access. The basic tool for this is ping. Use *ping* to establish that lower-level networking protocols are working, and then identify where the breakdown in sharing or availability is. Again, narrow the scope to identify whether it's a local or global problem, and if it's limited to one user or affects all users on a particular computer.

One area that we haven't touched on yet with regard to sharing issues is Windows Firewall or other, third-party firewalls. Windows Firewall has different settings depending on what kind of network you're on. Make sure that your network is listed as a domain network for all domain-joined computers on the SBS 2011 Essentials network, as shown in Figure 15-5.

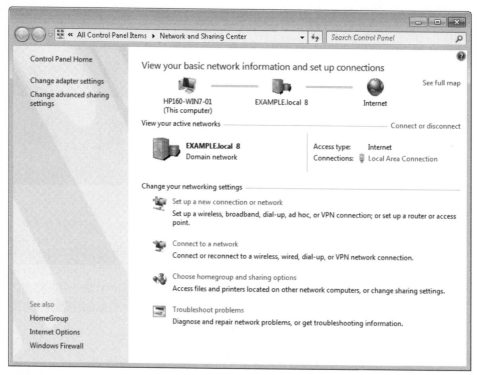

FIGURE 15-5 The Network And Sharing Center shows that the computer is on a Domain network.

A Windows 7 Home Premium computer will not have a domain network but should show Work or Home as the type of network. If the network is set as a Public network, sharing and file access will not work correctly.

Windows Firewall, shown in Figure 15-6, blocks all incoming connections to the client computer, and this can disrupt normal function and even troubleshooting if you are set to a Public network.

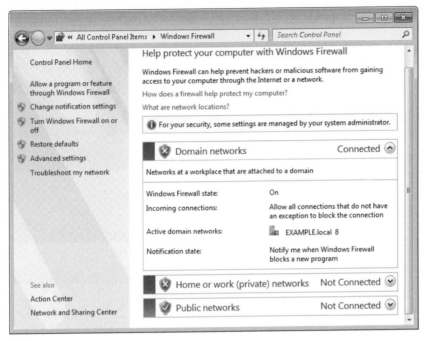

FIGURE 15-6 The Windows Firewall dialog box.

For more information on file sharing, see Chapter 8, "Managing Shared Folders." And for details on shared printers and how to troubleshoot them, see Chapter 12, "Installing and Sharing Printers."

Summary

In this chapter, we covered troubleshooting your SBS 2011 Essentials network, including the basic troubleshooting principles for all problem solving, along with specifics on troubleshooting installation issues, connectivity issues, remote access, and file sharing problems.

In the next chapter, we cover planning for your network to survive a disaster, as well as the details on how to recover your server in the event of failure.

Chapter 16
Disaster Planning and Server Recovery

Race car drivers wear Nomex fire-resistant undergarments and a helmet, and use sophisticated full-restraint systems. Schools and businesses have fire drills even though the vast majority of buildings never burn down. System administrators are no different—we do verified backups and write up disaster recovery plans we hope never to use. But we do them because there are only two types of networks: those that have experienced disaster and those that haven't—yet.

Disaster can take many forms, from the self-inflicted pain of a user or administrator doing something really, really unwise, to the uncontrollable, unpredictable, and unpreventable results of a natural disaster such as a flood or an earthquake. Whatever form your disaster takes, the future of your business will depend on how well you were prepared for the disaster, and how well you and your team respond to and recover from it.

This chapter covers both emergency preparedness and the specific steps required to recover a failed SBS 2011 Essentials server. It discusses creating a disaster recovery plan, with standardized procedures to follow in the event of a catastrophe. It also describes how to prepare for a disaster so that if (or when) one happens, you have the tools to recover.

Planning for Disaster

Some people seem to operate on the assumption that if they don't think about bad things, they won't happen. Unfortunately, life is not so easy. No business owner wants a disaster, but if you have one, you *really* don't want to start trying to build your recovery plan on the spot. Disaster recovery plans aren't exciting and sexy. But having a clear disaster recovery plan that has been thoroughly tested goes a long, long way toward providing assurance that your business will be one that survives.

There is no such thing as a final version of your disaster plan. The moment you finish creating the current version of it, it is time to start on the next version. A good disaster plan is one that you are constantly examining, improving, updating, and testing. Even the best disaster recovery plan needs to be constantly examined and adjusted or it quickly gets out of date.

Real World: Size Does Matter

Disasters happen to businesses of all sizes and types. Small businesses are no more insulated from them than large businesses are, but generally they don't have the same levels of resources to respond to them and recover from them. A large, multinational corporation with an IT staff of several hundred people worldwide certainly has more resources than a small accounting firm with an IT staff of one. As you work through the steps to build your disaster recovery plan, your decisions for planning and implementing it will vary depending on the size of your company and the resources available.

In the discussion of disaster planning that follows, many of the steps and the actions associated with those steps are quite formal and probably sound like a bit more than you can manage in your small business. And, in many cases, you're right—in a small business, one can often be substantially more informal. But do *not* make the mistake of ignoring something because it sounds too formal or involved. Rather, adjust the step and actions to fit within your smaller, but no less important, business. No matter how small your business is, if it uses and depends on Windows Small Business Server 2011 Essentials, you have valuable and business-critical assets on your server, so take the steps to protect them and your business before you have a disaster. You'll save money, time, and, most important, business reputation by being able to withstand and even grow in the face of disaster.

We've been through fires, earthquakes, crashed servers, and just plain egregious error, and we've learned the hard way that disaster recovery is something you can do a lot better if you've planned for it ahead of time. It's not sexy, and it's sometimes hard to sell to upper management, but it is worth the effort. If you're lucky, you'll never need to use all of your plans for worst-case scenarios, but if you do need them, you'll be really, *really* glad you have them.

Planning for disaster or emergencies is not a single step but an iterative, ongoing process. Systems are not mountains but rivers, constantly moving and changing, and your disaster recovery plan needs to change as your environment changes. To put together a good disaster recovery plan—one you can bet your business on—you need to follow these steps:

1. Identify the risks.
2. Identify the resources.
3. Develop the responses.
4. Test the responses.
5. Iterate.

Identifying the Risks

The first step in creating a disaster recovery plan is to identify the risks to your business and the costs associated with those risks. The risks vary from the simple to the horrible; from the deletion of an important file to the total destruction of your place of business and its computers.

To be ready for a disaster, you need to realistically assess the risks to your business and the potential costs and consequences of each disaster scenario. You need to decide both the likelihood of any specific disaster scenario and what resources you have to address it.

Identifying risks might seem like a one-time operation, but the reality is that it is constantly changing—first because your business is always changing and evolving, along with your use of technology, but also because some risks that seemed vanishingly remote a few years ago are now part of our everyday lives.

This isn't a job for a single person. You need to get as many people involved in the process of identifying the risks to your business as possible. Not only does this help ensure that you don't miss a critical risk, but it also helps to build the commitment and buy-in from everyone involved.

No matter how careful and thorough your risk assessment is, you'll miss something. Always include an "unknown risk" item in your list. Treat it just like any other risk: identify the resources available to address it, and develop countermeasures to take should it occur. The difference with this risk, of course, is that your resources and countermeasures are somewhat more generic, and you can't really test your response to the risk, because you don't yet know what it is.

Start by trying to list all the possible ways that your network could fail. Solicit help from everyone with a stake in the process. The more people involved in the brainstorming, the more ideas you'll get and the more prevention and recovery procedures you can develop and practice.

Next, look at all the ways that some external event could affect your system. (The current buzzword for this is *threat modeling*.) The team of people responsible for identifying possible external problems is probably similar to a team looking at internal failures, but with some important differences. For example, if your business is housed in a large commercial office building, you'll want to involve that building's security and facilities groups even though they aren't employees of your business. They will not only have important input into the possible threats to the business, but also they'll also have information on the resources and preventative measures already in place.

This risk identification phase is really made up of two parts: identification and assessment. They are different tasks. During the identification portion of the phase, you need to identify every possible risk, no matter how remote or unlikely. No risk suggested should be regarded as silly—don't limit or filter the suggestions in any way. Be careful at this stage in the process to not dismiss any idea or concern as trivial, unimportant, or unlikely. The idea is to get *all* ideas at this stage, however bizarre or unlikely. Then, when you have as complete a list as you can create, move on to the assessment task.

In the risk-assessment task, the goal is to understand and quantify just how likely a particular risk is. If you're located in a flood plain, for example, you're much more likely to think flood insurance is a good investment.

> **Note** Even in a very small business, where there might be only one person involved in disaster planning, it's a really good idea to get others involved somehow in at least the risk-identification task. Different people think up different scenarios and risk factors, and soliciting more and different viewpoints will improve the overall result of the process.

Identifying the Resources

After you've identified the risks to your network, you need to identify the resources available to address those risks. Resources can be internal or external, people or systems, hardware or software.

When you're identifying the resources available to deal with a specific risk, be as complete as you can, but also be specific. Identifying everyone in the company as a resource to solve a crashed server might look good, but realistically there are probably only one or two people who can actually rebuild the server, even with good documentation. Make sure that you identify who the key people are for each risk, as well as the more general secondary resources they have to call on, such as Microsoft Customer Support Services (CSS) and local Microsoft partners. For example, the primary resource available to recover a crashed server might consist of your hardware vendor to recover the failed hardware and your own IT person or primary system consultant to restore the software and database. General secondary resources could include Microsoft Support (*http://support.microsoft.com/oas/default.aspx?gprid=3208*), Microsoft partners in your area, and the Microsoft TechNet forum for SBS 2011 Essentials (*http://social.technet.microsoft.com/Forums/en-US/smallbusinessserver2011essentials/threads*).

An important step in identifying resources in your disaster recovery plan is to specify both the first-line responsibility (probably your internal IT person) and the back-end or second-tier responsibility (often a consultant or Microsoft partner). Make sure that everyone knows who to go to when the problem is more than they can handle or when they need additional resources. Also, clearly define *when* they should escalate. The best disaster recovery plans include clear, unambiguous escalation policies. This takes the burden off of individuals to decide when to notify someone and whom to notify, and it makes escalation simply part of the procedure.

Developing the Responses

An old but relevant adage comes to mind when discussing disaster recovery scenarios: When you're up to your elbows in alligators, it's difficult to remember that your original objective was to drain the swamp. This is just another way of saying that people lose track of what's important when they are overloaded by too many problems that require immediate attention. To ensure that your swamp is drained and your network gets back online, you need to take those carefully researched risks and resources and develop a disaster recovery plan. There are two important parts of any good disaster recovery plan:

- Standard operating procedures (SOPs)
- Standard escalation procedures (SEPs)

Making sure that these procedures are in place and clearly understood by everyone involved, *before* a disaster strikes, puts you in a far better position to recover gracefully and with a minimum of lost productivity and data.

Standard Operating Procedures

Emergencies bring out both the best and the worst in people. If you're prepared for the emergency, you can be one of those who comes out smelling like a rose, but if you're not prepared and let yourself get flustered or lose track of what you're trying to accomplish, you can make the whole situation worse than it needs to be.

It's just plain *hard* to stay calm and focused when you're in the middle of an emergency and there's a lot of extra stress being applied by everyone around you. Although no one is ever as prepared for a system emergency as they'd like to be, careful planning and preparation can give you an edge in recovering expeditiously and with a minimal loss of data. It's a *lot* easier to deal with the situation calmly when you know you've prepared for this problem and you have a well-organized, tested SOP to follow.

Because the very nature of emergencies is that you can't predict exactly which one is going to strike, you need to plan and prepare for as many possibilities as you can. The time to decide how to recover from a disaster is before the disaster happens, not in the middle of it when users are screaming and bosses are standing around looking serious and concerned. If you're lucky. (We seem to have been blessed by those who follow the more common adage, "When in trouble or in doubt, run in circles, scream and shout.")

Your risk-assessment phase involved identifying as many possible disaster scenarios and risks as you could; the resource-assessment phase identified the resources for those risks. Now you need to create SOPs for recovering the system from each of the scenarios. Having an SOP that details how to recover from a failed server makes that recovery a lot easier.

Reduce your stress and prevent mistakes by planning for disasters before they occur. Practice recovering from each of your disaster scenarios. Write down each of the steps, and work through questionable or unclear areas until you can identify exactly what it takes to recover from the problem. This is like a fire drill, and you should do it for the same reasons—not because a fire is inevitable, but because fires do happen, and the statistics demonstrate irrefutably that those who prepare for a fire and practice what to do in a fire are far more likely to survive the fire.

Even if you know you're the only resource the company has to recover from a disaster scenario, write down the basic steps to recover. You don't need to go into minute detail, but at the very least, outline the key steps. This might be something you do for real only once in your life, so don't count on being able to remember everything. Disasters, by their very nature, raise the overall stress level and cause people to forget important steps.

Your job as a system administrator is to prepare for disasters and practice what to do in those disasters—not because you expect the disaster, but because if you do have one, you want to be the hero, not the goat. After all, it isn't often that the system administrator or IT consultant gets to be a hero, so be ready when your time comes.

The first step in developing any SOP is to outline the overall steps you want to accomplish. Keep it general at this point—you're looking for the big picture here. Again, you want everyone to be involved in the process. What you're really trying to do is make sure you don't forget any critical steps, and that's much easier when you get the overall plan down first. There will be plenty of opportunity later to cover the specific details.

After you have a broad, high-level outline for a particular procedure, the people you identified as the actual resources during the resource-assessment phase should start to fill in the blanks of the outline. You don't need every detail at this point, but you should get down to at least a level below the original outline. This will help you identify missing resources that are important to a timely resolution of the problem. Again, don't get too bogged down in the details at this point. You're not actually writing the SOP, just trying to make sure that you've identified all of its pieces.

Remember that group of people that you went to when you were creating the list of risks to your network? Now is the time to get them involved again. When you think you've got all the steps of your SOP identified in the outline, get the larger group back together again. Go over the procedure and smooth out the rough edges, refining the outline and *listening* to make sure you haven't missed anything critical. When everyone agrees that the outline is complete, you're ready to add the final details to it.

The people who are responsible for each procedure should now work through all the details of the disaster recovery plan and document the steps thoroughly. They should keep in mind that the people who actually perform the recovery might not be who they expect. It's great to have an SOP for recovering from a failed router, but if the only person who understands the procedure is the IT person and she's on vacation in Bora Bora that week, your disaster recovery plan has a big hole in it. You need to make sure that the procedure can be read and understood by whomever the secondary resource is for that failed router.

When you create the documentation, write down everything. What seems obvious to you now, while you're devising the procedure, will not seem at all obvious in six months or a year when you suddenly have to follow it under stress.

Real World: Multiple Copies, Multiple Locations

It's tempting to centralize your SOPs into a single, easily accessible database. And you should do that, making sure that everyone understands how to use it. But you'll also need to have alternative locations and formats for your procedures. Not only do you not want to keep the only copy in a single database, you also don't want to have only an electronic version—how accessible is the SOP for recovering a failed server going to be when the server has failed? Always maintain a hard copy as well. The one thing you don't want to do is create a single point of failure in your disaster recovery plan!

Every good server room should have a large binder, prominently visible and clearly identified, that contains all the SOPs. Each responsible person should also have one or more copies of at least the procedures he or she is either a resource for or likely to become a resource for. We keep copies of all our procedures in several places so that we can get at them no matter what the source of the emergency or where we happen to be when the cell phone rings.

Even if you're the only resource, keep multiple copies of your procedures and key phone numbers of external resources. Don't rely entirely on electronic storage, because even external electronic storage might be difficult to access if the disaster is major. But don't ignore electronic storage, either. Most of the time, it's the fastest and easiest to get to, and the most likely to be completely up to date.

After you have created the SOPs, your job has only begun. You need to keep them up to date and make sure that they don't become stale. It's no good having an SOP to recover your ISDN connection to the Internet when you ripped the ISDN line out three years ago and put in a DSL line with five times the bandwidth at half the cost.

You also need to make sure that all your copies of an SOP are updated. Electronic ones should probably be stored in a database or in a folder on the SBS 2011 Essentials server that is available offline. However, hard copies of documents are notoriously tricky to maintain. A good method is to make yet another SOP that details who updates what SOPs, how often that person updates them, and who gets fresh copies whenever a change is made. Then put a version control system into place and make sure everyone understands his or her role in the process. Build rewards into the system for timely and consistent updating of SOPs—if 10 or 20 percent of someone's bonus is dependent on keeping those SOPs up to date and distributed, you can be sure that they'll be current at least as often as the review process occurs.

Standard Escalation Procedures

No matter how carefully you've identified potential risks, and how detailed your procedures to recover from them are, you're still likely to have situations you didn't anticipate. An important part of any disaster recovery plan is a standardized escalation procedure. Not only should each individual SOP have its own procedure-specific SEP, but you should also have an overall escalation procedure that covers everything you haven't thought of—because it's certain you haven't thought of everything.

An escalation procedure has two functions—resource escalation and notification escalation. Both have the same purpose: to make sure that everyone who needs to know about the problem is up to date and involved as appropriate, and to keep the overall noise level down so that the work of resolving the problem can go forward as quickly as possible. The *resource escalation procedure* details the resources that are available to the people who are trying to recover from the current disaster so that these people don't have to try to guess who (or what) the appropriate resource might be when they run into something they can't handle or something doesn't go as planned. This procedure helps them stay calm and focused. They know that if they run into a problem, they aren't on their own, and they know exactly who to call when they do need help.

The *notification escalation procedure* details who is to be notified of serious problems. Even more important, it should provide specifics regarding *when* notification is to be made. If a particular print queue crashes but comes right back up, you might want to send a general message only to the users of that particular printer, letting them know what happened. However, if the network card on your server has failed, and the server has been unreachable for more than half an hour, a lot of folks are going to be concerned. The SEP for replacing that network card should detail who needs to be notified when the server is unavailable for longer than some specified amount of time, and it should probably detail what happens and who gets notified when it's still down some significant amount of time after that.

This notification has two purposes: to make sure that the necessary resources are made available as required, and to keep everyone informed and aware of the situation. If you let people know that you've had a server hardware failure and that the vendor has been called and will be onsite within an hour, you'll cut down the number of phone calls, freeing you to do whatever you need to do to ensure that you're ready when the vendor arrives.

Testing the Responses

A disaster recovery plan is nice to have, but it really isn't worth a whole lot until it has actually been tested. Needless to say, the time to test the plan is at your convenience and under controlled conditions, rather than in the midst of an actual disaster. It's a nuisance to discover that your detailed disaster recovery plan has a fatal flaw in it when you're testing it under controlled conditions. It's a bit more than a nuisance to discover it when every second counts.

You won't be able to test everything in your disaster recovery plans. Even most large organizations don't have the resources to create fully realistic simulated natural disasters and test their response to each of them under controlled conditions, and even fewer small businesses have those kinds of resources. Nevertheless, there are things you can do to test your response plans. The details of how you test them depend on your environment, but they should include as realistic a test as feasible and should, as much as possible, cover all aspects of the response plan. The other reason to test the disaster recovery plan is that it provides a valuable training ground. If you've identified primary and backup resources, as you should, chances are that the people you've identified as backup resources are not as skilled or knowledgeable in a particular area as the primary resource. Testing the procedures gives you a chance to train the backup resources at the same time.

You should also consider using the testing to cross-train people who are not necessarily in the primary response group. Not only will they get valuable training, but you'll also create a knowledgeable pool of people who might not be directly needed when the procedure has to be used for real, but who can act as key communicators with the rest of the community.

Iterating

When you finish a particular disaster recovery plan, you might think your job is done, but it's not. Standardizing a process is actually just the first step. You need to continually look for ways to improve it.

You should make a regular, scheduled practice of pulling out your disaster recovery plan with those responsible and making sure it's up to date. A quarterly half-day off-site is a great way to both provide a structured review process and also set aside the time to actually do it. Use the occasion to look at the entire disaster recovery plan and see how you can improve on it. Take the opportunity to examine your environment. What's changed since you last looked at the plan? What equipment has been retired, and what has been added? What software is different? Are all the people on your notification and escalation lists still working at the company in the same roles? Are the phone numbers, including home phone numbers, up to date?

Real World: Understand and Practice Kaizen

Kaizen is a Japanese word and concept that means "small, continuous improvement." Its literal translation is, "Change (*kai*) to become good (*zen*)."

So why bring a Japanese word and concept into a discussion about disaster recovery? Because a good disaster recovery plan is one that you are constantly kaizening. When you really understand kaizen, it becomes a way of life that you can use in many ways.

The first thing to understand about kaizen is that you are not striving for major change or improvement. Small improvements are the goal. Don't try to fix or change everything all at once. Instead, focus on one area, and try to make it just a little bit better.

The second part of kaizen is that it is continuous. You must constantly look for ways to improve and then implement those improvements. Because each improvement is small and incremental, you can easily implement it and move on to the next one.

Kaizen is very much about teamwork. Good kaizen balances the load on a team and finds ways to build the strengths of the team as a whole. If you practice kaizen and continually look for small, incremental ways to improve your work, you will soon have a better and more enjoyable workplace. As a manager, if you find ways to encourage and reward those who practice kaizen, your team and you will grow and prosper.

Another way to iterate your disaster recovery plan is to use every disaster as a learning experience. After the disaster or emergency is over, get everyone together as soon as possible to talk about what happened. Find out what they think worked in the plan and what didn't. What tools did you not have that would have made the job go more quickly or better? Actively solicit suggestions for how the process could be improved. Then make the changes and test them. You'll not only improve your responsiveness to this particular type of disaster, but you'll also improve your overall responsiveness by getting people involved in the process and enabling them to be part of the solution.

Important   Do not use this post-disaster recovery discussion to assign blame or look for the cause of the disaster. This is about how to better respond to, and recover from, a disaster. And to do that, you need to *learn* from the experience so that you can do a better job planning for the next one. If everyone is trying to avoid blame, they won't have any energy for improving the process.

Preparing for a Disaster

As Ben Franklin was known to say, "Failure to prepare is preparing to fail." This is truer than ever with modern operating systems, and although SBS 2011 Essentials includes several exceptionally useful recovery modes and tools, you still need to prepare for potential problems. Some of these techniques are covered in detail in other chapters and are discussed here only briefly, whereas others are covered here at length.

Setting Up a Fault-Tolerant System

A fault-tolerant system is one that is prepared to continue operating in the event of key component failures. It's very useful for servers running critical applications. Here are a few of the many ways to ensure fault tolerance in a system:

- Use one or more redundant array of independent disks (RAID) arrays for system and data storage, protecting yourself from hard-disk failure. If a hard disk in the array fails, only that disk needs to be replaced—and no data is lost. See Chapter 2, "Planning Hardware," and Chapter 7, "Configuring and Maintaining Storage," for information about using RAID to provide fault tolerance for your disk subsystem.

- Use multiple disk array controllers to provide redundancy if a controller fails.

- Use an uninterruptible power supply (UPS) to allow the server to shut down gracefully in the event of a power failure.

- Use multiples of everything that is likely to fail, including power supplies and network cards.

- Keep key spares available so that you can quickly recover by replacing a failed part. If you have only a single power supply and it fails, you'll be back online a *lot* faster if you swap out a failed power supply yourself and then call your hardware vendor for a replacement for the failed one.

Backups

We've got a whole chapter on backups—Chapter 9, "Backing Up and Restoring"—but it's important to talk briefly about them here under disaster recovery because they're the backbone of any disaster recovery scenario. Having a backup of your critical system files is nice. Having backups of your data is nice. But having a *tested* backup of both of them is critical to a successful restore experience. By *tested*, we mean that you've actually restored the files in the backup and that you were able to read and use them.

Not every single backup will get tested for your ability to restore it. That's not realistic, and there's no point even pretending that it's going to happen. But you should have a regular schedule of testing backups to know that you can restore from them. We like to do ours at least once a week. We pick a couple of key subdirectories and restore them to a temporary location on the server.

Image backups, such as those done by Windows Server Backup, pose additional testing issues. It's a really good idea to test full system restores to ensure that your recovery scenario for a full hardware failure is viable—especially if you intend to do restores to dissimilar hardware, which is something not directly contemplated by Windows Server 2008 R2 Backup. If you want to be able to do a restore to dissimilar hardware, you're probably going to need to use a third-party backup utility, such as Acronis Backup & Recovery 11 Advanced Server SBS Edition (*http://www.acronis.com/backup-recovery/advanced-server-small-business/*) or StorageCraft ShadowProtect Server (*http://www.storagecraft.com*). Both of these products are designed to allow you to do backup and restore to dissimilar hardware, including physical-to-virtual (P2V) restores.

Restoring from Backup

The process of restoring your SBS 2011 Essentials server from backup is something you should test and do *before* you find yourself in the middle of a disaster. And yes, we know, we're repeating ourselves. But it's really important. One last time and then we'll let it go: The only good backup is a fully tested backup. And the only reliable way to test a backup is to restore it.

When disaster strikes your SBS 2011 Essentials network and you have to restore an entire server, you'll need the following:

- Your backup.

- Hardware to restore the backup to. If you're using the native Windows Server 2008 R2 Backup that is part of SBS, your hardware needs to be quite similar to the server you're replacing.

- The original Disk 1 from your SBS 2011 Essentials installation media, or another Windows Server 2008 R2 Standard DVD.

- Any drivers required for Windows Server 2008 R2 to "see" your hard disks or your backup media. These should be on a USB key or other medium that the target server can read.

After you have all the required components together, you're ready to restore your server by following these steps:

1. Insert Disk 1 of the SBS 2011 Essentials installation media, and turn on the server.

2. If the BIOS needs to be changed to allow the DVD drive to be the first boot device, go into the server's BIOS and make the change, and then restart the server.

3. If prompted, press any key to boot from the DVD drive and bring up the Installing Windows page of the Windows Small Business Server 2011 Essentials installation, as shown in Figure 16-1.

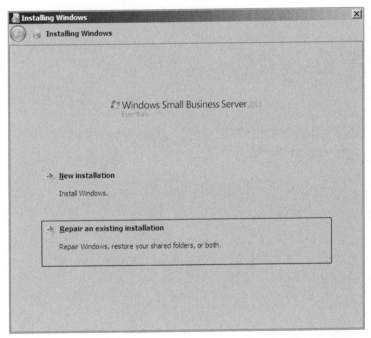

FIGURE 16-1 The Installing Windows page of the SBS 2011 Essentials installation.

4. Click Repair An Existing Installation to open the Re-Image Your Computer Wizard shown in Figure 16-2. If the repair does not find your server backup image, you'll have an option to load additional drivers.

5. If no image is selected or you want to load a different image than the one shown, choose Select A System Image. The wizard will let you load additional drivers or point to a network share for an image. Use this option *only* for situations where there is a problem with the default backup selected.

6. Click Next to continue to the Choose Additional Restore Options page of the Re-Image Your Computer Wizard, as shown in Figure 16-3.

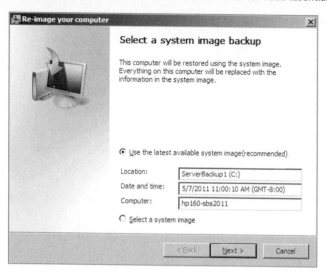

FIGURE 16-2 The Select A System Image Backup page of the Re-Image Your Computer Wizard.

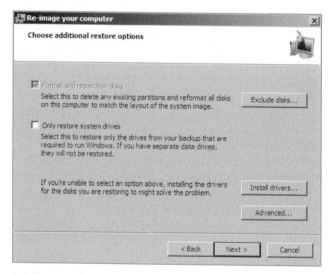

FIGURE 16-3 The Choose Additional Restore Options page of the Re-Image Your Computer Wizard.

7. You can choose to exclude disks from restoration or to only restore system drives on this page. If you are restoring from backup because your system drive failed, but all your other drives are fine, then you should choose Only Restore System Drives to protect your data. Click Exclude Disks to open the dialog box shown in Figure 16-4, in which you can restore a failed data disk without affecting the system disk or exclude data disks that you do not want completely re-imaged.

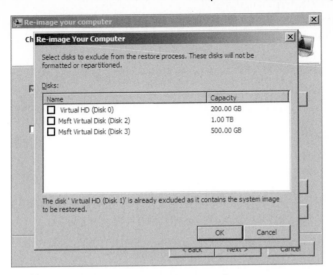

FIGURE 16-4 Excluding disks from the restoration process.

8. Click OK when you have selected disks to exclude, and then click Next to move to the confirmation page, as shown in Figure 16-5.

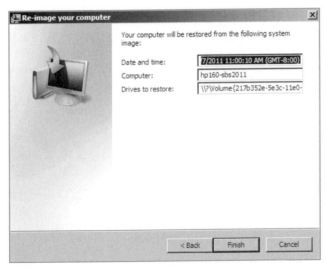

FIGURE 16-5 The confirmation page of the Re-Image Your Computer Wizard.

9. The Re-Image Your Computer Wizard will always enforce the Format And Repartition Disks option to be checked, as shown earlier in Figure 16-3. This means that *all* data on the target disks, except those that you have excluded, will be completely destroyed and the new image will replace the existing partitioning and data.

10. Click Finish to open a final confirmation dialog box, as shown in Figure 16-6. Click Yes and the restoration will begin.

FIGURE 16-6 Final confirmation before formatting disks and restoring your computer.

11. The restoration process can take a substantial amount of time. During the process, you'll see a progress dialog box, as shown in Figure 16-7.

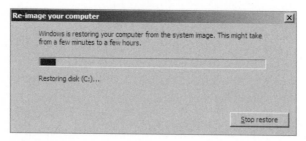

FIGURE 16-7 The progress dialog box of the Re-Image Your Computer Wizard.

12. After the restore is complete, you'll be prompted to restart the server. If any drives haven't been restored, you'll also see a message about that in the restart prompt, as shown in Figure 16-8.

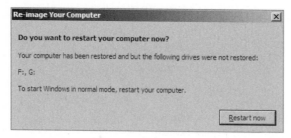

FIGURE 16-8 If some drives are not restored, you'll see a notification when the restore is complete.

Virtualization and Disaster Planning

The core of disaster planning is the same whether you're running SBS 2011 Essentials virtualized or on physical hardware. The five steps described at the beginning of this chapter are almost exactly the same. But there are differences when dealing with virtualized SBS. The two biggest differences to address are:

- No USB drive support inside the child partition.

- Hardware independence.

What do these differences mean for disaster planning? A few differences in the mechanics of backups and restores, primarily, with a possible change in the products used.

No USB Support

SBS 2011 Essentials is designed to back up to an attached USB hard disk, but Hyper-V doesn't support USB disks inside virtual machines (VMs). As discussed in Chapter 9, however, the native Windows Server Backup in Windows Server 2008 R2 supports additional backup target options, including remote shares and local hard disks. You can use these options without causing issues in the Dashboard.

One important advantage to a USB hard disk as a backup target is that you can remove a disk for offsite storage and attach another, something you can't do easily with a VM backup. A viable workaround, however, is to create a virtual hard disk (VHD) on the USB hard disk and attach the VHD to the SCSI controller of the SBS VM. The SCSI controller allows you to dynamically attach and unattach VHDs, and you can automate the entire process with Windows PowerShell. For more information on using Windows PowerShell to automate Windows Server Backup, see Charlie's blog at *http://blogs.msmvps.com/russel/2011/02/03 /windows-server-backup-with-powershell/*, or the TechNet wiki page he wrote at *http://social .technet.microsoft.com/wiki/contents/articles/windows-server-2008-r2-powershell-backup.aspx.*

Hardware Independence

The second difference with running SBS 2011 Essentials virtualized is all positive—hardware independence. Virtualization allows you to move VMs to different physical hardware almost transparently. Even when you haven't fully exported a VM, the rest is easy as long as you have copies of the VHD files—do a bit of configuration of the virtualization settings, and then create the virtual networks. After SBS 2011 Essentials is up and running, you will likely need to rerun the Set Up Remote Web Access Wizard.

This hardware independence gives you a lot of options as you plan for how you'll handle a disaster. Even if you don't immediately have an identical or even equivalent server available, most SBS 2011 Essentials servers can run without significant issues on a reasonably well-powered desktop computer with 2 to 4 gigabytes (GB) of RAM and a dual or quad-core processor. You wouldn't have the level of redundancy available that you would in a good server, and it's not a configuration we recommend using for any length of time, but it is more than adequate to get out of a disaster situation and get the business up and running.

Summary

Assume that disaster will eventually occur, and plan accordingly. Create standardized recovery procedures, and keep them up to date. When there's a lot of turmoil, as always happens in the case of a major failure, people forget important steps and can make poor decisions. Standardized procedures provide a course of action without the need for on-the-spot decisions. If you've planned for a disaster and practiced what to do in the event of one, you'll be able to recover much more quickly than if you haven't. And recovering quickly in the event of a major disaster can be a significant competitive advantage.

Part V
Appendices

Appendix A
Migrating to Windows Small Business Server 2011 Essentials

Many Windows Small Business Server 2011 Essentials networks will be installed in environments in which no central domain controller or server existed before. The administrators of these networks will not need to worry about migration. But other installations will replace an existing server and domain controller, and for those environments, installing in migration mode will allow the administrator to maintain the existing users and settings. This improves the experience for existing users and reduces the number of support calls following installation of SBS 2011 Essentials.

In this appendix, we'll primarily be covering the migration from Windows Small Business Server 2003, because that will be the largest group of migrations, but much of what we cover here is also applicable to migrations from Windows Small Business Server 2008, or from Windows Server. Whatever prior domain environment you're migrating from, we recommend that you read this appendix thoroughly before you begin, and follow the basic steps here. However, for environments other than SBS 2003, you'll use a slightly different document from Microsoft to refer to during the process, and you might have slightly different steps, though the overall process is essentially similar.

The Migration Process

Before you start your SBS 2011 Essentials migration, you should read and understand this appendix and the appropriate Microsoft migration guide. There are only two migration guides, and the one you'll need depends on which version of Windows Small Business Server you are migrating from. The two main guides are:

- "Migrating Windows SBS 2003 to Windows SBS 2011 Essentials" at *http://www.microsoft.com/downloads/en /details.aspx?FamilyID=288a1d8a-5620-4f20-ad67-20af97275a80.*

- "Migrating Windows SBS 2011 Essentials to New Hardware" at *http://www.microsoft.com/downloads/en /details.aspx?FamilyID=34199761-a812-42e5-b2ec-65d6ac3de15f.*

If you're currently running SBS 2008 and you want to migrate to SBS 2011 Essentials, there is no specific migration guide, but if you work from the "Migrating Windows SBS 2003 to Windows SBS 2011 Essentials" guide, you'll be able to adjust in those places where SBS 2008 is different without much difficulty. We'll refer to the guides generically as the *Microsoft migration guides*, and you should always refer to the appropriate one for your specific migration scenario.

The steps in a successful migration are as follows:

1. Prepare your existing SBS server for migration.

2. Use Notepad or another plain text editor to create a migration answer file.

3. Install SBS 2011 Essentials, using the answer file to run in migration mode.

4. Move the data and settings from your existing SBS server to your new SBS 2011 Essentials server.

5. When migration is complete, demote your existing SBS server to a domain member and then remove it from the domain. You must reformat the server before you can re-use it.

6. Perform optional post-migration tasks—including mapping users to computers and enabling folder redirection.

7. Run the Windows Server Solutions Best Practices Analyzer (SBS BPA).

Real World: A Migration Alternative

With SBS 2003, the Microsoft solution for migration was suboptimal and resulted in significant user disruption. It really was only a viable solution if you needed to change your SBS domain name for some reason, and were willing to touch every single client computer in the SBS network. In our book *Microsoft Windows Small Business Server 2003 R2 Administrator's Companion* (Microsoft Press, 2006), we recommended an alternative solution—Swing Migration (go to *http://www.sbsmigration.com*). Swing Migration uses a temporary domain controller to capture the Active Directory directory services, DNS, and other information from the existing domain controller (the source SBS server) and transfer that to the new SBS server, allowing the new SBS server to retain the exact same name and IP address as the original source SBS server. The result is an excellent and time-effective way to manage a migration and has several virtues over other methods, including:

- No disruption or change to SBS client computers.

- No disruption in network functions except for the final switchover, which can easily be done during normal downtimes. Most work is done offline and can be done on a flexible schedule.

- Full data and configuration protection.

- The ability to restart the process at any point in time with no risk of data loss if there is a problem.

With the release of Windows Small Business Server 2011 Standard and SBS 2011 Essentials, the Swing Migration packages have been updated to provide full support for migrations to the new products. The principal of SBSMigration.com, and the architect of the Swing Migration method, is Jeff Middleton, a Microsoft MVP for SBS. We've known Jeff for several years now, and we highly recommend using his Swing Migration, especially if your environment has anything unusual or a bit different than a completely standard SBS source server. With a Swing Migration, you get Jeff as your ultimate resource, and it just doesn't get any better than that.

Preparing Your Server

The most important part of any migration to SBS 2011 Essentials involves properly preparing your existing SBS server. The time and thought you spend on a full and careful preparation of your existing SBS server has a direct impact on the success of your migration. Don't just start a migration without first preparing. Read this entire appendix carefully, and read Microsoft's migration guide as well. Be sure you understand what will happen and what the requirements are before you start.

The steps for preparing your server are as follows:

1. Do a full and complete backup of the existing SBS server.

2. Install all current service packs and other updates on the server.

3. Configure your network for the migration.

4. Configure Active Directory.

5. Run the BPA to verify the health of the existing SBS network.

6. Clean up and optimize the current Microsoft Exchange Server mailboxes and prepare to migrate all email to a hosted solution.

7. Synchronize your existing SBS server to an external time source.

8. Update the Active Directory schema and extend the time that both versions of SBS can be running to 21 days.

9. Identify line-of-business applications running on the existing SBS server, and plan for their migration.

Before You Start

You're going to need certain tools during this process, and they might or might not already be on your source server. To simplify things and make sure you have everything ready and available, we suggest that you download the following ahead of time:

- Windows PowerShell 2.0 and the Management Framework Core from
  http://go.microsoft.com/FWLink/?Linkid=188528

- Microsoft Baseline Configuration Analyzer 2.0 (MBCA 2.0) from
  http://go.microsoft.com/FWLink/?Linkid=188529

- Microsoft .NET Framework 2.0 SP1 from
  http://go.microsoft.com/FWLink/?Linkid=153680

- Microsoft Windows Small Business Server 2003 Best Practices Analyzer from
  http://go.microsoft.com/FWLink/?Linkid=113752

- Software Update to Support "Join Domain" Migration of Windows Small Business
  Server 2003 Data and Settings to New Hardware from
  http://support.microsoft.com/kb/943494

- Microsoft IT Environment Health Scanner from
  http://www.microsoft.com/download/en/details.aspx?displaylang=en&id=10116

Also, collect any other tools you generally like to have available during the build process. If you create an ISO file of these or burn them to a DVD, they'll be available whenever and wherever you need them. For ISO creation, we like the simplicity of ISO Recorder (*http://isorecorder.alexfeinman.com/isorecorder.htm*). It's simple, it does the job really well, and it's free.

Go ahead and install Windows PowerShell 2.0, MBCA 2.0, and the BPA on your source server. They usually don't trigger a reboot.

Finally, before you start, you should uninstall or completely disable any third-party firewalls or antivirus software. These products can interfere with the operations that are required for a successful migration.

Back Up Your Existing SBS Server

The first and most important step in any migration is making sure that you have a full and verified backup. We all do backups, and we hope that we never need to use them. But if you aren't taking steps to actually verify that your backup can be restored, you don't really have a backup you can count on. Before beginning any SBS migration, it's essential that you establish a sound fallback position that will allow you to recover in case something goes wrong. Of course, nothing *should* go wrong, but we're firm believers in Murphy's Laws—after all, we wrote the books on them!

For details on how to back up your existing SBS 2003 server, go to *http://go.microsoft.com /FWLink/?Linkid=27140* or refer to Chapter 13, "Backing Up and Restoring Data," in our book *Microsoft Windows Small Business Server 2003 R2 Administrator's Companion*. (For SBS 2008, see Chapter 16, "Configuring Backup," in our book *Windows Small Business Server 2008 Administrator's Companion* [Microsoft Press, 2009] or, for SBS 2011 Essentials, see Chapter 9, "Backing Up and Restoring.")

In *addition* to doing a conventional backup using SBS Backup, we strongly suggest making an image backup of at least the system volume of your existing SBS server and any other volumes that are used to store core SBS data files. This will allow for a faster full recovery in the event that you have to cancel the migration for some reason. Products we've used for this image backup include those from StorageCraft, Acronis, and Microsoft (Windows Home Server). Currently we're using, and really liking, Windows Storage Server 2008 R2 Essentials to back up the virtual hard disks (VHDs) of SBS.

Whatever backup methods you use, you should *verify the integrity* of the backup by doing a test restore. For image backups, this means restoring the entire partition image to a disk of equal or greater size and, at a minimum, verifying that files can be read and opened. For an SBS Backup test, you should restore multiple files from different locations to an alternate location and verify that the files can be opened and read.

> **Important** Do not begin a migration without a **verified** backup. Really. Because once you start, there is no going back except to restore your backup, and that is *not* when you want to discover that you have a problem with restoring. We can't say this too many times—*test your backups!*

Install Current Updates

It seems obvious to us, but it bears repeating nonetheless—bring your current SBS server up to date, installing all current service packs and security updates. If you're running SBS 2003 R2 or later, with built-in Windows Server Update Services (WSUS), this should be happening automatically. But even if you're sure you are up to date, connect to Microsoft Update to verify.

The migration process expects minimum levels of service packs, and if your server is not fully "patched up," you might experience issues in the migration. Given that the migration is a one-way process, you really don't want to get well into it and find you have a blocker. We hope the tools in this preparation stage will enable you to catch any blockers, but it's still just a really good idea to get all your updates installed before you start.

Configure the Network

Before you can migrate to SBS 2011 Essentials, you need to configure your existing SBS server for a single network interface card (NIC). This means a significant change for most SBS 2003 networks, because the preferred configuration for SBS 2003 calls for two NICs—one connected to the external Internet and one connected to the internal SBS network. All traffic on the internal network actually passes through the SBS server to get to the Internet, as shown in Figure A-1.

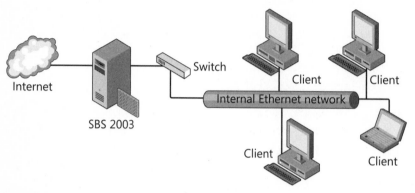

FIGURE A-1 Default two-NIC configuration for SBS 2003.

This configuration also uses SBS as the firewall for the SBS network—something it does quite well when running SBS 2003 Premium Edition with ISA 2004. Because SBS 2011 Essentials requires a single-NIC configuration, you need to change your SBS 2003 configuration before the migration. In a single-NIC configuration, as shown in Figure A-2, you'll need to add a router and firewall to your existing SBS network, along with reconfiguring the default gateway and other settings for your client computer and devices.

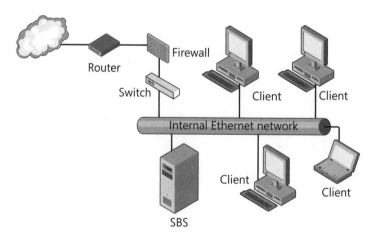

FIGURE A-2 Single-NIC configuration for SBS.

Most consumer-grade routers include minimal firewall capabilities, but they really aren't sufficient to properly protect an SBS network. You should either add a firewall appliance in addition or buy a true firewall router, such as one of the TZ series firewalls from SonicWALL (*http://www.sonicwall.com/us/products/TZ_Series.html*). Other possibilities include WatchGuard firewalls (*http://www.watchguard.com*) and NETGEAR ProSecure firewalls (*http://www.prosecure.netgear.com/products/prosecure-utm-series/models.php*).

The basic process of network reconfiguration uses the following steps:

1. Reconfigure the Dynamic Host Configuration Protocol (DHCP) for shorter lease times (optional), and save the DHCP database. In your final network, the DHCP will be the responsibility of the router/firewall, not your SBS server.

2. Disable or remove the Internet-facing NIC in your existing SBS server.

3. Run the Configure E-mail And Internet Connectivity Wizard (CEICW) to reconfigure networking.

4. Install a router/firewall and connect to the Internet.

5. Connect the router/firewall to a switch on the internal Ethernet.

6. Run the Remote Access Wizard to disable virtual private networks (VPNs) and reconfigure Routing and Remote Access (RRAS).

7. Reconfigure client computers and devices with fixed IP addresses and verify DHCP configuration.

Reconfigure DHCP

Although it's not absolutely required, you can simplify DHCP address reconfiguration on your SBS network if you shorten the lease time before beginning the migration. This will allow client computers and devices on your network to get updated network information without a reboot in a reasonable time frame. The default DHCP lease duration is eight days. To change the duration, follow these steps:

1. Log on to your existing SBS server with an account that has administrative privileges.

2. Open the DHCP console (dhcpmgmt.msc).

3. In the left pane, navigate to and select the scope you want to change.

4. Select Properties from the Action menu to open the Scope Properties dialog box shown in Figure A-3.

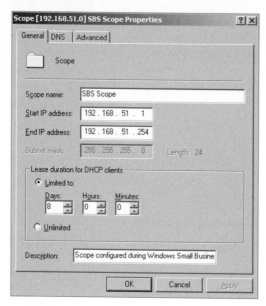

FIGURE A-3 The Scope Properties dialog box for a DHCP scope.

5. Change the Lease Duration For DHCP Clients values to a shorter time. We like to set an eight-hour lease here.

6. Click OK to close the Scope Properties dialog box and return to the DHCP console. Close the DHCP console.

Another useful step to take at this point is to document your DHCP configuration. If you are using a standard SBS DHCP with no reservations or other customizations, don't bother—the wizards will take care of it. But if you have done significant configuration, you should probably make a detailed documentation of the specifics of your DHCP settings so that they can be recreated after the migration.

Disable or Remove the Second NIC

Note You can skip this entire section if you're migrating from SBS 2008 or SBS 2011, because you're already configured for a single NIC with appropriate settings.

The first essential step in reconfiguring your SBS 2003 network from a two-NIC SBS network to a single-NIC network is to disconnect the externally facing NIC from your existing Internet connection and disable or remove the network card. You can get away with disabling it, but then you'll have more complaints from the SBS wizards, so we prefer removing it physically from the server. After you've removed the network card, you need to reconfigure your SBS network to the IP address range you'll use for your Internet connection.

Real World: Address Ranges

Because you're reconfiguring your network anyway, now is a good time to make a decision about the IP address range you want to use. The default range of many routers is 192.168.0.xxx or 192.168.1.xxx. The easy answer is to use whatever the default range of your new router/firewall is, and if you don't have branch offices or other specialized considerations, that's probably just fine. For our own use, however, we prefer to shift away from the default for most routers because it can cause complications down the road if we need to set up a static VPN to another network that has chosen that range. We prefer choosing pretty much any of the other possibilities in the private "C-class" range—anywhere from 192.168.2.xxx to 192.168.254.xxx. The default range for SBS 2003 is actually 192.168.16.xxx, and that's a good choice that doesn't seem to interfere with any other common ones we've seen. On our networks here, we have used 192.168.16.xxx and 192.168.51.xxx for our test networks. The one thing you *cannot* do is choose an address range in the 10.xxx.yyy.zzz private "A-class" range—the SBS wizards will not support that range.

After you've chosen the range for your new SBS network, you can complete the reconfiguration by following these steps:

1. Shut down the SBS server.

2. Disconnect the Internet-facing network cable from the server, open the server enclosure, and remove the network card.

3. Turn on the server. It will likely take a lot longer than usual to restart—be patient.

4. Log on to the server with the main administrator account.

5. In the left pane of the Server Management console, click Internet And E-Mail to display the Manage Internet And E-Mail page as shown in Figure A-4.

6. Click Connect To The Internet to open the CEICW.

7. Click Next to continue to the Connection Type page of the CEICW, as shown in Figure A-5.

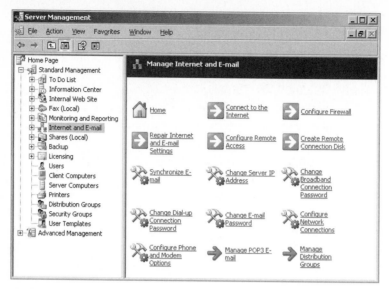

FIGURE A-4 The Manage Internet And E-Mail page of the SBS Server Management console.

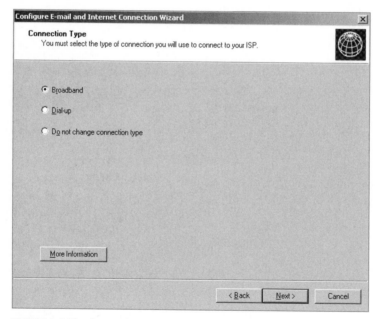

FIGURE A-5 The Connection Type page of the CEICW.

8. Select Broadband, and click Next to open the Broadband Connection page, as shown in Figure A-6. Select A Local Router Device With An IP Address from the My Server Uses list.

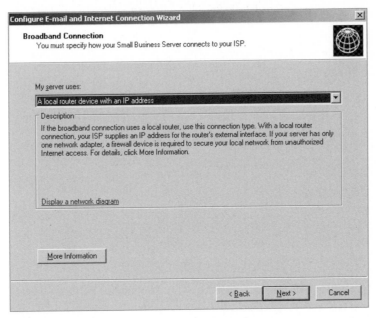

FIGURE A-6 The Broadband Connection page of the CEICW.

9. Click Next to proceed to the Router Connection page shown in Figure A-7. Type in the IP address you'll be using with your new router/firewall and the IP addresses for your ISP's DNS servers.

> **Note** If your router/firewall does DNS forwarding, you can use the IP address of the router/firewall for the Preferred DNS Server address and leave the Alternate DNS Server address blank. If you want to always use root hints for DNS, you can leave both addresses blank.

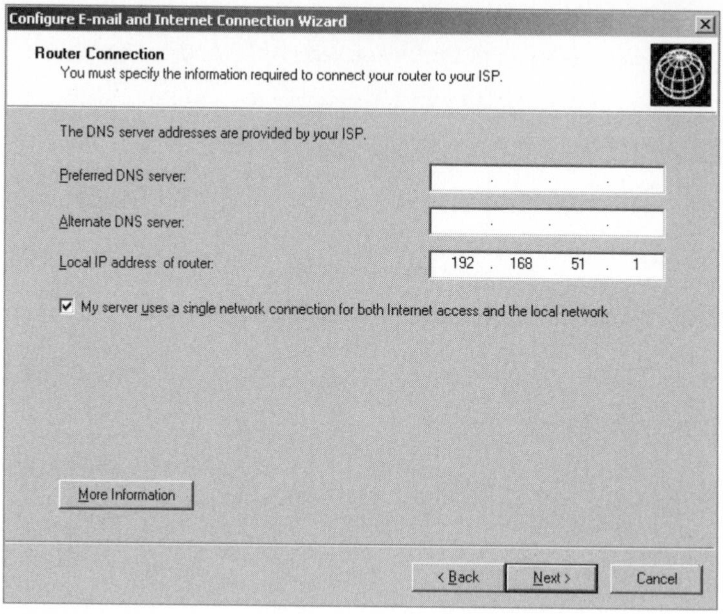

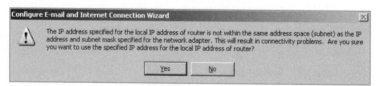

FIGURE A-7 The Router Connection page of the CEICW.

10. Select the My Server Uses A Single Network Connection For Both Internet Access And The Local Network check box.

11. Click Next. If the IP address of the router/firewall is in a different address range from your previous internal address, you'll see the message shown in Figure A-8.

FIGURE A-8 The warning message generated during network reconfiguration.

12. Click Yes to open the information message shown in Figure A-9. Because we're not connected to anything at this point, click No.

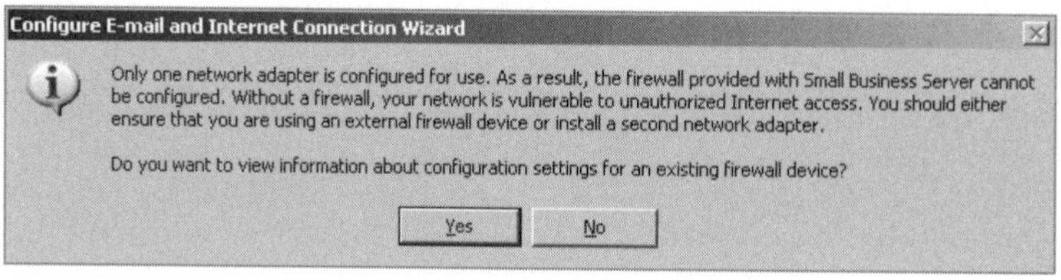

FIGURE A-9 The firewall informational message of the CEICW.

13. On the Web Services Configuration page, select the services that you want to be available when your existing SBS server is back online.

14. Click Next twice more, and then click Finish to complete the wizard.

15. Click Close when the CEICW finishes.

If you've chosen to use a different IP address range for your SBS network than the one you're currently configured to use, now is a good time to change it by following these steps:

1. On the Manage Internet And E-Mail page of the Server Management console, click Change Server IP Address to open the Change IP Address Tool dialog box shown in Figure A-10.

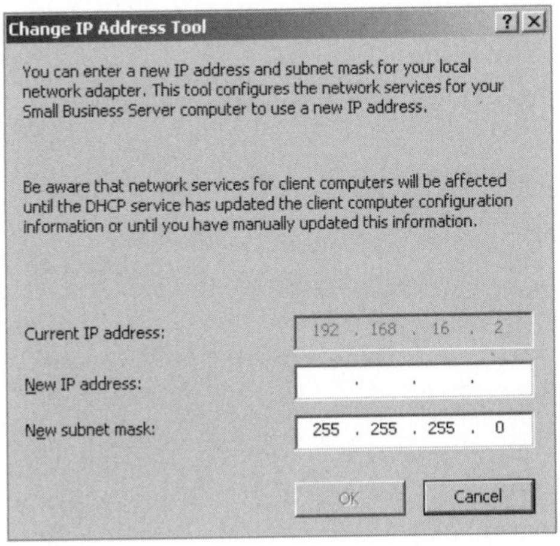

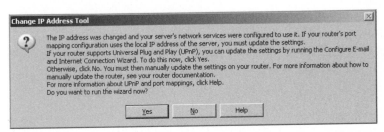

FIGURE A-10 The Change IP Address Tool.

2. Type in the new IP address for the server and click OK. When the tool completes, you'll see the message shown in Figure A-11.

FIGURE A-11 When you change the server's IP address, you are prompted to run the CEICW again.

3. Click No to complete the process and close the Change IP Address Tool dialog box. As shown in Figure A-12, the IP address has been reconfigured to point to the new router/firewall that we will install at 192.168.51.1.

```
Command Prompt                                                         _ □ ×
Microsoft Windows [Version 5.2.3790]
(C) Copyright 1985-2003 Microsoft Corp.

C:\Documents and Settings\Administrator>ipconfig

Windows IP Configuration


Ethernet adapter Local Area Connection:

        Connection-specific DNS Suffix  . :
        IP Address. . . . . . . . . . . : 192.168.16.2
        Subnet Mask . . . . . . . . . . : 255.255.255.0
        Default Gateway . . . . . . . . :

C:\Documents and Settings\Administrator>ipconfig

Windows IP Configuration


Ethernet adapter Local Area Connection:

        Connection-specific DNS Suffix  . :
        IP Address. . . . . . . . . . . : 192.168.51.2
        Subnet Mask . . . . . . . . . . : 255.255.255.0
        Default Gateway . . . . . . . . : 192.168.51.1

C:\Documents and Settings\Administrator>a_
```

FIGURE A-12 The IP address has changed on the server.

Note If you have fixed IP devices on your network, you'll need to manually reconfigure their default gateway. This won't matter for devices that don't need to connect to the Internet, such as printers, but if you have additional servers or workstations that use fixed IP addresses, you should reconfigure them now to point to the new router.

Install a Router and Firewall

After you've reconfigured your existing SBS server to use a single network card, you need to reconnect it to the Internet. If you don't already have a router, you need to insert one into the network and configure it for the network address range that you've chosen for your SBS network.

In many cases, you'll already have a router in place—we did. But that router is likely not a full-fledged firewall. Now is the time to replace it or add an additional firewall appliance. When you do, you'll need to configure the firewall for your SBS network. The ports SBS 2003 uses include:

- **25** Simple Mail Transfer Protocol (SMTP). Used by Exchange for incoming and outgoing email. This port is not needed after the completion of the SBS 2011 Essentials migration and should be closed when you're done.

- **80** Hypertext Transfer Protocol (HTTP). Outbound, this port is used to surf the web. Inbound, it can be used to initially connect to the Remote Web Workplace site.

- **443**   Hypertext Transfer Protocol Secure (HTTPS). This port is used outbound for connecting to secure websites and inbound for connecting to Remote Web Workplace.

- **444**   Companyweb. This port is used to connect to the Microsoft SharePoint Companyweb intranet site. Open this port only if your users connect to Companyweb when working remotely. This port is not needed after the completion of the SBS 2011 Essentials migration and should be closed when you're done.

- **3389**   Remote Desktop Protocol (RDP). This port is used only if you allow direct RDP connections from remote locations to your SBS server. If you do enable this for remote management, you should limit the IP addresses that are allowed to connect to specific, known IP addresses.

- **4125**   Remote Web Workplace (RWW). This port is used by RWW for connecting remote users to their desktops. This port is not needed after the completion of the SBS 2011 Essentials migration and should be closed when you're done with the migration.

Additional ports might be in use for specific applications on your network, but these are the basic incoming ports that are used by SBS 2003.

After you've installed and configured your router, connect it to your SBS network as shown earlier in Figure A-2. Verify that you have connectivity from the server and from your workstations to a known site. If a workstation doesn't have connectivity, reboot and try again. Verify that the DHCP-assigned IP address is in the correct range.

Disable VPNs

Before you begin the migration, you need to disable virtual private networking to the SBS server. If you need VPN access, you should choose a router/firewall that can act as a VPN endpoint. Ultimately, however, we think a better overall solution is to use Remote Web Access (RWA) and avoid VPNs whenever possible.

To disable VPNs on the existing SBS server, follow these steps:

1. Log on to the server with the main administrator account.

2. Open the Server Management console if it doesn't open automatically.

3. In the left pane of the Server Management console, click Internet And E-Mail. The Manage Internet And E-Mail page opens.

4. Click Configure Remote Access to start the Remote Access Wizard.

5. Click Next on the Welcome page to continue to the Remote Access Method page, as shown in Figure A-13.

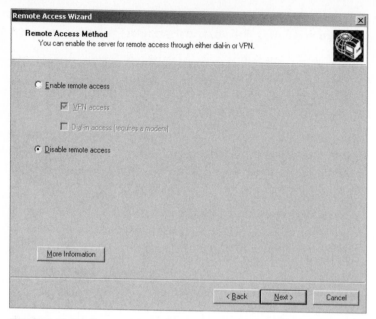

FIGURE A-13 The Remote Access Method page of the Remote Access Wizard.

6. Select Disable Remote Access, click Next, and then click Finish.

7. When the wizard completes, click Close to return to the Server Management console.

This completes the network reconfiguration for your SBS migration. Now is a good time to verify that all the computers and devices on your network are working as you'd expect and can connect properly. Pay particular attention to devices such as printers, wireless access points, and webcams that have a fixed or DHCP reservation address to make sure that they are communicating correctly with the rest of the network.

Configure Active Directory

Before you can complete the migration to SBS 2011 Essentials, you need to raise the domain and forest functional levels of your current SBS 2003 Active Directory. The migration requires that the Active Directory forest and domain functional level be Windows Server 2003. The default for SBS 2003 is the Windows 2000 functional level.

You can't move to a Windows Server 2003 functional level if there are any Windows 2000 or earlier domain controllers in your SBS domain. If there are, you must first demote them from being domain controllers. For Windows 2000, run Dcpromo.exe as a domain administrator to demote the Windows 2000 domain controller. If you still have Windows NT 4 domain controllers in your network, you'll need to rebuild these servers as non–domain controllers or remove them from the network entirely. Because Windows NT 4 is no longer supported by Microsoft and won't get any updates or security patches, you need to remove any remaining Windows NT 4 computers.

To raise the domain and forest functional level of your SBS 2003 Active Directory, follow these steps:

1. Log on to the SBS 2003 server with an account that has both Domain Admins and Enterprise Admins privileges. The administrator account is a good choice for this.

2. Click Start, click Administrative Tools, and then click Active Directory Domains And Trusts to open the Active Directory Domains And Trusts console shown in Figure A-14, or you can type **domain.msc** at the Run menu.

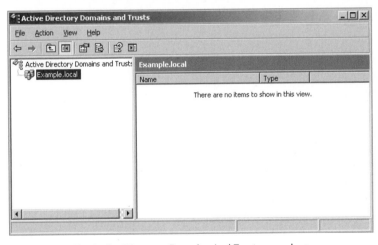

FIGURE A-14 The Active Directory Domains And Trusts console.

Note Raising the domain functional level is an irreversible change. You can't later lower the functional level.

3. Click the domain (example.local in Figure A-14), and select Raise Domain Functional Level from the Action menu to open the dialog box shown in Figure A-15.

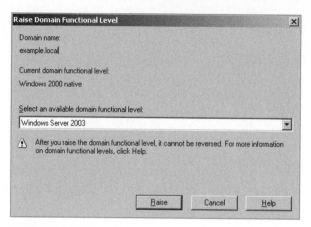

FIGURE A-15 The Raise Domain Functional Level dialog box.

4. Select Windows Server 2003 from the list (this should be the only choice in most SBS networks) and then click Raise to raise the domain functional level.

Note If the Current Domain Functional Level is shown as Windows Server 2003, you won't be able to change the functional level.

5. Click OK to accept the warning that this change can't be reversed, and click OK again at the success message. You will be returned to the Active Directory Domains And Trusts console and can now raise the forest functional level.

6. Click Active Directory Domains And Trusts in the left pane at the top of the tree.

7. Click Raise Forest Functional Level on the Action menu to open the Raise Forest Functional Level dialog box shown in Figure A-16.

Note Raising the forest functional level is also an irreversible change. You can't later lower the functional level.

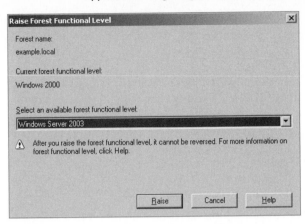

FIGURE A-16 The Raise Forest Functional Level dialog box.

8. Click Raise. You'll see the warning message that this change is irreversible, as shown in Figure A-17.

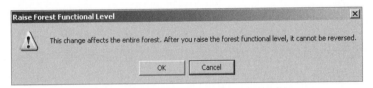

FIGURE A-17 Raising the forest functional level is irreversible.

9. Click OK. If the raise was successful, you'll see the informational message in Figure A-18.

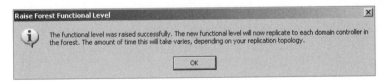

FIGURE A-18 The Raise Forest Functional Level success informational message.

10. Click OK to close the message, and then close the Active Directory Domains And Trusts dialog box.

Run the Best Practices Analyzer

The Best Practices Analyzer (BPA) is a useful tool to run against your SBS server regardless of whether you're planning on migrating to SBS 2011 Essentials immediately or later on. The BPA can identify all kinds of problems in an SBS environment with more than 200 errors, warnings, and informational messages about the health of your SBS network.

Before you can install the BPA, you need to install Windows PowerShell 2.0 if you don't already have it installed on your SBS 2003 server. You can download Windows PowerShell from *http://go.microsoft.com/FWLink/?Linkid=188528*.

You can download the BPA from *http://go.microsoft.com/FWLink/?Linkid=113752* and then install it on your SBS 2003 server. The Microsoft Knowledge Base article for the BPA is 940439. After you've downloaded the BPA, execute the SBS2003SP1-KB940439-x86-enu.exe file to install it. (The actual file name varies depending on the language.)

You can then run the BPA using the following steps:

1. Click Start, click All Programs, and select SBS Best Practices Analyzer Tool.

2. The first time you run the BPA, you'll be asked if you want to check for new versions every time you start it, and you'll be offered an opportunity to check now. Click Yes to receive automatic updates, and choose to check now—even with a fresh download, we still got a newer version after the check.

   From the welcome screen shown in Figure A-19, you can select the options to use for a scan or view a previous scan.

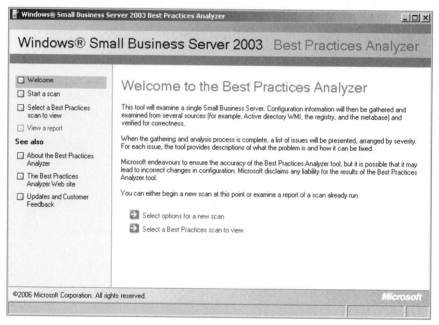

FIGURE A-19 The welcome screen of the SBS Best Practices Analyzer.

3. Click Select Options For A New Scan to open the Start A Scan page shown in Figure A-20.

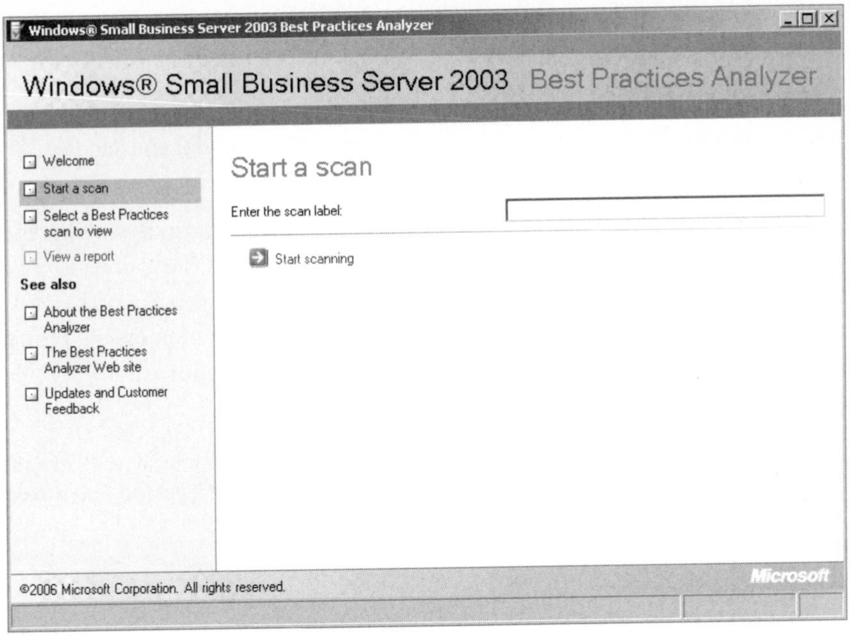

FIGURE A-20 The Start A Scan page of the SBS BPA.

4. Type a label for the scan, and click Start Scanning. When the scan completes, you'll see a summary of the results, as shown in Figure A-21.

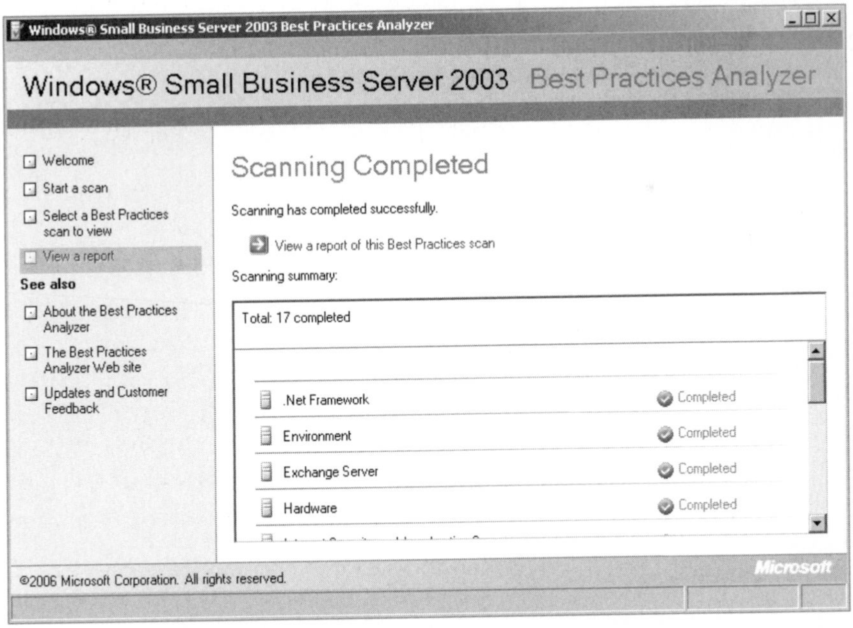

FIGURE A-21 The Scanning Completed summary page of the SBS BPA.

5. To view the results of the scan, click View A Report Of This Best Practices Scan. A typical report is shown in Figure A-22.

6. Click any listed issue to see more details on the issue, including links to Knowledge Base articles on how to correct the issue. The detail screen for the Receive Side Scaling issue shown in Figure A-22 is shown in Figure A-23.

7. After you've corrected the issues that could prevent a successful migration, run the BPA again by repeating steps 3 through 6 to verify that all the problems are corrected. At a minimum, you should correct all critical issues, and you should carefully evaluate the issues listed on the All Issues tab and correct any that are possible problems for your migration.

Important Do *not* proceed with your migration until all critical issues identified by the BPA have been resolved. Seriously. The migration *will* fail if you do. You should also carefully evaluate any additional issues shown on the All Issues tab and resolve as many as possible.

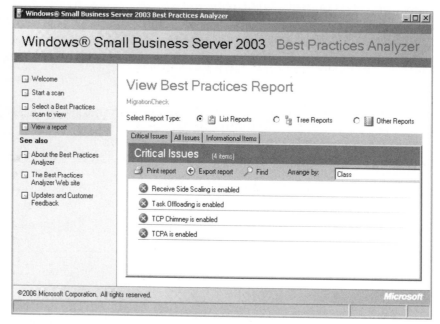

FIGURE A-22 A typical report from an SBS BPA scan.

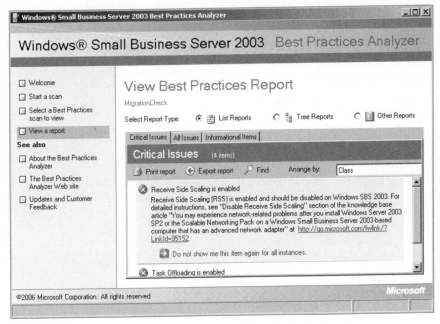

FIGURE A-23 The Receive Side Scaling issue details from the SBS BPA.

Optimize Exchange Mailboxes

You should have your users optimize their Exchange mailboxes to reduce the time it takes to migrate them to your new email solution. Whatever solution you use, the migration to your new email solution will be simpler and quicker if users reduce the size of their mailboxes now. If you've been enforcing strict mailbox limits, this likely isn't a major issue. However, if you've got a couple of users who are special and have seriously large mailboxes, now is a good time to try to get this under control. Anything that removes excess mail from the mailboxes is a good thing, but the most obvious steps are:

- Ask all users to empty their Deleted Items folders.

- Ask all users to empty their Junk E-mail folders.

- Ask all users to archive all mail items older than some reasonable date.

- Carefully inspect Public Folders, and remove or archive any out-of-date or unused contents to reduce the overall size of the Public Folders database.

- Make a separate archive (PST) of all active Public Folders as a backup.

When users have had a reasonable amount of time to clean up their mailboxes, it's usually useful to examine the mailbox store in Exchange to see whether any outstandingly large mailboxes remain. This allows you to have a more direct discussion with the owner of the mailbox to help reduce its size. You can check the size of mailboxes by opening the Exchange System Manager and navigating to Servers, then *servername*, then First Storage Group, then Mailbox Store, and then Mailboxes, as shown in Figure A-24.

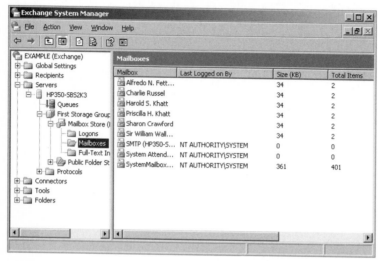

FIGURE A-24 A nearly empty Microsoft Exchange mailbox store.

Note The mailboxes listed in Figure A-24 are not typical of a working system but reflect what you would see on a brand-new system.

Synchronize Time

A critical step before you begin the installation of the SBS 2011 Essentials server is to synchronize the time on the existing SBS 2003 server with a known, reliable time source. The best way to do this is to configure SBS 2003 to use an external, authoritative Network Time Protocol (NTP) server. To configure SBS 2003 to use an external NTP server, use the following steps:

1. Log onto the SBS 2003 source server with the administrator account.

2. Open a cmd.exe window.

3. At the command prompt, type the following:

```
w32tm /config /update /manualpeerlist:"0.pool.ntp.org,0x8 1.pool.ntp.org,0x8
2.pool.ntp.org,0x8 3.pool.ntp.org,0x8" /syncfromflags:MANUAL
```

4. Stop and restart the W32Time service.

```
net stop w32time && net start w32time
```

This will set the SBS 2003 server to automatically set the domain time from the worldwide pool of NTP servers.

When you install SBS 2011 Essentials, you will also have an opportunity to set the clock for the new server. It *must* be set to the same time zone as the source server, and *must* be within five minutes of the same time as the source server. If you don't verify this, the migration will fail.

Note If you're installing SBS 2011 Essentials as a virtualized guest on Hyper-V, you should disable the Time Synchronization Integration Service for the virtual machine, as shown in Figure A-25. This will allow the SBS 2011 Essentials server to directly synchronize with an external time source.

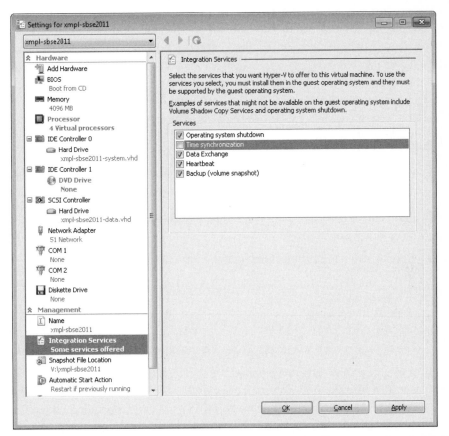

FIGURE A-25 Disable the Time Synchronization Integration Service if you are running virtualized.

Update the Active Directory Schema

There are two more tasks that need to be done on all SBS 2003 networks to prepare for the actual migration:

- Upgrade the Active Directory schema.

- Extend the time that two SBS servers can coexist in the same network.

> **Important** The first of these tasks, upgrading the Active Directory schema, is *irreversible*. After you have upgraded the schema, you can only return to your original state by restoring from backup. So, one last time—do you have a fully *tested* backup that you can fall back to if there are problems? If not, *stop now*, and make a backup and verify it.

Before you start the migration, you need to upgrade the Active Directory schema to align with the schema used by SBS 2011 Essentials. This is done by using the Adprep tool (adprep32.exe). To upgrade the schema, you *must* be logged on to the existing SBS server with an account that is a member of the Domain Admins, Enterprise Admins, *and* Schema Admins groups. The default administrator account (also known as "the 500 account") is in all three groups and is recommended for these procedures. To verify that the account you are using is in the necessary groups, open Active Directory Users And Computers and double-click the account you are using. Click the Member Of tab to see a list of groups to which the account belongs.

To run the Adprep tool, use the following steps:

1. Log on to your source server with an account that has Domain Admins, Enterprise Admins, and Schema Admins privileges.

2. Insert the original Disk 1 from your SBS 2011 Essentials installation media into the DVD drive of the source server.

3. Open a command prompt and type the following:

```
D:
cd support\adprep
adprep32 /forestprep
adprep32 /domainprep /gpprep
```

The *forestprep* step will take a while, but the *domainprep* step is quite quick.

4. If you haven't already downloaded the tool to extend your coexistence time, as referenced in *http://support.microsoft.com/kb/943494,* do so now and save it to a place you can easily find it. The exact name of this tool will vary depending on your language and versioning, but the one for our SBS 2003 server is WindowsServer2003-KB943494-v4-ENU.exe.

5. Execute the tool from your cmd prompt:

```
WindowsServer2003-KB943494-v4-ENU.exe
```

6. Reboot the SBS 2003 source server.

Plan to Migrate Line-of-Business Applications

A line-of-business (LOB) application is an application that is vital to running your business. For many existing SBS networks, these LOB applications run on the SBS 2003 server. Because the SBS 2003 server will be completely decommissioned and removed from the network as the last step of the migration, you need to plan where your LOB applications will run when the migration to SBS 2011 Essentials is complete. Because SBS 2011 Essentials is a 64-bit server, and SBS 2003 is a 32-bit server, there might be complications in migrating the LOB applications to the new server.

Most 32-bit applications run fine on 64-bit Windows, but you should contact your LOB vendor before moving forward with the migration to see if there are compatibility issues, or if they have a 64-bit version of the application that is a more appropriate choice. If there are issues with moving the application to 64-bit Windows, then you will need to plan to install a version of 32-bit Windows Server to support the LOB application. Your old SBS 2003 server hardware is a possible choice for the hardware required, but you will not be able to reuse the existing SBS 2003 license or software in the new network.

Creating a Migration Answer File

You must manually create a migration answer file (cfg.ini) to migrate from an existing Active Directory domain environment to your new SBS 2011 Essentials environment. When the installation process detects the answer file, it runs the installation in migration mode, enabling the migration of existing users to the SBS 2011 Essentials network.

The migration officially starts when the SBS 2011 Essentials setup detects the migration answer file and installs SBS 2011 Essentials in migration mode. You then have 21 days to complete the migration and decommission the existing SBS 2003 server.

There is no automated way to create the migration answer file. Use Notepad or any pure-text ASCII editor to create a file called cfg.ini with the following content:

```
[WinPE]
[InitialConfiguration]
AcceptEula=true
CompanyName=<CompanyName>
ServerName=<ServerName>
PlainTextPassword=<Password>
Settings=All
Migration=true
```

> **Note** Change "*<CompanyName>*" to your company's name, "*<ServerName>*" to the name you want for your server, and "*<Password>*" to the local administrator account password to use. Do not make any other changes in the text of this file.

Save the file as **cfg.ini.** Because this file contains your plain-text password, you need to protect the file against unauthorized access. You should completely delete all copies of the file when the migration is complete.

The cfg.ini file should be copied or moved to the root directory of a USB flash drive (or floppy disk if your server has a floppy drive). The USB or floppy disk must be present and the cfg.ini file must be detected during the initial installation of SBS 2011 Essentials for migration mode to be initiated.

Installing SBS 2011 Essentials

OK—we've prepared our server, we've created our answer file, and we're ready to go. Time to install SBS 2011 Essentials. We're going to follow the normal steps covered in Chapter 4, "Installing Windows Small Business Server 2011 Essentials," except that we're using the answer file we created earlier in this chapter. Insert the removable media with the cfg.ini, insert your installation DVD, and turn on the server.

> **Note** You won't actually need the answer file to be available until the Windows Server 2008 R2 portion of the installation completes.

You need to set your BIOS to boot from the DVD drive as the first option, to ensure that the server boots from the DVD. Then walk through the normal installation steps as covered in Chapter 4. You'll choose a new installation, select your installation disk, and add any necessary drivers, and then the installation of Windows Server 2008 R2 will proceed as it does for a new installation.

When the automatic part of the installation completes, you'll be in migration mode, as shown in Figure A-26.

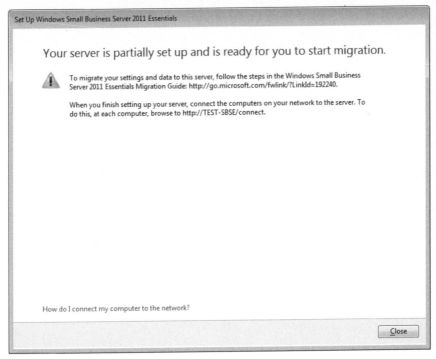

FIGURE A-26 After initial installation completes, the SBS 2011 Essentials server is in migration mode.

If you do *not* see the screen in Figure A-26, the cfg.ini file has not been detected. You should correct the problem and start the installation over again.

The actual migration of the existing domain to your new SBS 2011 Essentials server is not automated and has several steps that must be performed manually. These are:

- Set the DNS server IP address on the SBS 2011 Essentials server.
- Join the SBS 2011 Essentials server to the SBS 2003 domain.
- Install and restore the Certificate Authority on the SBS 2011 Essentials server.
- Transfer the Operations Masters roles to the SBS 2011 Essentials server.
- Import users and the SBS 2011 Essentials server into the Dashboard.
- Join existing domain computers to the SBS 2011 Essentials server.
- Move settings and data to the SBS 2011 Essentials server.
- Demote and remove the SBS 2003 server from the domain.
- Remove the legacy folder redirection Group Policy Objects (GPOs).

Set a DNS Address

The first task in the manual migration is to set a fixed IP address on your new SBS 2011 Essentials server. To do this, use the following steps:

1. Log on to the source SBS 2003 server and open a command prompt from the Start menu.

2. Type **ipconfig** and press Enter. The current network settings are displayed, as shown in Figure A-27.

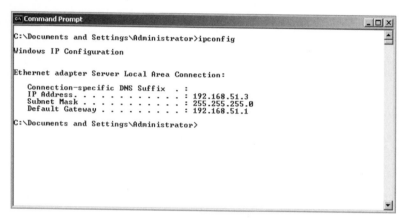

```
Command Prompt                                                      _ □ ×

C:\Documents and Settings\Administrator>ipconfig

Windows IP Configuration

Ethernet adapter Server Local Area Connection:

        Connection-specific DNS Suffix  . :
        IP Address. . . . . . . . . . . . : 192.168.51.3
        Subnet Mask . . . . . . . . . . . : 255.255.255.0
        Default Gateway . . . . . . . . . : 192.168.51.1

C:\Documents and Settings\Administrator>
```

FIGURE A-27 Use *ipconfig* to get the current network settings on the source server.

Make a note of the IP address shown (192.168.51.3 in our example).

3. Log on to the destination SBS 2011 Essentials server and open a command prompt from the Start menu.

4. Type **ncpa.cpl** and press Enter to open the Network Connections dialog box, as shown in Figure A-28.

5. Right-click Local Area Connection and select Properties from the menu to open the Properties dialog box for the network adapter.

6. Select Internet Protocol Version 4 (TCP/IPv4) and click Properties to open the Internet Protocol Version 4 (TCP/IPv4) Properties dialog box shown in Figure A-29.

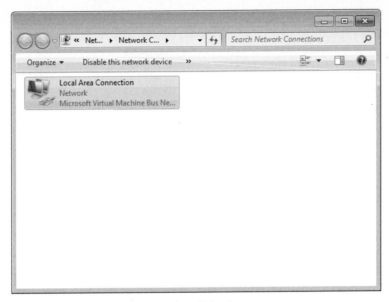

FIGURE A-28 The Network Connections dialog box.

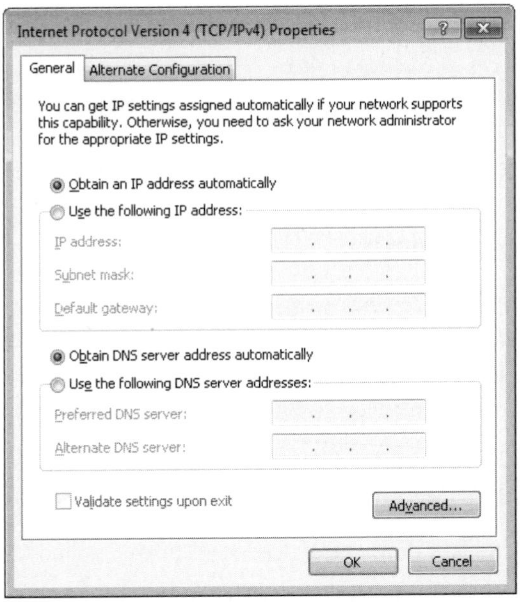

FIGURE A-29 The Internet Protocol Version 4 (TCP/IPv4) Properties dialog box.

7. Select Use The Following DNS Server Addresses and then enter the IP address of the SBS 2003 source server that you obtained in step 2 in the Preferred DNS Server field, as shown in Figure A-30.

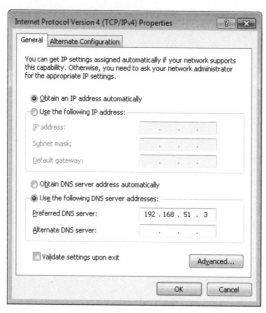

FIGURE A-30 Setting the Preferred DNS Server address to point to the SBS 2003 domain controller.

8. Click OK and then Close to change the DNS server address for the destination server.

Join the Server to the Domain

Before you actually join the new SBS 2011 Essentials server to your existing domain, you need to back up your existing Certificate Authority and remove it from the server. You'll restore this Certificate Authority after you've joined the SBS 2011 Essentials server to the domain and promoted the server to be a domain controller. To back up the Certificate Authority and remove it, use the following steps:

1. Log on to the destination SBS 2011 Essentials server.

2. Using Windows Explorer, create a new, empty folder on drive C called **CA_Backup**.

3. Select Certification Authority from the Administrative Tools menu to open the Certification Authority console, as shown in Figure A-31.

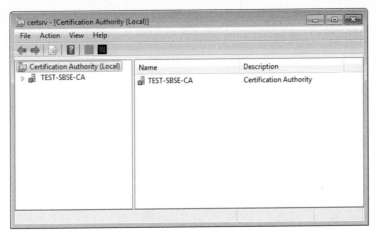

FIGURE A-31 The Certificate Authority management console.

4. Right-click *<ServerName>*-CA in the left pane, and select Back Up CA from the All Tasks menu, as shown in Figure A-32.

Note Substitute your SBS 2011 Essentials server name for *<ServerName>* in the step. For our server, this is TEST-SBSE.

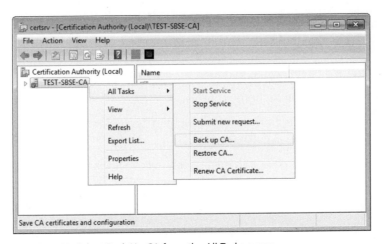

FIGURE A-32 Select Back Up CA from the All Tasks menu.

5. Click Next on the first page of the Certification Authority Backup Wizard to proceed to the Items To Back Up page, shown in Figure A-33.

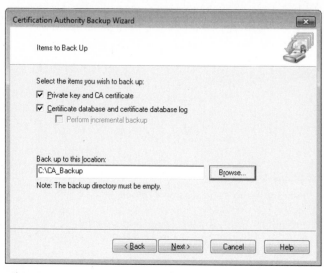

FIGURE A-33 The Items To Back Up page of the Certification Authority Backup Wizard.

6. Select both Private Key And CA Certificate and Certificate Database And Certificate Database Log, as shown in Figure A-33.

7. Click Browse and select the empty folder you created in step 2.

8. Click Next to open the Select A Password page. Enter a password and confirm it.

9. Click Next and then Finish to back up the Certificate Authority.

10. Close the Certification Authority console.

11. Select Server Manager from the Administrative Tools menu to open the Server Manager console shown in Figure A-34.

12. Click Roles in the left pane, and then select Remove Roles from the Action menu to open the Remove Roles Wizard.

13. Click Next to proceed to the Remove Server Roles page, as shown in Figure A-35.

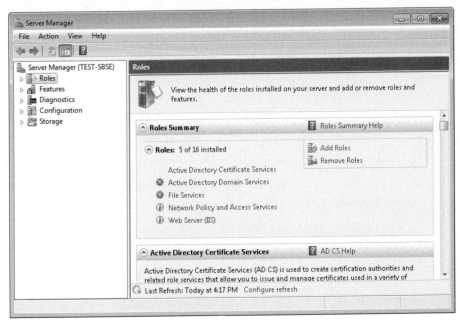

FIGURE A-34 The Server Manager console.

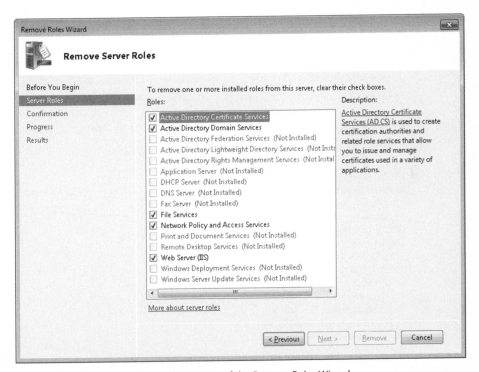

FIGURE A-35 The Remove Server Roles page of the Remove Roles Wizard.

14. Clear the check box for Active Directory Certificate Services. This is the first role listed.

15. Click Next and then Remove. When the removal is complete, click Close to close the wizard. A reboot should not be required.

Next you need to promote the SBS 2011 Essentials destination server to be a domain controller in the SBS 2003 domain. You must do this step within six days of installing SBS 2011 Essentials. To make the promotion, you need to use an unattend file. To create the file and promote the server to be a domain controller, use the following steps:

1. Open a command prompt on the destination SBS 2011 Essentials server.

2. In the command prompt window, type **cd desktop** and press Enter to change to the administrator's desktop directory, as shown in Figure A-36.

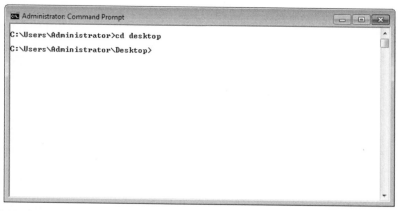

FIGURE A-36 Open a command prompt and change to the administrator's desktop directory.

3. Type **Notepad dc-cfg.ini** and press Enter. Click Yes to create the file.

4. Type the following information into the file:

```
[DCINSTALL]
UserName=<domain-admin-user-name>
Password=<domain-admin-password>
UserDomain=<domain>.local
DatabasePath=%systemroot%\ntds
LogPath=%systemroot%\ntds
SYSVOLPath=%systemroot%\sysvol
SafeModeAdminPassword=<domain-admin-password>
ConfirmGc=Yes
InstallDNS=yes
CreateDNSDelegation=No
CriticalReplicationOnly=no
ReplicaOrNewDomain=Replica
ReplicaDomainDNSName=<domain>.local
ReplicationSourceDC=<Source-Server-Name>.<domain>.local
RebootOnCompletion=No
ApplicationPartitionsToReplicate="""*""";
```

5. Replace *<domain-admin-user-name>*, *<domain-admin-password>*, *<domain>*, and *<Source-Server-Name>* in Notepad with the correct values for your SBS 2003 network. The values for our example network are shown in Figure A-37.

FIGURE A-37 The dc-cfg.ini file for our Example.local domain.

6. Select Save from the File menu and then Exit from the File menu to exit Notepad.

7. At the command prompt, type **dcpromo /unattend:"dc-cfg.ini"** as shown in Figure A-38, and then press Enter.

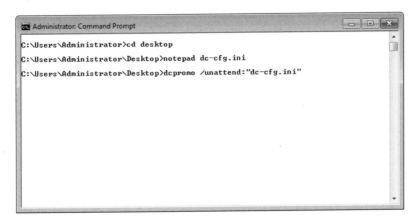

FIGURE A-38 The command to run dcpromo with an unattend file.

8. When the process completes, you'll see a status message in the command prompt window. Type **shutdown –t 0 –r** and press Enter to reboot the server.

9. When the server reboots, log on with a domain administrator account. The local administrator account will no longer be active.

10. Open Active Directory Users And Computers from the Administrative Tools menu, and navigate to the Domain Computers organizational unit, as shown in Figure A-39. Both the source SBS 2003 server and the destination SBS 2011 Essentials server should be listed and display GC in the DC Type column, indicating that they are global catalog servers.

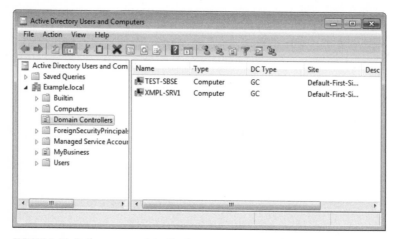

FIGURE A-39 Both source and destination servers are now domain controllers and global catalog servers.

11. You can close the Active Directory Users And Computers console.

Install and Restore the Certificate Authority

Now that your destination SBS 2011 Essentials server is a domain controller, you need to re-install the Active Directory Certificate Services role to the server and restore the Certificate Authority. To install the Active Directory Certificate Services role, use the following steps:

1. On the destination SBS 2011 Essentials server, open the Server Manager from the Administrative Tools menu.

2. Select Roles in the left pane and then Add Roles from the Action menu to open the Add Roles Wizard.

3. Click Next to proceed to the Select Server Roles page, as shown in Figure A-40.

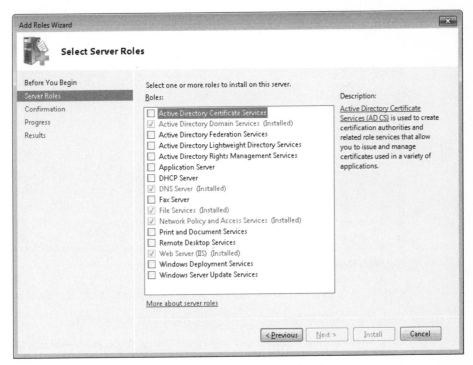

FIGURE A-40 The Select Server Roles page of the Add Roles Wizard.

4. Select Active Directory Certificate Services and click Next to proceed to the Introduction To Active Directory Certificate Services page. This page provides a brief overview of the role, along with specific notes and links to additional information.

5. Click Next to open the Select Role Services page shown in Figure A-41. On this page, you'll select Certification Authority and Certification Authority Web Enrollment.

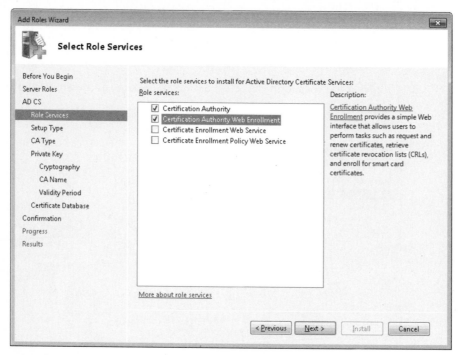

FIGURE A-41 The Select Role Services page of the Add Roles Wizard.

6. Click Next to proceed to the Specify Setup Type page. Select Standalone.

7. Click Next to go to the Specify CA Type page. Select Root CA.

8. Click Next to proceed to the Set Up Private Key page. Select Use Existing Private Key and then Select A Certificate And Use Its Associated Private Key, as shown in Figure A-42.

9. Click Next to open the Select Existing Certificate page, as shown in Figure A-43. Select the ServerName-CA certificate as shown. (Your server name will, of course, be different.)

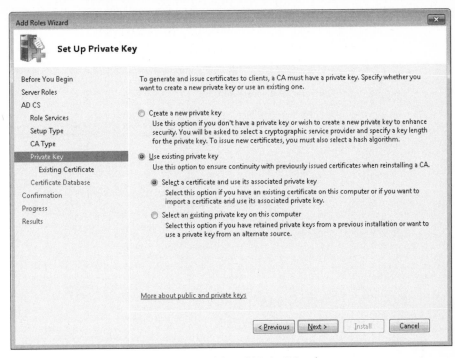

FIGURE A-42 The Set Up Private Key page of the Add Roles Wizard.

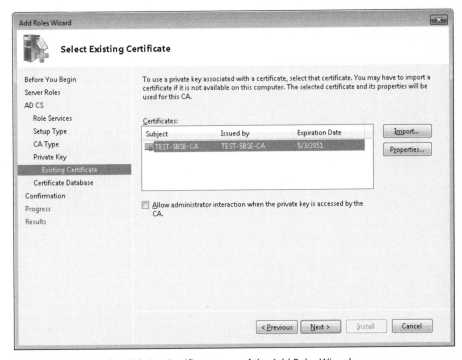

FIGURE A-43 The Select Existing Certificate page of the Add Roles Wizard.

10. Click Next to open the Configure Certificate Database page, as shown in Figure A-44. Accept the default locations or browse to change them.

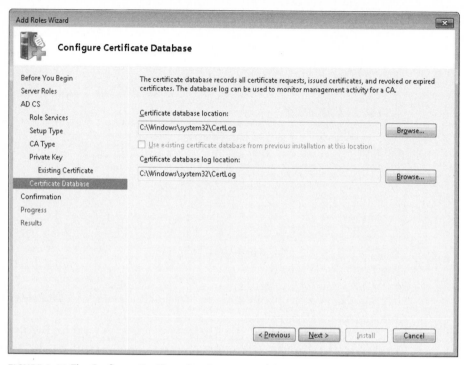

FIGURE A-44 The Configure Certificate Database page of the Add Roles Wizard.

11. Click Next to proceed to the Confirmation page and then Install to begin adding the role.

12. Click Close when the installation completes. Leave the Server Manager console open.

Next we need to restore the Certificate Authority that we saved before we promoted the SBS 2011 Essentials server to be a domain controller. To restore this authority, use the following steps:

1. In the left pane of the Server Manager console, navigate to *<ServerName>*-CA, as shown in Figure A-45 (where your server's name is substituted for *<ServerName>*).

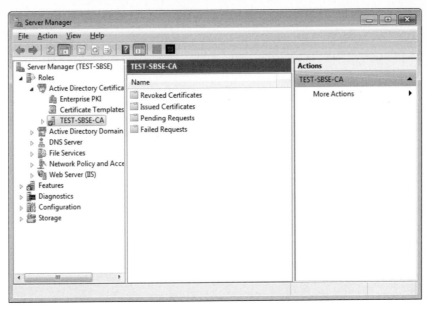

FIGURE A-45 The Certificate Authority is highlighted in the Server Manager.

2. Right-click the Certificate Authority and select Restore CA from the All Tasks menu, as shown in Figure A-46.

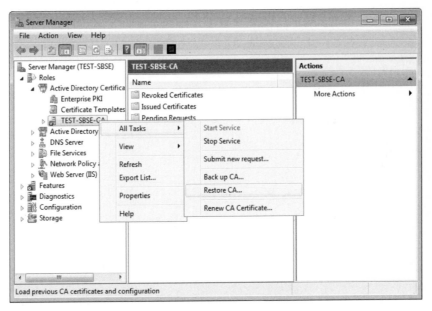

FIGURE A-46 Selecting Restore CA for the Certificate Authority.

3. Click OK on the Certification Authority Restore Wizard alert to stop Active Directory Certificate Services.

4. Click Next on the welcome page of the Certification Authority Restore Wizard.

5. Select both Private Key And CA Certificate and Certificate Database And Certificate Database Log on the Items To Restore page, as shown in Figure A-47.

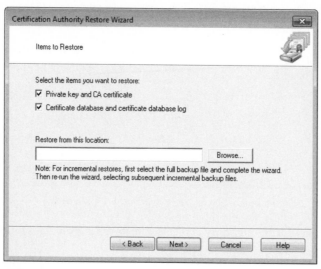

FIGURE A-47 The Items To Restore page of the Certification Authority Restore Wizard.

6. Click Browse and navigate to the C:\CA_Backup folder, as shown in Figure A-48.

FIGURE A-48 The Browse For Folder dialog box.

7. Click OK and then Next to open the Provide Password page.

8. Enter the password you used to protect the Certificate Authority.

9. Click Next to proceed to the Completing The Certification Authority Restore Wizard page.

10. Click Finish to restore the Certificate Authority. When prompted, click Yes to restart the Active Directory Certificate Services. Do not close the Server Manager—we're not quite done with it yet.

The final certificate action we need to perform is to configure the certificate revocation list (CRL) distribution list. To configure the CRL distribution list, use the following steps:

1. In the Server Manager, right-click *<ServerName>*-CA and select Properties to open the Properties dialog box for the certificate authority.

2. Click the Extensions tab and select the http:// entry, as shown in Figure A-49.

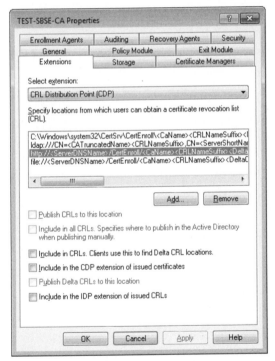

FIGURE A-49 The Extensions tab of the Certificate Authority Properties dialog box.

3. Select Include In CRLs and Include In The CDP Extension Of Issued Certificates.

4. Click Add to open the Add Location dialog box shown in Figure A-50.

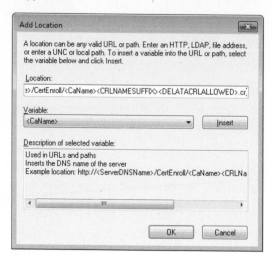

FIGURE A-50 The Add Location dialog box for the Certificate Authority Properties dialog box.

5. In the Location field, enter the following:

   ```
   http://<ServerDNSName>/CertEnroll/<CaName><CRLNAMESUFFIX><DELATACRLALLOWED>.crl
   ```

   Then click OK.

> **Important** Use the exact text shown in step 5; do not substitute your server name or CA name into the field.

6. Click Apply and then click Yes to restart the Active Directory Certificate Services.

7. Click OK to close the Properties dialog box. You can close Server Manager now.

Move the Active Directory Operations

Active Directory has five Flexible Single Master Operations (FSMO, pronounced *fizmo*) roles. These roles must always reside on the SBS server. In this section, we'll transfer the FSMO roles to the destination server, make sure that the destination server is a global catalog (GC) server, remove the GC from the source server, and turn on the UPnP beacon so that our clients can find the new server.

Transfer the FSMO Roles

To transfer the roles to the destination SBS 2011 Essentials server, log on to the destination SBS 2011 Essentials server using the administrator account, and then use the following steps:

1. Open a command prompt or Windows PowerShell window as administrator.

2. Type **netdom query fsmo** and press Enter. You should see a list of roles and the fully
qualified server name that holds each role, as shown in Figure A-51. All roles should be
pointing to the SBS 2003 server (xmpl-srv1.example.local in our test domain).

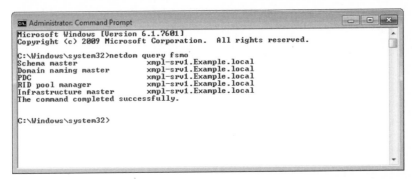

FIGURE A-51 Before transferring the FSMO roles, they all reside on the SBS 2003 server.

3. Type **ntdsutil** and press Enter to open the ntdsutil command prompt, as shown in
Figure A-52.

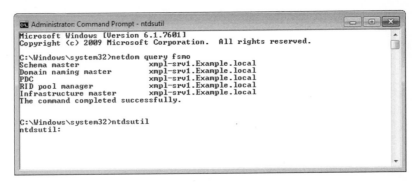

FIGURE A-52 At the ntdsutil prompt.

4. At the ntdsutil prompt, enter the following commands:

```
Roles
connections
connect to server <servername>
q
```

Note Substitute the name of your server for *<servername>*.

This will connect you to the SBS 2011 Essentials server and leave you at the fsmo maintenance prompt, as shown in Figure A-53.

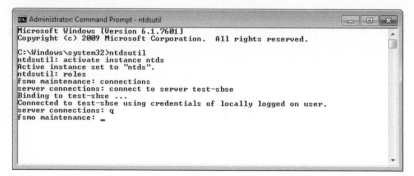

FIGURE A-53 At the fsmo maintenance prompt, ready to transfer roles.

5. Type **transfer PDC** and press Enter. Click Yes in the confirmation dialog box.

6. Type **transfer infrastructure master** and press Enter. Click Yes in the confirmation dialog box.

7. Type **transfer naming master** and press Enter. Click Yes in the confirmation dialog box.

8. Type **transfer rid master** and press Enter. Click Yes in the confirmation dialog box.

9. Type **transfer schema master** and press Enter. Click Yes in the confirmation dialog box.

10. Type **q** and press Enter.

11. Type **q** and press Enter to return to the command prompt.

12. At the command prompt, type **netdom query fsmo** and press Enter to see the current holder of the five FSMO roles. All of them should now point to your SBS 2011 Essentials server, as shown in Figure A-54.

```
Administrator: Command Prompt
Server "Test-SBSE" knows about 5 roles
Schema - CN=NTDS Settings,CN=TEST-SBSE,CN=Servers,CN=Default-First-Site-Name,CN=
Sites,CN=Configuration,DC=Example,DC=local
Naming Master - CN=NTDS Settings,CN=TEST-SBSE,CN=Servers,CN=Default-First-Site-N
ame,CN=Sites,CN=Configuration,DC=Example,DC=local
PDC - CN=NTDS Settings,CN=TEST-SBSE,CN=Servers,CN=Default-First-Site-Name,CN=Sit
es,CN=Configuration,DC=Example,DC=local
RID - CN=NTDS Settings,CN=TEST-SBSE,CN=Servers,CN=Default-First-Site-Name,CN=Sit
es,CN=Configuration,DC=Example,DC=local
Infrastructure - CN=NTDS Settings,CN=TEST-SBSE,CN=Servers,CN=Default-First-Site-
Name,CN=Sites,CN=Configuration,DC=Example,DC=local
fsmo maintenance: q
ntdsutil:
ntdsutil: q

C:\Users\Administrator.EXAMPLE>netdom query fsmo
Schema master                TEST-SBSE.Example.local
Domain naming master         TEST-SBSE.Example.local
PDC                          TEST-SBSE.Example.local
RID pool manager             TEST-SBSE.Example.local
Infrastructure master        TEST-SBSE.Example.local
The command completed successfully.

C:\Users\Administrator.EXAMPLE>
```

FIGURE A-54 All FSMO roles are transferred.

Set the Global Catalog

Now we need to verify that the destination server is a global catalog (GC) server, and then remove the GC role from the source server. Because the command prompt is already open, use the following steps:

1. At the command prompt, type **dssites.msc** and press Enter to open the Active Directory Sites And Services console, as shown in Figure A-55.

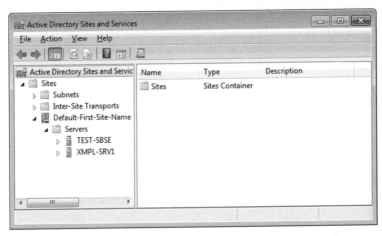

FIGURE A-55 The Active Directory Sites And Services console.

2. Navigate to the Servers container in the Default-First-Site-Name site. You should see two servers, the SBS 2003 source server and the SBS 2011 Essentials destination server, as shown previously in Figure A-55.

3. Expand the destination server container, and then right-click NTDS Settings. Select Properties from the menu to open the NTDS Settings Properties dialog box shown in Figure A-56.

FIGURE A-56 The NTDS Settings Properties for the destination server.

4. The Global Catalog option should be selected. If it is, proceed to step 5.

If the Global Catalog option is not selected, select it. Click OK to close the dialog box and restart the server, wait 15 minutes, and then return to the point of step 2. You can use the following commands to verify that replication is functioning correctly:

```
repadmin /replicate  <srcsrv> <targetsrv> dc=company,dc=com /full
repadmin /replicate  <srcsrv> <targetsrv> cn=Configuration,dc=company,dc=com  /full
repadmin /replicate  <srcsrv> <targetsrv>
    cn=Schema,CN=Configuration,dc=company,dc=com  /full
repadmin /replicate  <srcsrv> <targetsrv>  dc=DomainDnsZones,dc=company,dc=com  /full
repadmin /replicate  <srcsrv> <targetsrv>  dc=ForestDnsZones,dc=company,dc=com  /full
```

where each line is a *repadmin* command. (Books break command lines in awkward places sometimes.)

Note You can verify that the GC is properly recognized and replicating by opening the Event Viewer and searching for Event 1119 in the Directory Services log. The event should state that the destination server is now advertising as a global catalog server.

5. Expand the source server container, and then right-click NTDS Settings. Select Properties from the menu to open the NTDS Settings Properties dialog box.

6. Clear the Global Catalog check box, click OK, and then reboot the source server.

Set the DNS Server Address

Earlier, we configured the destination server to point to the source server for DNS, but now that we have moved all the FSMO roles to the destination server, we need to change the DNS settings so that the SBS 2011 Essentials server points to itself, using the following steps:

1. Log on to the destination SBS 2011 Essentials server and open a command prompt from the Start menu.

2. Type **ncpa.cpl** and press Enter to open the Network Connections dialog box.

3. Right-click Local Area Connection and select Properties from the menu to open the Properties dialog box for the network adapter.

4. Select Internet Protocol Version 4 (TCP/IPv4) and click Properties to open the Internet Protocol Version 4 (TCP/IPv4) Properties dialog box.

5. Select Use The Following DNS Server Address, and then enter **127.0.0.1** in the Preferred DNS Server field. Always use the special localhost address for DNS on the SBS 2011 Essentials server.

6. Click OK and then Close to change the DNS server address for the destination server.

Enable UPnP Discovery

To make it easier for clients to discover your destination server, you need to enable UPnP discovery on the SBS 2011 Essentials server. There are three services involved:

- SSDP Discovery
- UPnP Device Host
- Windows Server UPnP Device Service

To enable these services, log on to the destination server with an administrative account and use the following steps:

1. Open the Services console (services.msc).

2. Locate SSDP Discovery, as shown in Figure A-57.

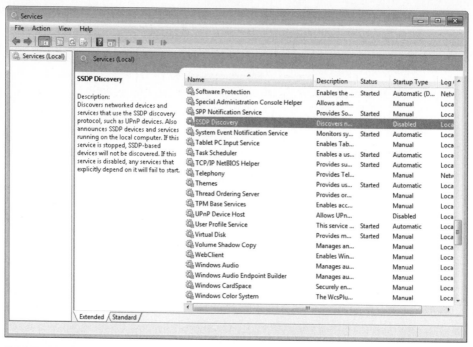

FIGURE A-57 The Services console, with SSDP Discovery highlighted.

3. Double-click SSDP Discovery, change Startup Type to Automatic as shown in Figure A-58, and click Apply.

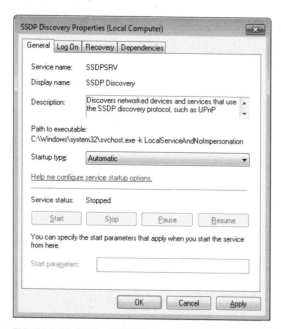

FIGURE A-58 Set the SSDP Discovery service to start automatically.

4. Click Start, and then click OK to start the service and return to the Services console.

5. Repeat the process in steps 3 and 4 for the UPnP Device Host service.

6. Scroll down to Windows Server UPnP Device Service and select it. The service should already be set to automatic start, but it won't have started yet because it depends on the two services you just enabled. Click Start The Service in the Extended pane to start the service.

7. Close the Services console. We're done with it for now.

Import Users into the Dashboard

Users from SBS 2003 are automatically migrated to SBS 2011 Essentials using Active Directory replication. But SBS 2003 users are not automatically added to the SBS 2011 Essentials Dashboard, and if you have more than 25 users, you need to reduce the total number of users. SBS 2011 Essentials supports a maximum of 25 users, whereas SBS 2003 supports up to 75 users. For SBS 2003 sites with more than 25 users, a migration to SBS 2011 Standard or to a native Windows Server 2003 R2 domain is recommended.

> **Note** In the following steps, we use Windows PowerShell to create groups. This differs from the published method used in the Microsoft migration guidance. But using Windows PowerShell is just easier.

First, create the new security groups that will be needed with SBS 2011 Essentials. To do that, use the following steps:

1. Log on to the SBS 2011 Essentials server as an administrative user.

2. Open a Windows PowerShell window using Run As Administrator.

3. In the Windows PowerShell window, type **Set-ExecutionPolicy RemoteSigned** and press Enter. Answer "Y" to the prompt.

4. Open Notepad or your favorite plain-text editor and create the following script:

```
# ScriptName: Create-SBSEGroups.ps1
#
# Script to create missing SBSE groups in a migration scenario
#     and add the 500 account (Administrator) from SBS 2003
#     to the SBSE Groups
#
# Uses: ActiveDirectory Module
#
# Created: 15/05/2011 by Charlie Russel
# ModHist:
#
# Copyright 2011 by Charlie Russel & Sharon Crawford. All rights reserved.
```

```
#    You may freely use this script in your own environment,
#      modifying it to meet your needs.
#    You may not, however, re-publish it without express permission,
#      and must, in all cases, provide attribution to the copyright holders.
#
Import-Module ActiveDirectory

# Modify the next line to use the correct Domain Name for your SBS Domain
$DomainName = "Example"

# If you've modified the name for the 500 account, change this next line
$AdminUser  = "Administrator"

# Create a list of SBS Essentials groups to create
$GrpList = "RA_AllowAddInAccess",`
           "RA_AllowComputerAccess",`
           "RA_AllowDashboardAccess",`
           "RA_AllowHomePageLinks",`
           "RA_AllowNetworkAlertAccess",`
           "RA_AllowRemoteAccess",`
           "RA_AllowShareAccess",`
           "WSSUsers"

# Set the type of security group to create
$GrpScope = "Universal"

# Location to create the groups
$SecGrpOU = "OU=Security Groups,OU=MyBusiness,DC=$DomainName,DC=local"

# Iterate through the list of groups and create them
ForEach ($GrpName in $GrpList) {
   New-ADGroup `
        -name             $GrpName `
        -sAMAccountName   $GrpName `
        -DisplayName      $GrpName `
        -GroupCategory    Security `
        -GroupScope       $GrpScope `
        -Description      "SBS 2011 Essentials Groups" `
        -Path             $SecGrpOU
   Add-ADGroupMember -Identity "$GrpName" -Members "Administrator"
}
```

5. Save the script as **Create-SBSEGroups.ps1**.

> **Note** This script is available online as part of the online companion content for this book (at *http://go.microsoft.com/FWLink/?Linkid=225701*) and is also available on Charlie's blog at *http://blogs.msmvps.com/russel/*.

6. Execute the Create-SBSEGroups.ps1 script, as shown in Figure A-59.

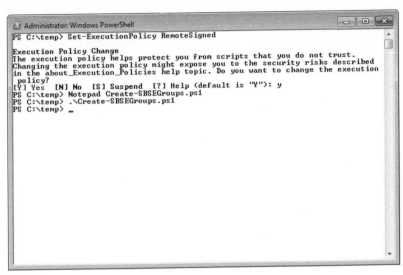

FIGURE A-59 Creating the default SBS 2011 Essentials security groups.

7. Leave the Windows PowerShell window open; you'll need it later.

Next, you need to add all of the users to the SBS 2011 Essentials Dashboard. SBS 2011 Essentials has a special Windows PowerShell environment for this. To add the users, execute the following steps:

1. In the existing Windows PowerShell window, type **& "$env:ProgramFiles\Windows Server\Bin\WssPowerShell.exe"** and press Enter to start the special WSS PowerShell environment for SBS 2011 Essentials.

2. In the Windows PowerShell window, type **Import-WssUser -name "Administrator"** and press Enter.

3. Repeat step 2 for each user you want to import into the Dashboard, substituting the user name for "Administrator" in the command.

An alternative approach, if you've got more than a couple of users, is to use a little script. First, create a text file with each user's logon name, one to a line. Save the file as **userlist.txt** and then run the following line of code in place of step 2 above:

```
Foreach ($user in (get-content userlist.txt)) { Import-WssUser -name "$user")
```

That seems a lot simpler and quicker if you have more than one or two users. And when you're done, you'll have all your users imported into the Dashboard, as shown in Figure A-60.

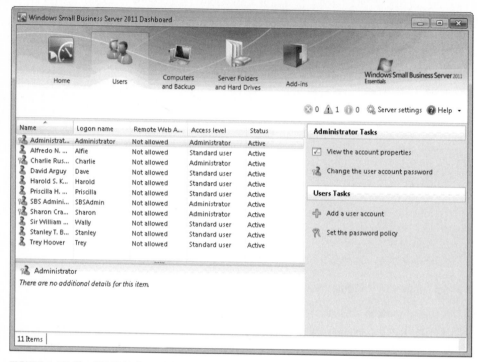

FIGURE A-60 The SBS 2011 Essentials Dashboard with users imported.

Join Existing Domain Computers

Not only do existing users not show up in the Dashboard until you import them, computers don't either. You need to add both the SBS 2011 Essentials server and the computers in your SBS network that you want to manage to the Dashboard. Adding the server to the Dashboard is easy: just run the following command in the WSS PowerShell window you have open from the previous step:

```
Import-WssLocalMachineCert
```

After you reboot the server, it will be recognized by the Dashboard. You'll actually see it immediately after you run the command, but it takes a reboot for it to fully integrate.

Unfortunately, there's no easy way to join client computers to the SBS 2011 Essentials network. You have to go to each individual computer and join it, just as you would with a brand-new SBS 2011 Essentials network. Follow the steps in Chapter 6, "Adding User Accounts," to join client computers to the SBS 2011 Essentials network.

There is one key difference for computers joined to an SBS 2011 Essentials network as compared to an SBS 2003 network. The first is that computers running a Home edition of Windows can be added to the SBS 2011 Essentials network. They aren't technically joined to the domain, because Home editions of Windows don't support domain join, but they are managed in the Dashboard and are backed up by the client backup of SBS 2011 Essentials.

Move Settings and Data

At this point, you should move any shared data or folders off of the source server and re-share them on the destination server. This is a mostly manual process. Start by reviewing a list of all the network shares on the source server, using the following command:

`Net share`

Save the output of this command into a text file for later referral. Document any special settings, and then recreate the shares on the SBS 2011 Essentials server.

To move the actual data, use the *robocopy* command. This command is part of SBS 2011 Essentials, so you should *pull* the data from the source server. Log on to the destination server with an administrative account and use the following command to move the data:

`Robocopy \\source\share \\destination\share /e /B /copy:DATSOU /log:c:\copyresults.log`

Repeat this for each shared folder.

Next, remove the netlogon script that SBS 2003 used. This doesn't work right with computers running versions of Windows after Windows Vista anyway, so it's time to get rid of it. From an elevated command prompt on the destination server, type **del \\localhost\netlogon*.bat** and press Enter.

Demote the SBS 2003 Server

It's now time to remove your old SBS server. You should demote it from a domain controller role to a simple member server, and then remove that server from Active Directory. After you remove the SBS 2003 server, you should not *ever* allow it to reconnect to the network until you have completely formatted the system disk and installed a new operating system on it.

To demote the SBS 2003 server, follow these steps:

1. Log on to the SBS 2003 server with an administrative account.

2. Open a command window. At the prompt, type **ncpa.cpl** and press Enter to open the Network Connections application, as shown in Figure A-61.

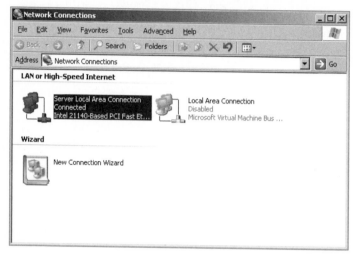

FIGURE A-61 The Network Connections application.

3. Right-click the remaining active network connection and select Properties.

4. Select Internet Protocol (TCP/IP), and click Properties to open the Internet Protocol (TCP/IP) Properties dialog box shown in Figure A-62.

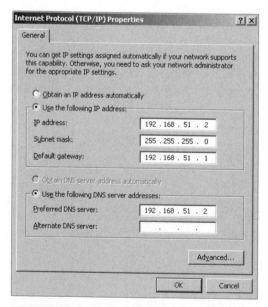

FIGURE A-62 The Preferred DNS Server address is still pointing to the source server.

5. Change the Preferred DNS Server address to the IP address of the destination server, as shown in Figure A-63. (The DNS address of your destination server will likely be different than that shown in this figure.)

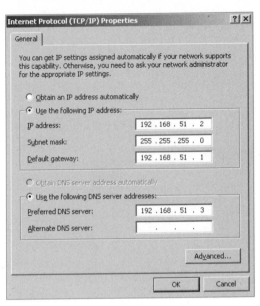

FIGURE A-63 Change the Preferred DNS Server to point to the destination server.

6. Open a command window. At the prompt, type **dcpromo** and press Enter to open the Active Directory Installation Wizard, as shown in Figure A-64.

FIGURE A-64 The welcome page of the Active Directory Installation Wizard.

7. Click Next. The global catalog server warning shown in Figure A-65 will be displayed if you didn't remove the global catalog from the server earlier.

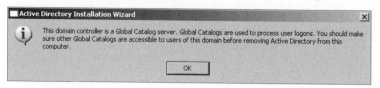

FIGURE A-65 The global catalog server warning that appears when you are demoting your source SBS 2003 server.

8. Click OK to continue to the Remove Active Directory page shown in Figure A-66.

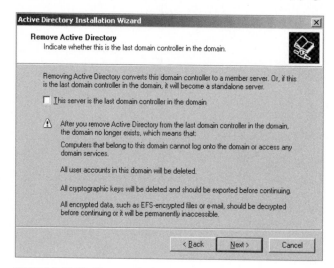

FIGURE A-66 The Remove Active Directory page of the Active Directory Installation Wizard.

9. Leave the check box cleared, and click Next to open the Administrator Password page.

10. Type a password, type it again to confirm it, and then click Next to open the Summary page shown in Figure A-67.

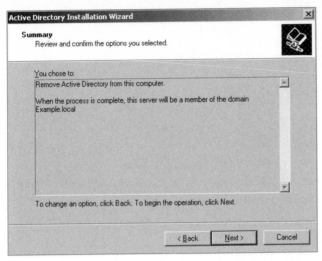

FIGURE A-67 The Summary page of the Active Directory Installation Wizard.

11. Click Next, and the wizard will remove Active Directory and demote the original SBS 2003 server to a domain member.

12. When the wizard completes successfully, click Finish and then click Restart Now.

> **Note** In some environments, the first running of *dcpromo* fails because of a timing issue—*netlogon* fails to stop in time. Simply wait a couple of minutes and then run *dcpromo* again.

13. On the Finish The Migration page of the Migration Wizard, select The Source Server Is No Longer A Domain Controller and click Next.

14. Disconnect the original SBS 2003 server from the network, and do not reconnect it until you have completely reformatted it and installed a new operating system.

Final Cleanup

We're almost there. You have a few cleanup tasks to do, however. These include:

- Enabling Remote Web Access (RWA).
- Setting the Remote Desktop Gateway certificate.
- Removing legacy Group Policy Objects.
- Mapping permitted computers to user accounts.

To enable RWA, follow the steps outlined in Chapter 14, "Managing Remote Access."

To set the RD Gateway certificate, open a command prompt as an administrator and type the following:

```
cd "C:\Program Files\Windows Server\bin"
configurerdp
```

There will likely be some leftover GPOs that are no longer appropriate. Because SBS 2011 Essentials allows computers running Windows Home edition on the network, you can't effectively use Group Policy to manage all the computers in a SBS 2011 Essentials network. However, if you do choose to require business-class Windows client computers, you can continue to use Group Policy to manage them. See Appendix B for more on Group Policy.

When we imported users into the Dashboard, they came in without having all their permissions set. You should now go into the Dashboard and set which computers each user is permitted to log on to, whether the user is allowed to use RWA at all, and which folders the user has permissions on. See Chapter 6 for details on these settings.

If your SBS 2003 Server was the DHCP server for the network, you need to enable DHCP on your router. Configuring RWA might have enabled this, but if it hasn't, you need to manually log on to your router and enable DHCP.

The final cleanup step is to run the Windows Server Solutions Best Practice Analyzer (WSS BPA) to identify any lingering problems. The WSS BPA is available from *http://www.microsoft.com /downloads/en/details.aspx?FamilyID=d40dcc5b-8f97-49e2-ae79-9c7a7a69dec4*.

> **Note** If that looks too long to type, you can always find a link to the current version of all SBS BPAs by going to *http://www.sbsbpa.com*. This site is maintained by Susan Bradley, an SBS MVP and the official SBS Diva, for whom we are all extremely grateful.

Appendix B
Using the Group Policy Add-In

For the most part, Group Policy is something that concerns administrators of large networks—and even then, not always. The default Group Policy settings are fine for many networks, and customizing them can add a layer of complexity that a smaller network does not need. Nevertheless, there are some highly desirable Group Policy settings that can easily be implemented on computers running Windows 7 Professional.

Group Policy in Windows Small Business Server 2011 Essentials

The Windows 7 Professional Pack add-in provides a way for you to make several Group Policy settings for your clients running Windows 7 Professional without requiring you to invoke Group Policy Management. With the add-in, you can set:

- Folder redirection (changing the location of folders from client to server).
- Settings for Windows Update.
- Security settings for Windows Defender.
- Security settings for the network firewall.

To implement the Windows 7 Professional Pack, open the Dashboard and follow these steps:

1. Select Computers And Backup.
2. In the right pane, under Computers And Backup Tasks, click Implement Windows 7 Professional Pack, as shown in Figure B-1.
3. Read the Getting Started information, and click Next.
4. On the Enable Folder Redirection Group Policy page, select the folders to be redirected, as shown in Figure B-2. (See the "Folder Redirection" sidebar for details.) Click Next.
5. On the Enable Security Policy Settings page, select the security settings you want to enable. Click Finish.

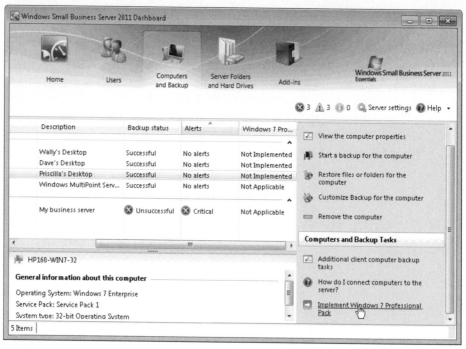

FIGURE B-1 Implementing the Windows 7 Professional Pack add-in.

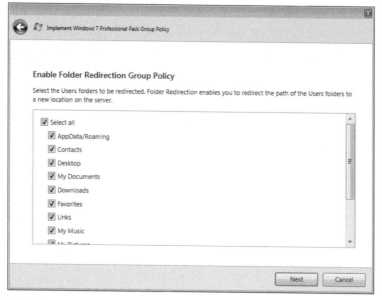

FIGURE B-2 Selecting folders to redirect.

Real World: Folder Redirection

Folder redirection allows you to save data in a location you choose and separates user data from profile data, which decreases the amount of time required to log on. Data is stored on a server, where it can be backed up. If the same redirection is applied to multiple users, all data is stored in that one location. Folder redirection also allows users to share data.

Although many folders can be redirected, the most important ones are the following:

- **AppData/Roaming**   Stores application information such as toolbar settings, custom dictionaries, and other information not stored in the registry. Redirect this folder when applications should operate in the same manner for a user whenever he or she utilizes a new computer. When the folder is redirected, the user does not need to be configured again when he or she changes computers.

- **Desktop**   Stores the contents of the user's desktop, including shortcuts, folders, and files.

- **My Documents**   Allows a user to access the same documents from any computer on the network.

- **Start Menu**   Stores the program groups and shortcuts from the user's Start menu. Allows user access to the Favorites and Printers And Faxes folders.

Redirect *all* folders if users frequently log on to different computers on the network.

Appendix C
Additional Resources

Books are great. They're easy to use and very portable. We love books. They are, however, somewhat static, and when you need information on the latest security threat or help with new applications, there's nothing like the Internet.

This appendix lists websites and blogs that are of use to Windows Small Business Server 2011 Essentials users and consultants. First are links to Microsoft resources, followed by websites and blogs maintained by other companies and knowledgeable individuals.

Microsoft Resources

http://blogs.technet.com/msrc/	Microsoft Security Response Center
http://blogs.technet.com/sbs/	Official Windows Small Business Server blog
http://blogs.technet.com/wsus/	Windows Server Update Services (WSUS) Product Team Blog
http://blogs.technet.com/mu/	Microsoft Update Product Team information
http://blogs.technet.com/sus/	The WSUS Support Team blog
http://blogs.msdn.com/ie/	IEBlog: The Windows Internet Explorer Weblog
http://www.microsoft.com/technet /security/advisory /RssFeed.aspx?securityadvisory	Microsoft TechNet Security TechCenter
http://feeds.feedburner.com /MicrosoftDownloadCenter	Microsoft Download Center
http://www.microsoft.com/mscorp /execmail/	Microsoft Executive E-mail: Insights about technology and public-policy issues important to computer users from Microsoft executives
http://blogs.msdn.com/MainFeed.aspx	MSDN blogs
http://windowsteamblog.com/	Windows Team blog
http://msexchangeteam.com	Microsoft Exchange Team blog
http://blogs.msdn.com/sqlblog/	Microsoft SQL Server Support Blog
http://www.youtube.com/user /SmallBusinessServer	Small Business Server 2011 YouTube channel

Other Resources for Windows Small Business Server Users and Consultants

All the sites listed here have been found by us to be informative and useful. However, as with all Internet resources, you must use your judgment and think critically about what advice to follow.

http://msmvps.com/bradley/	The SBS Diva blog. The first place we go for answers (and often the only place we need).
http://usingwindowshomeserver.com	Andrew Edney's blog. Devoted to Windows Home Server and Small Business Server.
http://connecteddigitalworld.com	Andrew Edney's other blog. Devoted to all things in the connected digital world.
http://www.eventid.net	Event details and general technical help.
http://feeds.feedburner.com /smbitprosposts	smbITPro: Small and Medium Business (SMB) IT professionals.
http://blogs.msdn.com/aaron_margosis/	Aaron Margosis' WebLog: The Non-Admin blog running with least privilege on the desktop.
http://msmvps.com/blogs/donna/rss.aspx	Donna's SecurityFlash: PC and Internet security blog.
http://blogs.iss.net/rss.php	Frequency X: Straight Dope on the Vulnerability du Jour from IBM Internet Security Systems.
http://computer.forensikblog.de/en /atom.xml	Int for(ensic)(blog;) Notes on computer forensics, international edition.
http://msinfluentials.com/blogs/jesper /rss.aspx	Jesper's Blog by Jesper Johansson, the author of the *Windows Server 2008 Security Resource Kit* (Microsoft Press, 2008).
http://titlerequired.com	Robert Pearman's blog. Small Business Server Tips & Tricks.
http://blog.loglogic.com/atom.xml	Everything about keeping and using security logs.
http://www.viruslist.com/en/rss /latestanalysis	All about Internet security.
http://msmvps.com/blogs/mainfeed.aspx	Blogs by current and former Microsoft Most Valuable Professionals (MVPs).

http://sbs.seandaniel.com/rss.xml	SBS and related technology.
http://www.symantec.com/content/en /us/enterprise/rss/securityresponse /srblogs.xml	Symantec Security Response blogs.
http://smallbizthoughts.blogspot.com /feeds/posts/default?alt=rss	Small Biz Thoughts; intended primarily for small business consultants.
http://feeds.trendmicro.com /MalwareAdvisories	Trend Micro's Malware Advisories.
http://www.smallbiztrends.com	Small Business Trends, an online publication for small business owners, entrepreneurs, and the people who interact with them.
http://blogs.msmvps.com/russel	Charlie Russel's blog. Devoted to server issues in general, with a healthy dose of Windows PowerShell thrown in.
http://social.technet.microsoft.com /wiki/contents/articles /windows-powershell-survival-guide.aspx	The Windows PowerShell Survival Guide.

Appendix D
Understanding TCP/IP v4

The protocol wars have ended, and TCP/IP is the winner. After years of proprietary protocols vying for popularity, TCP/IP emerged as the only protocol needed by most networks. Every modern computer supports TCP/IP, as do a growing number of other devices such as printers, network appliances, personal digital assistants (PDAs), and cell phones. What is different is that version 6 of the TCP/IP protocols (IPv6) is beginning to be a part of our everyday world and will eventually replace the ubiquitous version 4 of TCP/IP (IPv4).

The TCP/IP Protocol Suite

Whole books have been written about TCP/IP, and justifiably so. Although most administrators don't need to know every detail about programming a TCP connection or what to expect as a return value from a *gethostbyname* call, they do need to understand enough to configure the protocol and make it work properly.

The key thing to remember about TCP/IP is that it *isn't a single entity*. TCP/IP is short for Transmission Control Protocol/Internet Protocol, but these are only two of the protocols included in the TCP/IP suite. There are a variety of other protocols, each with its own specialized area of importance and use.

TCP/IP isn't proprietary and isn't controlled by any one company or vendor, unlike other protocols such as Internetwork Packet Exchange/Sequenced Packet Exchange (IPX/SPX) and the now-obsolete NetBEUI protocol. TCP/IP is an open standard controlled by the Internet Engineering Task Force (IETF) and by the users of the Internet itself in the form of RFCs (requests for comments). Anyone can submit an RFC for consideration and inclusion into the written definitions of the protocols and policies of the Internet and TCP/IP.

Internet Protocol

Internet Protocol (IP) is the core protocol of the TCP/IP suite. To quote from RFC 791, "The Internet Protocol is designed for use in interconnected systems of packet-switched computer communication networks." IP performs only one basic function: it delivers a packet of bits (called a *datagram*) from point A to point B over any network "wire" it happens to encounter along the way.

> **Note** The term *wire* is used loosely here and elsewhere to indicate the actual—usually physical—network connection between two points. In fact, that wire can just as easily be a piece of optical fiber or even a radio or infrared signal. In all cases, it functions as the transmission medium through which the packets travel.

IP doesn't in and of itself know anything about the information in the datagram it carries, nor does it have any provision beyond a simple checksum to ensure that the data is intact or that it has reached its destination. That is left to the other protocols in the TCP/IP suite.

Transmission Control Protocol

According to RFC 793 (the defining RFC for the protocol), Transmission Control Protocol (TCP) is "a connection-oriented, end-to-end reliable protocol designed to fit into a layered hierarchy of protocols which support multinetwork applications." That's nice, but what does all that really mean? The following list should help:

- **Connection-oriented**   TCP provides for the communication of packets between two points, sending the datagram specifically from one computer or device to another, and sending an acknowledgment back to the sending computer on receipt of intact packets.

- **End-to-end**   Each TCP packet designates a specific endpoint as its destination. Packets are passed along the wire and ignored except by the actual endpoint of the packet and any device that needs to direct it.

- **Reliable**   This is the key point of TCP. When a program or application layer protocol such as File Transfer Protocol (FTP) uses TCP for its transport protocol, TCP takes responsibility for the reliability of the communications. The protocol itself provides for interprocess communication to ensure that packets that are sent out not only get there, but also that they get there in the order in which they were sent. If a packet is missed, the protocol communicates with the sending device to ensure that the packet is resent.

  Because TCP has to create a reliable connection between two devices or processes, each packet involves substantially more overhead than is needed with other, less reliable protocols within the suite. But by the same token, the programmer writing the application that uses TCP doesn't have to include a lot of error checking and handshaking in the application itself.

User Datagram Protocol

The User Datagram Protocol (UDP), another protocol in the TCP/IP suite, is a connectionless, transaction-oriented protocol designed to send packets with a minimum of protocol overhead. It provides no guarantee that its intended recipient received the packet, or that packets were received in the order in which they were sent. UDP is frequently used in broadcast messages where there is no specific intended recipient, such as Boot Protocol (BOOTP) and Dynamic Host Configuration Protocol (DHCP) requests, but it can also be used by applications that prefer to ensure reliable delivery internally rather than in an underlying protocol. UDP is defined in RFC 768.

Many parts of the TCP/IP suite of protocols and programs can use either TCP or UDP as their transport protocol. The choice of which to use will depend on the reliability and security of the network you're on and whether there are routing issues. An example of a protocol that can use either TCP or UDP is the Network File System (NFS) protocol.

Windows Sockets

Windows Sockets (commonly referred to as *Winsock*) is a Microsoft technology that provides a consistent way for applications to communicate with a TCP/IP stack without having to consider any underlying variations in the TCP/IP stack implementation.

In the distant past, there were many vendors of TCP/IP protocol and applications suites for MS-DOS–based computers, each slightly different from the others. This situation made it extremely difficult to write an application that required TCP/IP and yet worked with all the TCP/IP implementations that existed. Winsock was designed to get around this problem by providing a uniform set of application programming interface (API) calls that would be the same regardless of the underlying differences in the actual implementation of TCP/IP.

The original Winsock version 1 had a fair number of difficulties, and version 1.1 was released soon after its initial implementation. The current version of Winsock supported by Windows Server 2008 R2 and Windows 7 is version 2, which provides for full backward compatibility with earlier versions while offering improved functionality and support for additional features and expandability. Note that Winsock 2 has been around since Windows NT 4, so applications are widely available that use this API.

NetBIOS

NetBIOS is a networking API used by legacy applications and operating systems to communicate across a network using the NWLink (IPX/SPX-compatible), NetBEUI, or TCP/IP protocol.

Until the advent of Windows 2000, NetBIOS was the primary networking API used by all Microsoft operating systems. NetBIOS names were used for name resolution within Windows-based networks. Any time a computer wanted to communicate with another computer on the network, it had to resolve the NetBIOS name for the other computer either by querying a Windows Internet Naming Service (WINS) server, by using a NetBIOS broadcast, or by referring to the computer's local Lmhosts file.

With Windows 2000, Microsoft changed the Windows networking infrastructure to one based on TCP/IP, with no NetBIOS support required. Networks based on Windows Server 2003 or Windows 2000 can use DNS to resolve network names, and network applications can use the Winsock interface to communicate using a network.

Unfortunately, because earlier versions of Windows require NetBIOS support to function properly on a Windows-based network, most companies still need to support NetBIOS over TCP/IP and provide WINS services for earlier clients and servers. Even in a pure Windows Server 2008 R2 and Windows 7 network, NetBIOS and WINS might be required, depending on what other applications and servers are on the network.

Requests for Comments

Requests for comments (RFCs) come in many guises, but all of them have the same intent and a somewhat similar format. They are designed to provide a way for an extremely diverse group—the users of the Internet—to communicate and agree on the architecture and functionality of the Internet. Some RFCs are official documents of the IETF, defining the standards of TCP/IP and the Internet; others are simply proposals trying to become standards; and still others fall somewhere in between. Some are tutorial in nature, others are quite technical, and some are even humorous (such as RFC 2324, "Hyper Text Coffee Pot Control Protocol"). But all are a way for the Internet, an essentially anarchic entity, to organize, communicate, and evolve.

There's no need for us to list all the RFCs here, and you certainly don't need to read them all, but you should know where to find them and be aware of the most important ones. You can find listings of RFCs in several places, including *http://www.ietf.org/rfc.html* and the official RFC editor site, *http://www.rfc-editor.org*. Table D-1 lists some important RFCs and their subject matter.

TABLE D-1 Some Key RFCs* and What They Cover

RFC Number	Subject
RFC 768	User Datagram Protocol (UDP)
RFC 791	Internet Protocol (IP)
RFC 792	Internet Control Message Protocol (ICMP)
RFC 793	Transmission Control Protocol (TCP)
RFC 821	Simple Mail Transfer Protocol (SMTP) (Obsoleted by RFC 2821)
RFC 822	Standard for the Format of Advanced Research Project Agency (ARPA) Internet Text Messages (Obsoleted by RFC2822)
RFC 854, 855	Telnet Protocol
RFC 959	File Transfer Protocol (FTP)
RFC 1001, 1002	Network Basic Input/Output System (NetBIOS) over TCP/IP
RFC 1011	Official Internet Protocols
RFC 1034	DNS Concepts and Facilities
RFC 1035	DNS Implementation and Specification
RFC 1166	Internet Numbers
RFC 1542	Clarifications and Extensions for the Bootstrap Protocol
RFC 1886	DNS Extensions to Support IP version 6 (Obsoleted by RFC 3596)
RFC 1918	Address Allocation for Private Internets
RFC 2131	Dynamic Host Configuration Protocol (DHCP)
RFC 2136	Dynamic Updates in the DNS System (Dynamic DNS)
RFC 2251	Lightweight Directory Access Protocol (LDAP)
RFC 2460 through 2463	Internet Protocol version 6 (IPv6) Specifications
RFC 2661	Layer Two Tunneling Protocol (L2TP)
RFC 2782	A DNS Resource Record (RR) for Specifying the Location of Services (DNS SRV)
RFC 3007	Secure DNS
RFC 3011	A DHCP server on one subnet can respond to an address from another subnet.

* As in any such list, some of these RFCs are currently standards, some are proposed, and some might never be fully adopted. An RFC is only a request for comment. The comments might lead to it becoming a standard or might lead to it withering away.

IP Addresses and What They Mean

Your IP address is to the Internet (or to the other computers on your local network) what your street address is to your mail carrier. It uniquely identifies your computer by using a simple, 32-bit (or 128-bit, with IPv6) addressing scheme. This scheme, which originated in the late 1960s and early 1970s, uses four octets (for IPv4) separated by dots, in the form *w.x.y.z* (we'll use these letters to represent each octet throughout this appendix, to describe both the network's address and the local machine's address on that network). Each octet is represented by a single decimal number but is called an octet because it requires eight bits to describe it.

> **Note** IPv6 addresses use hexadecimal notation, with blocks separated by colons. For IPv6 addresses, the first half (64 bits) of the address is a network-specific and routing-specific prefix, and the second 64 bits comprise the actual address of the device. Each IPv6 device can have multiple, scope-specific, addresses.

In terms of IPv4 addresses, all networks fall into one of three classes: A, B, or C. These different classes describe networks (sometimes referred to as *licenses*) of different sizes and complexities. The licenses to use a range of IP addresses are controlled by the Internet Corporation for Assigned Names and Numbers (ICANN).

> **Note** The use of the word *class* to describe the size of an IPv4 network is officially deprecated, and we're not supposed to use it any more. But it's still commonly used and will undoubtedly continue to be used as long as there are IPv4 networks in common use.

Class A Networks

A class A network has an address that begins with a number from 1 through 127 for the first octet—the *w* portion of the address. This octet describes the network itself, and the remainder of the address is the actual local device's address on that network. A class A network with the network address of 10 (the *w* portion) contains all IP addresses from 10.0.0.0 to 10.255.255.255.

The class A address 127 has a special meaning and isn't available for general use. This means that there are a total of 126 possible usable class A addresses in the world (from 1 through 126), and that each class A network can contain more than 16 million unique network devices.

The class A addresses were spoken for long ago and are assigned to such entities as the United States Department of Defense, Stanford University, and Hewlett-Packard.

> ## Real World: 127—The Loopback Address
>
> All IP addresses that begin with the network number 127 are special. Your network card interprets them as loopback addresses. Any packet sent to an address beginning with 127 is treated as if it got to its intended address, and that address is the local device. So packets addressed to 127.0.0.1 are treated the same as packets to 127.37.90.17; both are actually addressed to your current machine, as are all the other 16 million addresses in the 127 class A network. (You too can have your very own class A network. Of course, you can talk only to yourself, but who cares?)

Class B Networks

A class B network uses the first two octets, *w* and *x*, to describe the network itself, and the remainder of the address is the actual local device's address on that network. The first octet in a class B network must begin with a number from 128 through 191, resulting in 16,384 class B networks, each of which can have 65,534 unique addresses. This is still a pretty large network, and most of the class B networks were assigned long ago to large organizations or companies such as Rutgers University and Toyota Motor Corporation.

Many addresses in the class B address space have subsequently been divided into smaller groups of addresses and reassigned. Large Internet service providers (ISPs), for example, use this technique to more efficiently use the available address space.

Class C Networks

A class C network has an address that begins with a number from 192 through 223 for the *w* octet of the address and uses the first three octets (*w.x.y*) to describe the network itself. The last octet, *z*, describes the actual local device's address on that network. This arrangement makes for roughly 2 million class C networks, each of which can have a maximum of 254 devices on the network. That's enough for a small business or a department, but not for a major corporation.

> **Note** Because Internet-accessible IPv4 addresses are in such short supply these days, a new method of dividing up Internet IP addresses was created—Classless Inter-Domain Routing (CIDR). CIDR allows IP addresses to be leased out in smaller chunks than entire classes so that companies can lease a more suitable number of IP addresses than if they had to lease an entire class A, B, or C network. CIDR uses variable-length subnet masks to accomplish these smaller address chunks.

Class D and Class E Addresses

An IP address with a number from 224 through 239 for the *w* octet of the address is known as a class D address, which is used for multicast addresses. With multicast addresses, several computers can share a single multicast address, in addition to their normal IP addresses. This makes it easy to send identical data to multiple hosts simultaneously—just send the data to the shared multicast address, and every member of the multicast group receives it.

The IP address space that uses the numbers 240 through 247 for the *w* octet is referred to as a class E address. This space is reserved for future use.

Real World: IP Addresses for Networks That Use Firewalls or Internet Gateways

Organizations and companies today use routers, proxy servers, and firewalls between the computers in their organization and the public Internet. The addresses of the computers within the organization are *translated* by that router or firewall, a process called Network Address Translation or NAT, and are never directly propagated onto the Internet. Addresses within the organization, then, need to be unique within the organization, but not necessarily globally unique, because no other organization will see them. Should you use just any old address then? No, you really shouldn't. There is a special set of network addresses reserved for just such uses. These addresses are defined in RFC 1918, and by using these addresses you can comfortably employ a substantially larger address space than you are otherwise able to access.

Using these special network addresses also protects the integrity of the Internet. Because these special addresses are designated exclusively for private networks, they are automatically filtered at routers, protecting the Internet. The following is a list of these special addresses:

- 10.0.0.0 through 10.255.255.255 (a single 24-bit block of addresses or a class A network)

- 172.16.0.0 through 172.31.255.255 (16 contiguous 20-bit blocks of addresses or class B networks)

- 192.168.0.0 through 192.168.255.255 (256 contiguous 16-bit blocks of addresses or class C networks)

You should always use addresses from this group of addresses for your internal IPv4 network. Only machines directly connected to the public Internet should use globally unique IPv4 addresses. All other devices on your network should use these RFC 1918 addresses, which will be hidden by the router or firewall from public view using NAT. Windows Server 2008 can provide NAT directly, or you can choose to use a full-featured firewall such as Microsoft Forefront Threat Management Gateway. When you use a firewall or proxy server, you require "real" IP addresses only for machines that are outside your firewall and are visible to the Internet as a whole, which helps conserve the global IPv4 address space.

Routers and Subnets

If every computer on the Internet had to know the location of every other computer on the Internet and how to get from here to there, the entire Internet would have come to a grinding halt long ago. Early on, it became apparent that some method was needed to filter and route packets to allow users to not only print to their network printers easily, but also to reach any other computer on the Internet without having to know a whole lot about how to get there. Enter subnets, routers, and gateways.

What Is a Subnet?

A *subnet* is simply a portion of the network that operates as a separate network, without regard to what happens outside and without affecting the rest of the network. A subnet is usually a separate physical "wire" that has only a single point of contact with other areas of the network, through a router or bridge—although even when two subnets share the same physical wire, they still require a router to connect to each other.

Setting up a subnet involves using what is known as a *subnet mask* to allow computers in a subnet to see and directly communicate only with other computers in the same subnet. A subnet mask is a special number, again in *w.x.y.z* form, that masks or blocks areas outside the subnet from sight. The mask works by letting you see only those portions of the IP address space that aren't masked by a 1. (Remember that each octet is actually an 8-bit binary value. To "mask by 1" means to ensure that the appropriate bit has been set to a value of 1.) For example, if you have a class C address of 192.168.0.17, and your subnet mask is 255.255.255.0 (a typical class C subnet), as shown in Figure D-1, you can see only addresses in the last octet of the address (the *z* portion).

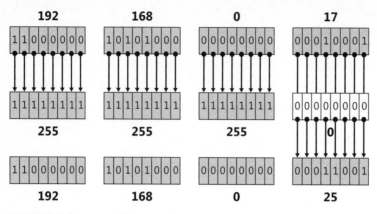

FIGURE D-1 Subnet masking.

If your IP address is 192.168.0.17, the address at 192.168.51.25 is hidden from you by your subnet mask of 255.255.255.0. You can send a packet to that address only by first passing that packet to a gateway or router that knows both where you are and either where the other network is or how to find it. If, on the other hand, you send a packet to a printer with the IP address 192.168.0.129 or to a computer at 192.168.0.50, you have no problem. The system can see that address, and the packet goes directly to its destination.

If you can assign an entire class of addresses to a subnet, it's easy to figure out what your mask is; however, if you can assign only a portion of a class (as is the case when leasing Internet IP addresses using CIDR), you need to sit down with your binary-to-decimal conversion tables and determine exactly what the correct subnet mask should be. (Remember that this is all done in binary.) If you understand how it works, you can customize your subnet mask or figure out what the one you have is actually doing. Custom subnet masks are also called *variable-length subnet masks* and are often referred to in so-called *slash notation*, where the network number is specified, followed by the number of bits used in the subnet mask. For example, 192.168.1.0/26 has a subnet mask of 255.255.255.192, allowing a single class C network to be broken into four subnets, with a maximum of 62 hosts per subnet.

> **Note** Use the default subnet mask for your network class unless you have a specific reason not to. For a class A network, this is 255.0.0.0; for a class B network, it's 255.255.0.0; and for a class C network, use 255.255.255.0.

All the subnet masks on a single portion of your network must be the same. If they aren't, this causes all sorts of problems. One machine might be able to send a packet to another, but the other might not be able to send the packet back.

Real World: Physical vs. Logical

Throughout this appendix, we talk about subnets as being separate physical segments on the network. And usually that is the case. But there can be occasions when different subnets need to share the same physical segment of "wire." Sometimes that's an actual Ethernet cable they're sharing, but it could also be a wireless network. You can have different physical networks even with wireless, by using different frequencies. For example, 802.11a and 802.11g are on different wireless frequencies and cannot see each other. Thus, an 802.11a and an 802.11g network have some of the same characteristics as two separate Ethernet cables. Regardless of whether two subnets are on the same physical wire, however, they can't see each other because of the subnet masking without the intervention of a router. But in this case, the router would have two connections (virtual or physical) to the same physical network.

Often you'll have two different wireless networks sharing the same "wire"—that is, the same frequency and same general physical location. But even here, subnets and subnet masks help to hide one network from another. If you have a public, unsecured 802.11g wireless network and a private, secured 802.11g wireless network, you should assign a different subnet to each network. Traffic that must cross from one to the other will still need the services of a router.

Gateways and Routers

A gateway can have different functions on a network, but for the moment you're going to focus on the subnet and routing functions. As already mentioned, if you have a subnet mask of 255.255.255.0 and the *y* octet of your IP address is 222, you can't see an IP address on the network with a *y* octet of 223.

How, then, do you get to an IP address on another subnet? The answer is a *gateway* or *router*. A *router* is a device (usually an external box, but sometimes a computer with more than one network adapter) that connects to more than one physical segment of the network and sends packets between those segments as required. For example, it would take your packets from the 222 subnet and send them over to the 223 subnet for delivery to the address on that subnet. Thus, it acts as a gatekeeper between the two separate portions of the network, keeping the traffic with 222 addresses in the 222 subnet and letting only traffic with 223 addresses cross over to the 223 segment.

If a router doesn't know where to direct a packet, the router knows which entity to ask for directions—another router. It constantly updates its routing tables with information from other routers about the best way to get to various parts of the network.

> **Note** Although the terms *gateway* and *router* are often used interchangeably, strictly speaking, a gateway is a device or computer that translates between networks of different architectures, such as IPX/SPX and TCP/IP. A router is a device or computer that sends packets between two or more network segments as necessary by using logical network addresses (typically IP addresses).
>
> In addition to gateways and routers, there are also *bridges*. These are devices or computers that direct traffic between two network segments based on physical (media access control) addresses, and they are generally used to isolate two sections of a network to improve performance. Bridges are cheaper and less capable than routers.

Address Resolution and Routing Protocols

Detailed information about how address resolution and routing protocols work and the algorithms involved in routing and address resolution are beyond the scope of this book, but it's useful to know what some of the protocols are, if only to recognize some of the acronyms when they're thrown about. In that spirit, the following list consists of the most common TCP/IP address resolution and routing protocols:

- **Address Resolution Protocol (ARP)**   Maps the IP address to the physical hardware address [the media access control (MAC) address] corresponding to that IP address, permitting you to send something to an IP address without having to know what physical device it is.

- **Routing Information Protocol (RIP)**   A distance-vector–based routing protocol that is mostly provided for backward compatibility with existing RIP-based networks. As with most distance-vector–based routing protocols (which make extensive use of broadcasts to discover which other devices and routers are nearby), RIP is being replaced by newer routing protocols that scale better and have lower network traffic overhead.

- **Open Shortest Path First (OSPF)**   A link-state routing protocol that is suitable for use in large and very large networks, such as those common in large enterprises. Link-state routing protocols maintain a map of the network topology that they share with other routers. As the topology changes, routers update their link-state database and then inform neighboring routers of the topology change, reducing the amount of network bandwidth consumed when compared to vector-based routing protocols.

> ## Real World: Routing Flaps
>
> The Internet has grown exponentially since the early 1990s and continues to grow, stretching the technology for resolving addresses and calculating routes to the limit, and sometimes past the limit. When a major router on the Internet goes down—even momentarily—all the other routers on the Internet have to tell one another about it and recalculate new routes that bypass that router. This adjustment results in large numbers of packets passing back and forth, causing traffic to become so heavy that the routing updates can't occur properly because the information doesn't make it through the traffic. Such a situation is called a *routing flap*, and it can cause a large portion of the Internet to come to a virtual halt.
>
> Routing flaps don't happen very often, but they are becoming more and more of a problem. In addition, current router technology is reaching the limit of its ability to calculate the best route from all the possible routes when major changes are caused by the failure of a key router. The next generation of TCP/IP (known as IPv6) will help, as will new algorithms for performing the routing calculations.

Name Resolution

As useful as the 12-decimal–digit IP numbers (192.168.101.102) are when it comes to computers recognizing other computers, they're not the sort of information that human minds process very well. Not only is there a limit to how many 12-digit numbers one can memorize, but such numbers can easily change.

Even worse, IP version 6 (IPv6) addresses are 128 bits expressed in strings that can have as many as 32 hexadecimal characters, although they're often shorter. (Actually, IPv6 addresses can even be written as 128 ones and zeroes, but that's not likely to catch on.)

Obviously, easy-to-remember names are preferable to strings of numbers or strings of characters and numbers. This section looks at how names are handled in the TCP/IP and Internet world.

The Domain Name System

The Domain Name System (DNS) was designed in the early 1980s, and in 1984 it became the official method for mapping IP addresses to names, replacing the use of "hosts" files. With Windows 2000, DNS became the method clients use to locate domain controllers by using the Active Directory directory service. (Clients use Lightweight Directory Access Protocol [LDAP] to actually access the data stored in the Active Directory database.) Although there have been modifications to the overall structure of DNS, the general result is still remarkably like the original design.

> **More Info** See RFC 1591 for a high-level description of DNS, and RFCs 1034 and 1035 for the actual specification. RFCs 3007, 4033, 4034, and 4035 provide the specification for dynamic updates (Dynamic DNS), with which Windows Server 2008 R2 and Windows 7 comply.

The Domain Namespace

The *domain namespace* describes the tree-shaped structure of all the domains from the root ("." or "dot") domain down to the lowest-level leaf of the structure. It is a hierarchical structure in which each level is separated from those above and below with a dot, so you always know where you are in the tree.

Before the Internet moved to DNS, a single master file (Hosts.txt) had to be sent using FTP to everyone who needed to convert from numbers to names. Every addition or change required a revised copy to be propagated to every system. This obviously created enormous overhead even when the Internet was still quite small.

DNS overcomes the limitations of Hosts.txt files by maintaining a distributed database that is extensible to add information as needed. It permits local administration of local names while maintaining overall integrity and conformance to standards.

Top-Level Domains

The top-level domains are the first level of the tree below the root. They describe the kinds of networks that are within their domain in two, three, or now four letters, such as *.com* for commercial domains and *.edu* for educational domains. The original top-level domains were functionally based and had a decidedly American slant. That's not surprising, given that most of the namespace was originally set up and administered by the United States Department of Defense.

As the Internet grew, however, this approach made less and less sense, especially with a distributed database such as DNS that allowed for local administration and control. Geographical top-level domains were added to the functionally based ones, such as *.ca* for Canadian domains, and so on.

How Names Are Resolved into Addresses

When you click a link to *http://www.microsoft.com* and your browser attempts to connect to that site, what actually happens? How does it find *www.microsoft.com*? The short answer is that it asks the primary DNS server listed in the TCP/IP Properties dialog box on your workstation. But how does that DNS server know where the site is?

Real World: Where Domain Names Come from and How You Get One

These days, virtually every business (and many individuals) wants its own domain. The keeper and distributor of domain names used to be Network Solutions, formerly called InterNIC. Recently this task was opened up to competition, and there are now a myriad of companies that will register your domain name for you. The list is too big and volatile to include here—for a complete listing, visit the ICANN website at *http://www.icann.org/registrars/accredited-list.html*. You can link to any of the accredited registrars from this site and perform a search to find out if your chosen name is taken.

> **Note** Have alternative names in mind as well; you'll probably need them. After you re-search existing names and choose one that isn't taken, register the name with your chosen registrar. Pay between $15 and $35 (U.S.) per year or you lose the name.

After you acquire a domain name from a registrar such as Network Solutions, you need to properly set up the DNS hosting for the domain name. If you acquired the domain name through your web hosting company, this is probably done automatically for you. Otherwise, follow the directions provided by your registrar to enter the addresses of two DNS servers that have DNS records for your domain name. If you're using a web hosting company, these are probably that company's DNS servers. If you're hosting your website on your own server or servers, you'll need to either host your own DNS records or contract with a company that specializes in DNS to host them for you. This could be your ISP or a company such as ZoneEdit (*www.zoneedit.com*) that specializes in DNS.

Long ago, domain names were free and lasted forever, but those days are gone. If you don't pay your bill from your registrar, your domain name is put up for grabs, and chances are that someone else will claim it before you're able to reregister it. The avail-able short names are disappearing at a rapid rate, and many people are finding that they need to think up longer versions to find something that isn't taken.

When a TCP/IP application wants to communicate with or connect to another location, it needs the address of that location. However, it usually knows only the name it's looking for, so the first step is to resolve that name into an IP address. The first place it looks for the name is in the locally cached set of names and their IP addresses that it has resolved recently. After all, if you asked about *http://www.microsoft.com* just a few minutes ago, why should it go through all the trouble of looking up that name again? It's not likely that the IP address will have changed in that time.

Suppose, however, that you haven't been on the Internet for a couple of days, and your computer doesn't have the address for *http://www.microsoft.com* cached. In this case, Windows queries your primary DNS server (specified in the connection properties for your Internet connection). If your DNS server doesn't have any recent information about *http://www.microsoft.com*, the DNS server asks around to see whether anyone else knows the IP address.

This can happen in a couple of ways. The default method is to use recursion, in which the DNS server queries the root server of the domain, which passes back the location of the DNS server that is authoritative regarding the next level down in the domain, which the original DNS server then queries. This process recurs until it reaches a DNS server that contains the IP address of the desired host in its zone data.

> **Note** You might want to disable the use of recursion on your DNS server if it is in use on an internal network and you want your clients to fail over to a secondary DNS server that handles name resolution for hosts outside your local network.

If you disable recursion on the DNS server, or if the client doesn't request the use of recursion, the DNS entry for the desired host is found by iteration. When using iteration, the DNS server checks its zone and cache data, and when it finds that it cannot complete the request, it sends the client a list of DNS servers that are more likely to have the host name in their zones. The client then contacts those servers, which might in turn respond with their own list, possibly even to the point that the client might query the Internet root servers looking for the appropriate DNS server.

Reverse Lookups

In most cases, you have a host name for which you need to locate the IP address, but in some instances you might have only an IP address, for which you need to look up the host name. Reverse lookup was added to the DNS specification for this reason. The only problem with creating reverse lookups is the difference between the way the DNS namespace is organized and the way in which IP addresses are assigned. DNS names go from specific to general, beginning with the host name and ending with the root of the domain [the period at the end of a fully qualified domain name (FQDN)]. IP addresses work in reverse fashion, so to facilitate the lookup of a host name from an IP address, a special domain, the *in-addr.arpa* domain, was created.

In the in-addr.arpa domain, the octets of an IP address are reversed, with in-addr.arpa appended to the address. For example, the IP address 10.230.231.232 is queried as 232.231.230.10.in-addr.arpa.

The reverse lookup zone is maintained as a separate database within the DNS database. The resource records (RRs) in the reverse lookup zone are of the type PTR (pointer). Much like pointers in common programming languages, or shortcuts in Windows, these PTR RRs refer to a different record—the associated A (address) record in the forward lookup zone. For example, the following list describes two records that a host might have:

- **A record (forward lookup zone)**   hp350-dc-02.example.local IN A 192.168.51.2
- **PTR record (reverse lookup zone)**   2.51.168.192.in-addr.arpa. IN PTR hp350-dc-02.example.local

You can perform a reverse lookup of an IP address by typing **nslookup** followed by the IP address you want to look up at a command prompt. For example, if you type **nslookup 192.168.51.2**, the DNS server responds with the name and address of the DNS server, followed by the name and address of the host.

Dynamic DNS and Active Directory Integration

Dynamic DNS, introduced in Windows 2000 Server, makes DNS more flexible by permitting clients to update their DNS records dynamically. This capability eliminates the need to update DNS entries manually when clients change IP addresses. Unfortunately, the standard dynamic DNS service described in RFC 2136 allows for only a single-master model, in which a single primary DNS server maintains the master database of zone data (the addresses and host names for a particular domain). This database can be replicated with secondary DNS servers, but only the primary server can manage dynamic updates to the zone. If the primary server goes down, client updates to the zone aren't processed.

The dynamic DNS server in a Windows Server can overcome the limitations of a single-master model and use Active Directory to store its zone data, permitting a multiple-master model. Because the Active Directory database is fully replicated to all Active Directory–enabled domain controllers, any domain controller in the domain can update DNS zone data. Using Active Directory to store the zone data also allows for added security features and simplified planning and management, as well as faster directory replication than is possible using a single-master model, because Active Directory replicates only relevant changes to the zone.

Zone Storage and Active Directory

A DNS server is required to support the use of Active Directory, so if a DNS server can't be found on the network when a server is being promoted to domain controller, the DNS service is installed by default on the domain controller. After Active Directory is installed, the storage and replication of your zones is integrated directly into Active Directory, and replication is managed as part of Active Directory replication.

Lightweight Directory Access Protocol

LDAP is used to access data in the Active Directory database. Once again, DNS is used to locate domain controllers, and LDAP is used to access the Active Directory data. LDAP runs on top of TCP/IP, and Active Directory supports both versions 2 and 3 of LDAP. Any LDAP product complying with these specifications can be used to access data in Active Directory.

Dynamic Host Configuration Protocol

One of the problems traditionally faced by organizations using TCP/IP is deciding how to manage internal IP addresses. The chore of managing and maintaining all the IP addresses in an organization can quickly become an administrator's nightmare, especially with the number of intermittently connected computers such as laptops, PDAs, and remote computers. DHCP provides a simple way to manage addresses for computers, and it allows for greatly simplified administration and management of addresses and configuration. If you need to make a change to the TCP/IP settings for your entire organization, you need to make the change only to the DHCP server, and it will be automatically propagated to all the DHCP clients. This is a *lot* simpler than having to go around to all of the computers in the organization and change their settings.

DHCP allows the administrator to assign IP addresses only as required. A mobile user can connect a laptop to the network when necessary and be assigned an appropriate address automatically. Likewise, a dial-in user doesn't need a permanent IP address; one can be assigned when the connection is made to the network, and when the connection is broken, the address is made available for someone else's use.

How DHCP Works

To receive an IP address, the client computer sends a DHCP discover broadcast, which a DHCP server picks up and responds to by offering the client an IP address for its use. The client responds to the first offer it receives and sends back to the DHCP server a request for the IP address offered. The DHCP server sends an acknowledgment telling the client that it succeeded in leasing the IP address for the amount of time specified by the DHCP server.

DHCP clients attempt to renew their leases at boot-up, as well as after 50 percent of the lease time has passed. In this renewal process, the discover stage is skipped and the client simply begins with a request. If the renewal of the lease fails at the 50 percent mark, the client waits until 87.5 percent of the lease has passed and then attempts to acquire a new IP address by sending out a DHCP discover broadcast and starting the IP lease process again.

Appendix E
Introduction to Networks

If you've ever made a phone call or used a bank ATM, you've already experienced using a network. After all, a *network* is simply a collection of computers and peripheral devices that can share resources. The connection can be a cable, a telephone line, or even a wireless channel. The Internet itself is a network—a global network made up of all the computers, hardware, and peripherals connected to it.

Your bank's ATM consists of hardware and software connected to central computers that know, among other things, how much money you have in your account. When you call cross-country or just across town, telephone company software makes the connection from your phone to the phone you're calling by using multiple switching devices. It's something we do every day, without thinking about the complicated processes behind the scenes.

Both the telephone networks and the ATM networks are maintained by technicians and engineers who plan, set up, and maintain all the software and hardware; however, the assumption underlying Windows Small Business Server 2011 Essentials is that there isn't anyone dedicated full time to maintaining the network and its operating system. Instead, Windows Small Business Server 2011 Standard provides the Windows Small Business Server 2011 Standard Console (generally shortened to *Windows SBS Console*)—a unified administrative interface designed to meet the needs of small businesses and simplify your choices. For SBS 2011 Essentials, the central management console is known as the Dashboard.

Servers

A *server* is a computer that provides services. It's really just that simple. The difficulty comes when people confuse the physical box that provides the service with the actual service. Any computer or device on a network can be a server for a particular service. A server doesn't even need to be a computer in the traditional sense. For example, you might have a print server that is nothing more complicated than a device connected to the network on one side and connected to a printer on the other. The device has a tiny little brain with just enough intelligence to understand when a particular network packet is intended for it and translates those packets into something that the printer can understand.

In SBS 2011 Essentials, usually a single computer acts as the physical server box (though you can have secondary servers), but that box provides a variety of services to the network, including the usual file and print services. These services meet your core business needs, including authentication and security, an Internet connection, remote access, backup, sharing, and even database services with the Windows Small Business Server 2011 Premium Add-on.

Clients

A *client* is anything on the network that avails itself of a server's services. Clients are usually the other computers on the network. Users and applications on the client computers typically print to network printers, read email, work on shared documents, connect to the Internet, and generally use services that aren't available on the client computer itself. Clients aren't usually as powerful as servers, but they're perfectly capable computers on their own.

Media Connecting Servers and Clients

Another portion of a network is the actual network media that connects the various servers and clients to each other. This media includes both the network cards that are part of the server or client and the physical wire (or wireless connection) between them, as well as the various other components involved, such as hubs, routers, and switches. When all these media components work as they should, we pretty much forget about this portion of the network and take it for granted. But when a failure of one component of the network media occurs, we face troubleshooting and repairs that can be both frustrating and expensive—a good reason to buy only high-quality network components from vendors and dealers who support their products.

Features of the Windows Operating System

The Windows Server 2008 R2 operating system that underlies SBS is a proven, reliable, and secure operating system with all the features needed to run a business of virtually any size. With SBS 2011 Essentials, the operating system and server components have been specifically tuned to support from 2 to 25 users in a small business environment, with all the server functions residing on a single computer.

Some of the features that make Windows Server 2008 R2 ideal for a small business server include:

- Easy installation that is almost fully automated in SBS.
- A robust yet easy-to-administer security model using Active Directory directory services.
- The NTFS file system, which fully supports long file names, dynamic error recovery, shadow copies, user space limitations, and security.
- Support for a broad range of hardware and software.

Domains and Workgroups

Microsoft provides for two different networking models in their operating systems: workgroups and domains. SBS supports only the domain model of Microsoft networking, but it's worthwhile to go over why this decision makes sense, even in a very small business.

Do Workgroups Work?

Microsoft introduced the concept of the workgroup in 1992 with Windows for Workgroups. The *workgroup* is a logical grouping of several computers whose work or users are connected and who want to share their resources with each other. Usually, all the computers in a workgroup are equal, which is why such setups are referred to as *peer-to-peer networks*.

Workgroup networks are appealing because they're easy to set up and maintain. Individual users manage the sharing of their resources by determining what will be shared and who will have access. A user can allow other users to use a printer, a CD-ROM drive, an entire hard drive, or only certain files. The difficulty arises when it's necessary to give different levels of access to different users. Passwords can be used for this purpose in a limited way, but as the network gets larger, passwords proliferate and the situation becomes increasingly complicated. Users who are required to have numerous passwords start using the same one over and over or choose passwords that are easy to remember and therefore easy to guess, and there is no way to enforce a minimum password quality level. If someone leaves the company to work for the company's biggest competitor, passwords have to be changed and everyone in the workgroup has to be notified of the new passwords. Security, such as it is, falls apart.

Another problem that occurs when a workgroup becomes too large is that users have difficulty locating the resources they need. The informal nature of workgroups also means that centralized administration or control is nonexistent. Everything has to be configured computer by computer. This lack of central administration and control, along with the limited security, makes the workgroup model a bad choice for all but the home network.

Domains

To provide a secure and easy-to-manage environment that takes full advantage of Active Directory, Microsoft made the decision to use a domain-based networking environment. Management is simplified and centralized on the server, reducing the complexity and security problems caused by having to manage users, resources, and passwords across multiple clients.

A *domain* is really just a type of workgroup that includes a server—but a server that manages and administers all of the users and computers in the network. It is a logical grouping of users who are connected by more than the cables between their computers. The goal of a domain is to let users share resources within the group and to make it easier for the group to work. However, the key difference is that Active Directory—and the server it runs on—manages, catalogs, and secures the users, groups, computers, and resources for the entire network, providing a single point of administration and control.

Additional Users

When adding a new user to the domain, you won't need to go around to each computer and enter all the information. As the administrator, you can simply connect to the server and add the new user, using the Dashboard. You can set up a home folder, add the user to security and distribution groups, set up disk quotas, and even configure a client computer—all with only a few clicks and the entering of the user name and password. The change will be immediately seen across the entire domain.

All users, including the newest, can get at their resources no matter which computer is being used. Permission to access resources is granted to individual users (or a group of users), not to individual computers. And when you need to restrict access to a sensitive document or directory, you need to log on to only a single workstation to make the change across the entire domain. You can easily and quickly grant or restrict access by individual user or by groups of users.

Access Control

In a workgroup, there are limitations on sharing your computer's resources with the rest of the workgroup. At the simplest level, you can either share the resource or not share it. Beyond that, you can require a password for a particular level of access to the resource. This enables only a very limited ability to control access to the resource, and virtually none if your computer is physically accessible to anyone but yourself.

SBS provides *discretionary access control*, which allows, for example, some users to create a document or make changes to an existing one while other users can only read the document and still other users can't even *see* it. You can set access for:

- An individual file or files within a directory.
- The entire directory.

SBS lets you make selections as fine or as coarse as needed and makes the administration of security easy to manage.

Domain Components

An SBS domain has at least two main components and an optional third component:

- Domain controller
- Member server (optional)
- Workstations or clients

Let's take a look at these components.

The Domain Controller

The main computer in the SBS domain is the *domain controller*. In many, if not most, SBS domains, the domain controller is the only server. It hosts Active Directory and all the components of SBS, as well as acting as the file and print server and the backup server for the domain. All computers in the domain connect and authenticate to the domain controller, and all domain security is controlled by it.

Member Servers

In some larger SBS domains, additional Windows Server 2008 R2 computers might be in the domain. SBS 2011 Essentials includes a second server as part of the Premium Add-on. These computers can be used to spread some of the network's resource load around so that the domain controller doesn't carry the whole load, and the Premium Add-on includes Microsoft SQL Server 2008 R2 for Small Business, which can be installed on either the second server or the main SBS server.

Another reason you might have an additional member server in your SBS domain is to host Windows Remote Desktop Services (RDS). RDS allows you to use inexpensive, easily managed desktop computers and terminals whose only function is to run applications directly on the Remote Desktop (RD) Session Host computer. The RD Session Host provides the disk space and all the applications that the user has, while the terminal or computer of the user is merely a display and console (keyboard and mouse). Centralizing applications onto an RD Session Host can dramatically reduce costs and simplify administration in some scenarios. However, for security reasons, RDS cannot be run from the main SBS server, so if you use RDS, you'll need at least one additional server on your network.

Workstations or Clients

All the Windows clients of an SBS network must be running Windows XP SP3, Windows Vista, or Windows 7, but in most networks, they will be running Windows 7. If you have any workstations running versions of Windows earlier than Windows XP, they are no longer supported and should be upgraded. You can also have Mac and even UNIX or Linux clients, but their ability to integrate fully with the SBS network will be limited.

Ideally, Windows clients should be running a business-class version of Windows—specifically, Windows XP Professional, Windows XP Tablet PC Edition, Windows Vista Business, Windows Vista Enterprise, Windows Vista Ultimate, Windows 7 Professional, Windows 7 Enterprise, or Windows 7 Ultimate. However, SBS 2011 Essentials supports Home editions of Windows, with some limits to functionality, such as no remote logon through Remote Web Access.

Index

Symbols

About the Authors

Charlie Russel is the author of more than two dozen books on operating systems and enterprise environments and is an information technology consultant, specializing in interoperability and virtualization. He is also a Microsoft MVP for Windows PowerShell. Together with Sharon Crawford, Charlie authored *Windows Server 2008 Administrator's Companion* and *Windows Small Business Server 2011 Administrator's Companion*.

Sharon Crawford is a veteran writer of computer books. Together with Charlie Russel, Sharon authored *Windows Server 2008 Administrator's Companion* as well as the *Windows Small Business Server 2011 Administrator's Companion*.

Andrew Edney is a Microsoft MVP for Windows Home Server, MCSE, CISSP, MSc, and CEH. He has a wide range of experience in virtually all aspects of Microsoft computing solutions, and he has designed and architected large enterprise solutions for government and private-sector customers. Andrew is the author of *Windows Home Server User's Guide* (Apress, 2007) and other books.

Windows Server 2008—
Resources for Administrators

Windows Server® 2008 Administrator's Companion

Charlie Russel and Sharon Crawford

ISBN 9780735625051

Your comprehensive, one-volume guide to deployment, administration, and support. Delve into core system capabilities and administration topics, including Active Directory®, security issues, disaster planning/recovery, interoperability, IIS 7.0, virtualization, clustering, and performance tuning.

Windows Server 2008 Administrator's Pocket Consultant, Second Edition

William R. Stanek

ISBN 9780735627116

Portable and precise—with the focused information you need for administering server roles, Active Directory, user/group accounts, rights and permissions, file-system management, TCP/IP, DHCP, DNS, printers, network performance, backup, and restoration.

Windows Server 2008 Resource Kit

Microsoft MVPs with Microsoft Windows Server Team

ISBN 9780735623613

Six volumes! Your definitive resource for deployment and operations—from the experts who know the technology best. Get in-depth technical information on Active Directory, Windows PowerShell® scripting, advanced administration, networking and network access protection, security administration, IIS, and more—plus an essential toolkit of resources on CD.

Internet Information Services (IIS) 7.0 Administrator's Pocket Consultant

William R. Stanek

ISBN 9780735623644

This pocket-sized guide delivers immediate answers for administering IIS 7.0. Topics include customizing installation; configuration and XML schema; application management; user access and security; Web sites, directories, and content; and performance, backup, and recovery.

Windows PowerShell 2.0 Administrator's Pocket Consultant

William R. Stanek

ISBN 9780735625952

The practical, portable guide to using *cmdlets* and scripts to automate everyday system administration—including configuring server roles, services, features, and security settings; managing TCP/IP networking; monitoring and tuning performance; and other essential tasks.

ALSO SEE

Windows PowerShell 2.0 Best Practices
ISBN 9780735626461

Windows® Administration Resource Kit: Productivity Solutions for IT Professionals
ISBN 9780735624313

Windows Server 2008 Hyper-V™ Resource Kit
ISBN 9780735625174

Windows Server 2008 Security Resource Kit
ISBN 9780735625044

Microsoft®
Press

microsoft.com/mspress

Windows Server 2008 Resource Kit— Your Definitive Resource!

Windows Server® 2008 Resource Kit

Microsoft® MVPs with the Microsoft Windows Server Team

ISBN 9780735623613

Your definitive reference for deployment and operations—from the experts who know the technology best. Get in-depth technical information on Active Directory®, Windows PowerShell® scripting, advanced administration, networking and network access protection, security administration, IIS, and other critical topics—plus an essential toolkit of resources on CD.

ALSO AVAILABLE AS SINGLE VOLUMES

Windows Server 2008 Security Resource Kit

Jesper M. Johansson et al. with Microsoft Security Team

ISBN 9780735625044

Windows Server 2008 Networking and Network Access Protection (NAP)

Joseph Davies, Tony Northrup, Microsoft Networking Team

ISBN 9780735624221

Windows Server 2008 Active Directory Resource Kit

Stan Reimer et al. with Microsoft Active Directory Team

ISBN 9780735625150

Windows® Administration Resource Kit: Productivity Solutions for IT Professionals

Dan Holme

ISBN 9780735624313

Windows Powershell Scripting Guide

Ed Wilson

ISBN 9780735622791

Internet Information Services (IIS) 7.0 Resource Kit

Mike Volodarsky et al. with Microsoft IIS Team

ISBN 9780735624412

Get Certified—Windows® 7

Desktop support technicians and administrators—demonstrate your expertise with Windows 7 by earning a Microsoft® Certification focusing on core technical (MCTS) or professional (MCITP) skills. With our 2-in-1 *Self-Paced Training Kits*, you get a comprehensive, cost-effective way to prepare for the certification exams. Combining official exam-prep guides + practice tests, these kits are designed to maximize the impact of your study time.

EXAM 70-680

MCTS Self-Paced Training Kit: Configuring Windows 7

Ian McLean and Orin Thomas

ISBN 9780735627086

EXAM 70-685

MCITP Self-Paced Training Kit: Windows 7 Enterprise Desktop Support Technician

Tony Northrup and J.C. Mackin

ISBN 9780735627093

EXAM 70-686

MCITP Self-Paced Training Kit: Windows 7 Enterprise Desktop Administrator

Craig Zacker and Orin Thomas

ISBN 9780735627178

Great for on the job

Windows 7 Resource Kit

Mitch Tulloch, Tony Northrup, Jerry Honeycutt, Ed Wilson, and the Windows 7 Team at Microsoft

ISBN 9780735627000

Windows 7 Inside Out, Deluxe Edition

Ed Bott, Carl Siechert, Craig Stinson

ISBN 9780735656925

Windows 7 Administrator's Pocket Consultant

William R. Stanek

ISBN 9780735626997

What do you think of this book?

We want to hear from you!
To participate in a brief online survey, please visit:

microsoft.com/learning/booksurvey

Tell us how well this book meets your needs—what works effectively, and what we can do better. Your feedback will help us continually improve our books and learning resources for you.

Thank you in advance for your input!